S0-EJU-805

3 0050 01614 9105

DATE DUE

HIGHSMITH #45115

AUTOBIOGRAPHY AND GENDER IN EARLY MODERN LITERATURE

Early modern autobiographies and diaries provide a unique insight into women's lives and how they remembered, interpreted, and represented their experiences. Sharon Seelig analyzes the writings of six seventeenth-century women: diaries by Margaret Hoby and Anne Clifford, more extended narratives by Lucy Hutchinson, Ann Fanshawe, and Anne Halkett, and the extraordinarily varied and self-dramatizing publications of Margaret Cavendish. Combining a fresh account of the development of autobiography with close and attentive reading of the texts, Seelig explores the relation between the writers' choices of genre and form and the stories they chose to tell. She demonstrates how, in the course of the seventeenth century, women writers progressed from quite simple forms based on factual accounts to much more imaginative and persuasive acts of self-presentation. This important contribution to the fields of early modern literary studies and gender studies illuminates the interactions between literature and autobiography.

SHARON CADMAN SEELIG is Professor of English at Smith College. She is the author of *The Shadow of Eternity: Belief and Structure in Herbert, Vaughan, and Traherne* (1981) and *Generating Texts: The Progeny of Seventeenth-Century Prose* (1996), as well as numerous articles on seventeenth-century English literature.

AUTOBIOGRAPHY AND GENDER IN EARLY MODERN LITERATURE

Reading Women's Lives, 1600–1680

SHARON CADMAN SEELIG

CAMBRIDGE
UNIVERSITY PRESS

CAL STATE EAST BAY
UNIVERSITY LIBRARY

CT
25
.S44
2006

CAMBRIDGE UNIVERSITY PRESS

Cambridge, New York, Melbourne, Madrid, Cape Town, Singapore, São Paulo

Cambridge University Press
The Edinburgh Building, Cambridge CB2 2RU, UK

Published in the United States of America by Cambridge University Press, New York

www.cambridge.org
Information on this title: www.cambridge.org/9780521856959

© Sharon Cadman Seelig 2006

This book is in copyright. Subject to statutory exception
and to the provisions of relevant collective licensing agreements,
no reproduction of any part may take place without
the written permission of Cambridge University Press.

First published 2006

Printed in the United Kingdom at the University Press, Cambridge

A catalogue record for this book is available from the British Library

ISBN-13 978-0-521-85695-9 hardback
ISBN-10 0-521-85695-7 hardback

Cambridge University Press has no responsibility for the persistence or accuracy of URLs for external
or third-party internet websites referred to in this book, and does not guarantee that any content on
such websites is, or will remain, accurate or appropriate.

CAL STATE EAST BAY
UNIVERSITY LIBRARY

For my father, 1902–1972
And my mother, 1905–

Contents

Preface

My awareness of seventeenth-century women's writing began with poetry
(by Mary Wroth, Katherine Philips, and Aemilia Lanyer), with drama
(by Elizabeth Cary), and with fiction (by Aphra Behn and Margaret
Cavendish). But my interest in a wider variety of texts was awakened by
the brief selections of first-person narratives in the volume entitled *Her
Own Life* and by the larger, complete texts made available, first in hard
copy and later online, by the Brown Women Writers Project. And
gradually I turned to nonfiction prose – to diaries, memoirs, and other
autobiographical texts – as forms of self-representation and as a window
on a period I had long studied with attention to its male writers. Along the
way, I met with occasional discouragement. In 1996, while on sabbatical
in Europe, I was poring over the diary of Lady Margaret Hoby in somewhat constrained working conditions. Our sixteen-year-old son, looking
over my shoulder at the text, and aware that pleasure as well as work
should attend such a leave, said, "You're on sabbatical, right? You could
read anything you want, right?" Then, in response to my affirmative, he
said, "I think that's just sick." We've continued that conversation since,
and though I can't claim to have converted him to the reading of early
modern women's diaries, I'm the more inclined to explain why I keep
reading these texts and what I think can be learned from them.

I take pleasure in acknowledging help, support, and advice I have
received from generous friends and colleagues: most especially I thank
Betsey Harries, Bill Oram, and Naomi Miller, who read drafts of the
whole and made many valuable suggestions; and Andrea Sununu and
Carrie Klaus, who as co-organizers of a workshop at the conference on
Early Modern Women helped develop some of the ideas of the study. I
gratefully remember Ron Macdonald, who turned out not to be a skeptic
but a supporter of this project. Participants in several conferences at which
these ideas were presented have helped with their questions and further
suggestions: the meeting of the Margaret Cavendish Society at Wheaton

College in 2001 and the conference on Attending to Early Modern Women at the University of Maryland in 2000. Members of the Smith College faculty heard earlier drafts of several chapters, and participants in a Kahn Institute Project on Life Writing in 2003–4 provided insight and encouragement. My students at Smith College let me try out texts and ideas on them and responded with interest, enthusiasm, and a lively diversity of views. I gratefully acknowledge a grant from Smith College that allowed me to travel to England to answer scholarly questions and survey landscapes, and a summer grant from the National Endowment for the Humanities that enabled me to bring this study to its conclusion. I wish to thank two anonymous readers for Cambridge University Press for their warm endorsement of my project and their thoughtful challenges to it. To my family, my husband, and now grown children, who have sustained, nourished, and even distracted me during the gestation of this book, my love and deepest thanks. Finally, I owe much to my mother who, like Anne Clifford, kept a diary as long as she was able, and who demonstrates many of the qualities of the women of this study: persistence and piety; a love of detail and a devotion to family history; a sense of adventure and drama; a desire to be well dressed; and better handwriting than the Duchess of Newcastle. But I owe no less to my father, for like Anne Clifford, I have aspired to be my father's daughter, and am pleased when others see some resemblance.

Introduction: mapping the territory

The question posed by Margaret Cavendish at the end of *A True Relation*, "Why hath this lady writ her own life?", has proved provocative enough to stay with us over the centuries and even to inspire a number of recent titles.[1] Why indeed hath this lady writ her own life? Quite often, of course, she did not, preferring instead to write someone else's life – most frequently her husband's – and to define her role within their mutual destiny; often, early modern women wrote no life at all. But despite Virginia Woolf's famous assertion that there were almost no women writers in this period (because "any woman born with a great gift in the sixteenth century would certainly have gone crazed, shot herself, or ended her days in some lonely cottage outside the village, half witch, half wizard, feared and mocked at"), a remarkable number of women did record aspects of their lives in diary, autobiography, poetry, confession, or tract.[2] In the case of Cavendish, as I shall argue, the writing of her life seems to have been an act of self-preservation of the most elemental and perhaps desperate kind. And Anne Clifford, who began compiling a family history to establish her place among her distinguished ancestors and to justify her inheritance, continued keeping records until the day she died. In fact, the reasons behind these early self-presentations or self-constructions are nearly as many as the writers themselves: to record daily events; to monitor one's own activities; to present a record to the world; to justify oneself; to place oneself in the midst of past and present events and persons; to place oneself in a more favorable or dominant or more subordinate role than one perhaps occupied; to find or create a pattern, a meaning in life itself; to go beyond the details of life to the trajectory of fiction.

In this book I'm concerned with the autobiographical impulse, with the desire to represent oneself as it is seen in a variety of forms – diary, memoir, autobiography, fantasy – in texts by six early modern British women. Although these texts differ strikingly from one another, they do share a common enterprise: they construct the self in written form; they present particular images or conceptions of the self, whether in isolation or in connection with others, whether intended to be shared or kept to oneself. They range from brief notation to extended narration; they move from the factual and documentary to more fully elaborated and persuasive accounts. They represent, as James Olney puts it, that "act of autobiography [that] is at once a discovery, a creation, and an imitation of the self."[3]

But just because Cavendish, Clifford, and other early modern women felt strongly about these attempts at self-representation does not mean that we should. I want to ask not only why early modern English women wrote their own lives, in forms from diary and autobiography to lyric verse to mother's testaments to utopian fiction and romance, but also why we read these lives. Although I began by wanting simply to know which texts existed, I grew increasingly interested in their remarkable range and variety. I have furthermore been intrigued by the very fact and degree of their appeal. For the terrain is uneven: these texts can be perplexing, frustrating, inconsistent, forbidding. What keeps us reading; what are our expectations and assumptions? What are we looking for in these texts, and what do we find there? To what extent do our assumptions and experiences shape or illuminate what we read?

Early and late I had questions about how to read: do these texts merit the kind of detailed attention I have given them? Is such a mode of reading useful or rewarding? Does it distort the object of attention? Are these texts in which we might look for coherence, linearity, and consistency? Are these expectations of ours something alien to the writer or something shared by her? There are related questions about women's lives: are women's autobiographical texts less unified than those of their male counterparts, as has been claimed? If so, is it because women's lives are less coherent, or is it rather that women are more likely to conceive of their role as subordinate or dependent, less driven by individual ego?

In considering a variety of texts and their ways of recording and interpreting life experiences, I have tried to notice generic clues without imposing rigid generic expectations. One of my first concerns was accurate description: what kinds of diaries or life records are these? How often did the writer record? What kinds of things did she include? What did she omit? Why did she do so? For whom was she writing? Who in fact might have read this text and why? Such questions, though they have received some attention, remain important because these diaries and autobiographies are so different from what we would understand by the terms. We so often think of life-writing as confessional that we may not know what to make of contrary examples. We may mistake generic differences for temperamental differences, aspects of function for matters of choice or expression (or failure of expression).

While attending to these questions, I shall pay relatively little attention to several other important issues raised by recent studies of early modern women – female literacy and the right to write. That is because questions of literacy, in particular differential rates of literacy for men and women, and the disjunction between the teaching of reading and writing, though of great value to our general understanding of the period, are not crucial to the writers of this study.[4] If the upper-class women I've considered did not enjoy the level of education offered to their brothers (Margaret Cavendish makes the point; Lucy Hutchinson is the exception), they all had easy access to books, whether read alone or in the company of others. Margaret Hoby frequently read with her chaplain, Anne Clifford more often with members of her household. Clifford was tutored by no less than the poet Samuel Daniel, and in the great portrait she commissioned, she chose to be pictured with her books, significantly disordered as if by use; she refers frequently to reading that ranges from Augustine, Josephus, and the Bible to Sidney and Ovid, Spenser and Montaigne; she credits her beloved Chaucer with keeping her from melancholy in the North. Lucy Apsley Hutchinson loved books more than playmates her age; her learning was one of the things that, in her telling, most attracted her future husband. And Margaret Cavendish, for all the gaps in her formal education, conversed with Thomas Hobbes and Pierre Gassendi.

I do not, moreover, share the preoccupation of many earlier critics with the cultural constraints that discouraged women from publishing. By their very nature these diaries and autobiographies – with the notable exception of Cavendish's *A True Relation* – were not meant for publication; at most they were intended for distribution within the family. The diary of Margaret Hoby can have been intended for no one but herself, and the daybooks of Anne Clifford, though they may have been used as a basis for later narrative constructions, also seem like a way of speaking to herself. Clifford's annual summaries, apparently based on more detailed daily records, move from private to public as part of a family chronicle; and the narratives of Lucy Hutchinson, Anne Halkett, and Ann Fanshawe either emerge from or move toward narratives grounded in the family. With regard to these writers, general questions of what women might or might not write, or what they might or might not publish, have seemed less important than attention to what they did write, why, and to whom. As J. Paul Hunter notes, "Personal writings were in the seventeenth century private writings, and they were legion."[5] And the kind of self-scrutiny and self-examination Hunter refers to was practiced by women as well as by men.

In turning from seventeenth-century texts to ways of reading them, one quickly discovers that the study of autobiographical texts and theory has within the last thirty years become not only a growth industry but also the site of considerable disagreement[6] – disagreement over the texts to be included and the methodology to be used; over whether general conclusions may be drawn from specific examples; whether texts by men and by women diverge absolutely or whether they may fruitfully be considered together; whether authors exist, and if they do not, what becomes of the recent discovery of texts written by women.[7] I want briefly to review some of this discussion in order to locate my concerns within its context.

The writing of autobiography, it has been argued, is connected with the heightened sense of history and self-consciousness associated with the early modern period. In his seminal essay Georges Gusdorf maintains that "autobiography is not possible in a cultural landscape where consciousness of self does not, properly speaking, exist," and that autobiography depends on the conscious awareness of each individual life.[8] Although we are less likely than Gusdorf or his predecessor Georg Misch to speak of "the Renaissance" or to assume that it was a period of general awakening, it is certainly the case that there were very few autobiographies in our modern sense before the seventeenth century and that, after 1640, the number of such texts increased sharply.[9] As Paul Delany writes in his study of British autobiographies, "Fundamental to the autobiographical urge is a sense of one's importance as an individual; in the twentieth century this is usually taken for granted, but in the seventeenth it was neither taken for granted – except in so far as men claimed significance because they lived under God's providence – nor supported by a general theory of democratic individualism as it is today. The seventeenth-century autobiographer tends to claim individual significance by virtue of some specific quality or accomplishment, or because he has been a witness to the affairs of the great; hence the variety of motivation and subject-matter in his works."[10]

But arriving at valid or even useful definitions of autobiography has proved extremely difficult. James Olney, who uses the term in a very broad sense, points out that autobiography includes the simplest and commonest of literary forms as well as the most elusive; it is a genre for which no general critical rules are available: either autobiography vanishes before our eyes, or everything turns into autobiography.[11] Moreover, descriptions of the nature of autobiography, or of the autobiographical impulse, are likely to be particularly problematic in the case of texts written by women. Part of the difficulty is that critical discussion of autobiographical forms has focused so largely on those written by men that they are considered the norm, and those by women the exception, even an aberration.[12] For example, the chief forms of seventeenth-century British autobiography, both secular and sacred, have been carefully catalogued by Paul Delany, but of his 175-page study, only one brief chapter is devoted to texts written by women. The very useful series of essays edited by James Olney, *Autobiography: Essays Theoretical and Critical*, also puts women's autobiographical writings in a separate category, devoting only one essay to them.[13] And a study by Susanna Egan, *Patterns of Experience in Autobiography*, includes no women because "female autobiography . . . deserves a study of its own."[14] It is a great oddity, as Domna C. Stanton notes, that even though women's writing is often seen as autobiographical, their work is so largely excluded from studies of autobiography.[15]

If many studies give insufficient attention to texts written by women, even those that deal primarily with women's autobiography struggle to arrive at accurate descriptions or generally valid principles. According to Estelle Jelinek and Sidonie Smith, the genre as so often defined – a story of a success, the achieving of a goal, a picture of a representative life, a life that gives us as well a sense of the times in which it was lived – does not often apply to the autobiographical texts written by women.[16] The question is perhaps usefully problematized – though not resolved – by using terms like *self-writing* or *life-writing*, which convey the multiplicity of forms involved and the lack of adherence to certain predetermined generic types. Smith argues that it is virtually impossible for a woman to be representative of her period and to write; that kind of authority would come closer, in fact, to making her representative of men of her period. Rather, she asserts, women's autobiographical writings tend to be about personal encounters or about family life; insofar as they are about a broader social experience, a number of these were undertaken to inform their children about their fathers' character and accomplishments. Mary G. Mason sees a difference between the prototypical male autobiographies and those written by women, asserting that in contrast to the self-revelatory approach of Augustine or Rousseau, "the self-discovery of female identity seems to acknowledge the real presence and recognition of another consciousness, and the disclosure of female self is linked to the identification of some 'other.'"[17] Estelle Jelinek argues that male "autobiographers consciously shape the events of their life into a coherent whole," constructing "a chronological, linear narrative . . . by concentrating on one period of their life, one theme, or one characteristic of their personality." By contrast she sees women's autobiographies as characterized by "irregularity rather than orderliness, . . . not chronological and progressive but disconnected, fragmentary, or organized into self-sustained units rather than connecting chapters."[18]

These comments assume a significant difference between the experience of men and women, one that translates into differences in the texts they create. But while it is useful to reject the notion of a single (male) model and to broaden the range of works considered in an analysis of the genre, it is surely not the case that all autobiographies written by men are linear and unified, and all those written by women are discursive and fragmentary.[19] Jelinek's assertions about the characteristics of male and female autobiography, although based on a fairly broad temporal spectrum, seem to me too categorical, true in some but not all cases, based in part on more recent texts than those that concern me. But her comments do raise important questions about the relationship between women's lives and the texts that represent them. If in fact women's life experiences are less coherent than those of men, will the narratives women construct likewise be less coherent? *Are* women's lives less unified than those of their male counterparts, or is it rather that women are more likely to conceive of their role as subordinate or dependent, less driven by individual ego? Such a view of the self as part of a larger social order may well affect the kinds of narratives women construct. And yet, given the examples in this study, I would not want to advance the notion of female textual subordination as universal; for as I write, several ghostly figures rise up to contradict or qualify such a view: Anne Clifford, whose life and writing were powerfully focused on the image of herself as heir to George Clifford, daughter to Margaret Russell, and rightful owner of the family's property; Margaret Cavendish, intensely ambitious of renown; Anne Halkett, determined to defend her reputation for integrity; Lucy Hutchinson, taking a starring role in her biography of her husband.[20]

In articulating the differences between early modern forms and present-day self-representation, and the necessity of bearing these differences in mind in any critical analysis or even description of texts, the comments of Sara Heller Mendelson and Elspeth Graham are particularly helpful. In her consideration of what she calls "serial personal memoranda" from the Stuart period, Mendelson points out that "seventeenth-century memoirs had not yet crystallized into their modern-day forms, the diary and the autobiography. Instead, they represent a continuum from one genre to the other, ranging from the daily journal to a variety of sporadic memoranda."[21] Elspeth Graham concurs, suggesting a useful approach to generic questions: "Rather than attempting to 'sort out' forms by considering what they later become, we should perhaps focus on the significances of fluidity itself . . . It is not surprising . . . in this context of general generic instability, that self-narratives are enormously variable in structure and focus."[22] Hence, at least for the early modern period, some of the quality of discursiveness or fragmentary construction that might be attributed to female authorship or to the particular nature of women's lives may well be a matter of broader generic instability.[23] In my analysis of diaries, annual summaries, memoirs, family and personal narratives, and fantastic self-fashioning, I've found it less helpful to assign individual texts to a particular generic category than to use those categories to understand the contexts in which a text may be read. My goal is not to arrive at an absolute definition of these forms, but rather to notice how individual texts are related, and how distinguished from each other. I'm concerned not just with autobiography as we currently understand it, but also with the autobiographical impulse more broadly understood, with the variety of forms and conceptions for which "modes of self-representation" might be a more accurate designation.

Even as we qualify Jelinek's generalizations about men's and women's lives and the texts they construct, her comments prompt useful questions about what we should be looking for in these autobiographical texts. Are coherence, linearity, consistency, and progressivity especially to be prized or seen as the mark of literary excellence? Should we be looking for literary excellence? Are these literary texts? In fact her assessment should make us more open to a variety of writing, just as we are open to a variety of recorded life experiences. Such openness, vital to the reading of autobiography, is even more essential in the reading of journals and diaries, as we attempt to describe the text and to take account of the reader's response to it. Although these texts were in fact not intended as *belles lettres* by their authors, it is perhaps inevitable that we will look for coherence, unity, and purpose in them, without necessarily assigning a definitive value to such qualities.

As Mendelson points out, a number of the texts I consider predate the categories we associate with autobiography, most especially the spiritual diary and the daily records kept by Hoby and Clifford. But without forcing early modern texts into a procrustean bed, some awareness of the generic possibilities open to these writers is helpful. One of the models available for mid-seventeenth-century autobiography, adopted by both women and men, is the conversion narrative, the account of one's spiritual existence that assumes a particular direction, a plot in which prior experience, often of perceived dissipation or at least of spiritual lethargy and insensitivity, is seen as the prelude to new insight and a new way of life. Since, as Delany points out, the writer of an autobiography must have some reason to believe his or her life worth recounting, such a spiritual transformation supplies that rationale, even, or perhaps especially, for members of the middle or lower classes.[24] Although none of the autobiographies I consider follows this pattern throughout, the account of one's spiritual journey, broadly conceived rather than being defined by a single incident, is important in several of them – as Anne Halkett, although rejecting the notion of a misspent youth, presents a case for her integrity; or as Anne Clifford, coming into her property, celebrates her vindication by the God of Isaiah, Psalms, and Proverbs; or as Lucy Hutchinson sees Providence bringing her and her future husband together. For these writers the spiritual autobiography may be a touchstone rather than a model.

Another frequent justification for writing one's life is the wish to present a family history, to preserve a record of parents or grandparents for the next generation, an enterprise concerned not simply with facts or deeds but with values and principles. This particular rationale dominates the life stories of Fanshawe and Halkett, while in the case of Hutchinson and Cavendish the family addressed is the world at large.[25] In some of these texts, the self is represented primarily as an individual carrying out spiritual obligations; in other cases its significance is seen in relation to the husband and the family whose story the writer preserves; in still others it is more closely linked with a community, justified before the law of the state or of God. In Anne Halkett's autobiography, with its vivid depictions of particular scenes and its assertions of faithful accuracy, there are strong resemblances to such fictional forms as romance or drama. Thus, while early modern texts do not display the generic form that we, on the basis of our own literary experience, might expect, a single text may partake of a number of generic models, models that were available and useful, though not definitive and determinative for early modern women writers.

The amount of recent scholarship devoted to autobiography indicates the importance attached to it and the sophistication with which it is now read. But the question may still persist: why should we read the diaries, memoirs, and self-representations of early modern women? What will we find in them? That the particular texts I have chosen have been published, often in more than one very good modern edition, suggests that although most were never intended for public circulation and waited long to appear, they are a source of considerable interest today. Part of the reason may be rarity or accessibility: since so few diaries by early modern women remain to us, why not choose to transcribe and edit those that are extant? For historians as well as literary scholars, these are very useful sources of information about social conditions, attitudes, and behavior. Yet a number of these texts are both strangely recalcitrant as a source of information and persistently intriguing. This is especially true of the diaries, which, while recording the events of particular days of the writers' lives, also seem to leave so much unsaid.[26] Throughout this study I have asked: what purpose does the diary serve for its author; what assumptions of our own affect or distort our reading? Such questions pertain as well to the longer narratives I consider and even to Cavendish's remarkable fiction, which seems to adhere to few or none of the generic rules familiar to us.

Women readers and critics have been understandably eager to connect with these early writers, to know about the circumstances of their lives, their attitudes and beliefs, the reasons why they wrote. Germaine Greer, for example, expresses the hope that by careful study of earlier authors, we will be able to "grasp what we have in common with the women who have gone our chosen way before us."[27] But therein also lies the difficulty: in our enthusiasm for the rediscovery of the texts and lives of early modern women, we run the risk of confusing their attitudes and aspirations with our own, or at least viewing them not only as forebears but forerunners of who and what we are, seeing them as particularly repressed and perhaps eager to break out of these restraints to join us in a fully empowered existence. As Margaret Ezell asks, "Are we actually seeing all that there is to see in the past, meeting all our relatives, in our genealogical sweeps? Or are we so concerned with establishing continuity that our vision of the life of a woman writer, before 1700 in particular, is exclusive and selective? Have we, to use Jerome McGann's terms, gerrymandered the past in order to support a particular present concept of the woman writer?"[28]

While it is certainly true that early modern women faced cultural assumptions and received hortatory advice at considerable variance from what is in fashion today – amply evidenced in pamphlets, homilies, and works of controversy – and that they were repeatedly urged to modesty and silence, we now know that sixteenth- and seventeenth-century women wrote a good deal and in many forms. Perhaps ironically, two early studies that contributed greatly to our awareness of women's writing – Suzanne Hull's *Chaste, Silent, and Obedient* and Margaret Hannay's *Silent but for the Word* – have to some extent perpetuated in their very titles some of the misconceptions that the authors themselves complicate or challenge.[29] Although Hull emphasizes the limitations on what women were expected or encouraged to read, the lists she provides also indicate the great increase in books for women between 1570 and 1640 (127–39). Hannay's volume demonstrates the ways in which religion, despite a patriarchal bias that silenced women's original speech, also gave them opportunities for expression. Taking the point further, Margaret Ezell contests the idea that seventeenth-century notions of femininity "had sufficient force to control the extent of female participation in the intellectual world and the forms in which women could 'safely' write."[30] And in response to the oft-cited paucity of works by women, she underscores the role of manuscript circulation and correspondence networks for both men and women, noting that a reluctance to see one's work in print was not "a peculiarly female trait, but a manifestation of a much more general, and much older, attitude about writing, printing, and readership."[31] Ezell takes an important step toward seeing seventeenth-century women writers in a historically accurate context, arguing for a definition of private and public more appropriate to the period and urging us to consider the full range of women's writing before 1700, not just those genres congenial to us or those more obviously related to those of subsequent periods.[32]

If, with the help of historically based criticism of seventeenth-century texts, we escape seeing them simply through a particular set of contemporary lenses, we must also guard against another limitation of perspective – reading these texts as transparent, as simply conveying information, without regard to generic shaping or experimentation.[33] While the diaries and autobiographies of early modern women are indeed useful sources of information about their lives, experiences, and attitudes, if we take them simply at face value, we may reach inappropriate conclusions about what these texts say or mean. In the case of Margaret Hoby, for example, we might think that she had no life outside the rigorous devotional practice she records. Or in the case of Ann Fanshawe we might conclude that the daring young woman of the early years "dwindled into a wife," that she had few interests or experiences beyond those connected with supporting her husband as ambassador to Spain and Portugal.

In this study I have considered both the kind of writing, the genre, however unfamiliar it may be to us, and the experience of the text itself; I have tried to encounter each text on its own terms, without being too categorical at the outset about what those terms might be. I have taken into account the sort of generic considerations I've outlined above, while approaching each text on its own, noting its effect on me as a reader. Reading the writing of early modern women, as I might that of early modern men (like Donne, Burton, or Browne), I have asked: what happens to me when I read? What patterns do I find in this text? Are they of my making or the author's? If the author's, where do they come from? If mine, how do these affect or distort my reading? This clearly involves something of a balancing act – being aware of genre without engaging in rigid categorization, and maintaining sensitivity to nuance and detail without losing sight of historical context. But one of the fascinating aspects of this study for me has been the way in which these writers, and I as reader, search for meaning in their lives and in their texts. As Domna Stanton notes, autobiography, because it "can never inscribe the death of the speaking subject . . . [is] necessarily un-ended, incomplete, fragmentary, whatever form of rhetorical closure it might contain."[34] And just as the writer is reading her life as she writes it, so the reader may participate in shaping the text she reads.[35]

From the considerably larger body of possibilities, I have chosen texts by six seventeenth-century English women written over the course of the seventeenth century, from 1599 to roughly 1678. These are the diary of Margaret Hoby, compiled during 1599–1605; the terse diaries and extended annual summaries of Anne Clifford, which begin in 1603 when she was thirteen, and conclude in March 1676 just before her death; the narrative autobiographies of the royalists Anne Murray Halkett and Ann Harrison Fanshawe, written c. 1676–78; the brief life of Lucy Hutchinson, a fragment unpublished in her lifetime, set against her comprehensive life of her husband (c. 1674), in which she plays a part not adequately indicated by the number of pages devoted to it; and Margaret Cavendish's several self-representations – in the *True Relation of My Birth, Breeding and Life* (1656) and the science-fiction fantasy *The Blazing World* (1666). These texts display an array of strategies for self-understanding and self-presentation. Taken together, they trace a progression from fairly factual documentation of events to more consistent and conceptualized narratives, to extravagant and romantic self-depiction and self-construction. While there were diaries late in the period and life stories earlier than those I consider, nevertheless the movement toward a stronger sense of self and a willingness to put oneself – or some version thereof – in a prominent position in a text, even if not intended immediately for publication, is striking. It suggests not only the increasing variety and complexity of women's self-representation but also its increasing decisiveness and even flamboyance.[36]

The first text, the diary of the Puritan Lady Margaret Hoby, is the very reverse of confessional. Early in her third marriage Hoby began keeping a record of her spiritual observances – prayer, devotional reading, conversations with her chaplain, useful activities – a record so dense and complete that it nearly crowds out all secular activities. Part of my project here is understanding genre and purpose – but also attempting to get a picture of Hoby's life experience through the diary's very specific focus. Hoby details the occasions but not the content of her spiritual life, and yet, if one persists, the text conveys a sense of its author, her independence and interdependence. The diary of Lady Anne Clifford, although in some ways equally restrained, conveys the greater breadth of the writer's activities and interests; like Hoby's, it records daily events in brief notes rather than narrative form, yet it creates a far stronger sense of an inner life. The juxtaposition of Clifford's earlier and later writing highlights the differences in form and effect in two kinds of self-representation – the tersely dramatic entries of 1616–19 when she was under extreme pressure to give up claim to her inheritance, and the narrative summaries compiled for the years 1650–75, when, as Dowager Countess of Dorset, Pembroke, and Montgomery, Clifford took full possession of her northern castles. Both demonstrate Anne Clifford's vigorous attempts to control textual and material circumstances, and the writing itself is so constant a part of her experience that it shapes not only our understanding of her but her life itself.

The next four texts – those by Lucy Hutchinson, Anne Halkett, Ann Fanshawe, and Margaret Cavendish – are all more fully developed narratives than these early diaries and are properly termed autobiographies or autobiographical fragments. Although varying greatly in scope, style, and persona, they are usually longer, more coherent, and to some extent more focused, even more tendentious, than the diaries of Hoby and Clifford. Hutchinson appears both in an autobiographical fragment and in her account of the life of her husband; in each case she places herself in a larger context that justifies her narrative and lends it weight. Anne Murray Halkett's account, perhaps the most interesting in its own right, combines a remarkable range of narrative material and conceptions – from the familial and religious to the romantic and dramatic – as she strongly asserts the integrity of her actions. Ann Fanshawe, whose life seems to have been rich with adventure, juxtaposes such scenes with others considerably more prosaic, as she represents herself maturing into the role of a wife. Margaret Cavendish's autobiographical sketch *A True Relation,* although it precedes her biography of her husband by eleven years, places her throughout in the context of marital and familial relations on the one hand and the watching world on the other. Cavendish returns in the fantasy of *The Blazing World* to embody all her wishes in print.

Since the texts I discuss range from the sometimes painfully factual to the extravagantly inventive, I have been concerned with the various strategies by which they are shaped; and since a number of the autobiographical narratives strongly resemble passages of fiction, I have found it appropriate to look beyond life-writing for the models or conceptions that may have inspired them. As William J. Howarth asserts, autobiography is a self-portrait in which the author simultaneously poses and paints; "autobiography is thus hardly 'factual,' 'unimaginative,' or even 'nonfictional,' for it welcomes all the devices of skilled narration and observes none of the restrictions – accuracy, impartiality, inclusiveness – imposed upon other forms of historical literature."[37] It would be hard to overstate the difference between the two texts that begin and end this book – the realm of fact and spiritual observance in Hoby's diary, and the realm of invention in which Cavendish stars in multiple roles. In one text the self as we presently understand it is barely evident; in the other, the writer engages in a lavish self-presentation that involves fictional characters, wit and satire, self-indulgence and self-display. And yet in both, as throughout this book, I want to trace the connection between the self and the representation of that self, the autobiographical impulse in a wide variety of forms, from stubborn fact to wildest fancy. In so doing I find a continuum that represents the range of possibilities for self-fashioning and demonstrates the development of women's writing within the seventeenth century.

Although one might conclude from this study (as from others of male authors of the period) that "autobiography was in its infancy," to speak in those terms is to assume a particular end, and to see other kinds of texts as partial and perhaps only partially successful. I began my study inductively, eager to know what kinds of texts existed, but I quickly gained an appreciation of each of them in its own terms: some are marked by enigmatic pithiness and restraint, others by detail and richness; some insist or dwell on fact, others create drama and revel in fiction. If I came armed with a sensibility born of the twentieth century, a set of expectations that influence what I find when I read, I have also become aware of ways in which these writers are themselves shaping their work, using sometimes quite formal or rigid patterns, at other times more thematic or generic ones. Without blurring the lines between writer and reader, it has seemed to me that we are engaged in parallel tasks. The seventeenth-century writers of diaries and autobiographical texts were striving to record but also to comprehend their daily lives and their place in the larger scheme of things. They themselves engaged in acts of memory and of interpretation, even of argument and dramatic presentation. And the reader, confronted with texts that are uneven, ranging from the pedestrian to the exotic, sometimes physically fragmented, sometimes obscure and elliptical, also looks for structure and meaning. This is not a matter of conscious expectation (since I have learned not to expect of the seventeenth century what the intervening centuries have produced) but rather a habit of mind, a tendency to look for pattern, to move from the parts to the whole. And so, as I have outlined in the chapters to come, the pleasures of these texts are in what they reveal – about the lives, the thoughts, the formal possibilities and constraints of seventeenth-century women writers – and in what they conceal. The pleasures of finding – and of seeking – are here in rich measure.

CHAPTER I

Margaret Hoby: the stewardship of time

The diary of Lady Margaret Hoby is the earliest, and in many ways the least fully developed of the texts I consider; at times simply a sketch of her daily activities and religious observance, it is at the other end of the scale from the narratives with which I conclude this study. For the historian as well as the literary scholar, diaries are very useful sources of information about social conditions, attitudes, and actions. But Margaret Hoby's text, for all that it may convey about the life of a woman of her era, is both strangely resistant as a source of information and yet persistently and curiously intriguing. Since Hoby's diary is so different from anything that might bear that title today, it raises important questions about genre itself.[1] I want to consider what this text tells us, in the most direct and factual of terms, and, equally fascinating, what it withholds.[2]

Margaret Hoby, born to Thomasine and Arthur Dakins in 1571, received her education in the strongly Puritan household of the Countess of Huntingdon.[3] She was married three times: first at the age of eighteen to Walter Devereux, brother of Robert, Earl of Essex; second, after his death in 1591, to Thomas Sidney, brother of Sir Philip Sidney and Mary Sidney, Countess of Pembroke; and finally, after Sidney's death in July 1595, to Sir Thomas Posthumous Hoby, who had been an eager suitor four years earlier.[4] Much of the interest in Margaret Dakins's hand may be attributed to her considerable inheritance, which included the manor of Hackness and surrounding property in the predominantly Roman Catholic East Riding of Yorkshire, where she and her husbands lived.[5] During the years 1599–1605 Margaret Hoby compiled a diary, quite certainly not intended for publication or wider distribution, which is now preserved in the British Library.[6] Although most of the manuscript is in good condition, the first page and the last two are torn, making it impossible to know just how much is missing. Nevertheless, the dates of the remaining manuscript suggest, intriguingly, that Margaret Hoby began keeping a diary on the third anniversary of her marriage to her third husband, and continued to that date six years later.

Besides missing an indeterminate amount of material, the diary is partial in another sense as well. Despite the title of the most recent edition, *The Private Life of an Elizabethan Lady: The Diary of Lady Margaret Hoby 1599– 1605*, it offers remarkably little intimate revelation. Lady Hoby's diary was not a place for her to tell all; it contains almost no expression of feelings or attitudes; it seems personal only in the sense of providing a record of her daily activities, devotional, domestic, and social.[7] Nor does it resemble the meditative poetry and prose of her near contemporaries, for example the intensely introspective reflections of Donne's *Devotions upon Emergent Occasions*, which places his illness in the context of the sickness of sin, or George Herbert's *The Temple*, described by its author as "a picture of the many spiritual Conflicts that have past betwixt God and my Soul, before I could subject mine to the will of Jesus my Master."[8]

Margaret Hoby's is a spiritual diary, not in the sense of recording the content of her spiritual exercises but rather their very existence. In other words, it is a form of self-monitoring, of record keeping apparently undertaken as a spur to devotional observance.[9] Sara Heller Mendelson, in a very helpful account of the writing associated with godly self-examination, notes some key features of the genre, taking as one example John Featley's *A Fountain of Tears* (1646), which includes

a list of thirty-eight questions for women to ask themselves each night before going to sleep, in order to scrutinize every aspect of the day's activities.

At what time . . . did I arise from my bed?
What first did I?
How devoutly prayed I?
What Scripture read I?

The catechism continues through the day's household business, dinner, company, recreation ('Was it not affected with too much delight?'), to the final evening prayers. When we look at actual female spiritual diaries, we can watch their authors ticking off these points one by one.[10]

Many of the entries in Margaret Hoby's diary fit just this pattern, so much so that an example might be chosen almost at random. Here, for instance, is the first complete entry for a weekday, that of August 13, 1599:

In the Morninge after priuat praiers and order taken for diner, I wrett some notes in my testament tell :10: a clock : then I went to walk, and, after I retourned home, I praied priuatly, read a chapter of the bible, and wrought tell dinner time : after I walked a whill with Mr Rhodes and Then I wrought, and did som things about the house tell :4: then I wrett out the sarmon into my book preached the day before, and, when I had again gone about in the house and giuen order for supper and other thinges, I retourned to examination and praier : then I walked tell supper time, and, after Catichisinge, medetated awhill of that I had hard, with mourninge to god for pardon both of my omition and Commition wherin I found my selfe guilte, I went to bed."

Or the entry for October 5, 1599:

After priuat praier I went about the house, then I wrett notes in my testement : then Mr Hoby Came home, with whom I talked tell diner time: after diner I was busie about presaruing quinces, and, a Litle before supper time, I walked about the house: then I examened my selfe and praied, then I went to supper : after to the lector, and, sonne after that, to bed[.]

Or the entry for July 24, 1600:

After priuat praers I wrett in my testement and reed : after, I went about and wrought, and, when I had Called vpon god, I went to diner : after, I went to work and then I went about the house, hard Mr Rhodes read, and, after I had walked a whill, I went to priautt medetation and praier : after, I went to supper, then to the lecture : after, I wrett to Mrs Carington, and then I praied and went to bed[.]'[12]

These entries differ in some respects from those recommended by Featley: they are less specific about the time of arising, the particular passage of scripture read, the content of other reading, and even the degree of energy or devotion involved in prayer and self-examination. But we can glean this information from some of the earliest entries, which tend to be more specific than later ones. For example, August 15, 1599: "In the morninge at :6: a clock I praied priuatly"; or August 14: "In the morning I praied priuatly and wrett notes in [page torn] tement tell :7: a clocke : then I took order to diuers thinges touchinge the house, and, after I had brekfast . . . " Margaret Hoby does not usually detail the content of her reading, though she mentions it often enough that we have a good sense of it. There are references to Thomas Cartwright, scholar and popular Puritan preacher; to George Gifford's sermons on the Song of Solomon; and to a host of other similarly inclined preachers and scholars – Richard Greenham, Hugh Broughton, Hugh Latimer, and Foxe's ever popular *Book of Martyrs*.

Nor does Margaret Hoby normally detail the specifics of her prayer life, although the earliest pages of the diary suggest this form of self-examination as a chief motivating factor in her writing.[13] The very first entry, on a page partially torn away, reads: "day was deadnes in praier, and my greatest offence was want of sorow for the same: the Lord of his mercie increase true and fervant mourninge vnto god that he neuer take his spiritt from me amen amen." Subsequent entries continue this concern with the quality of her spiritual observance: on August 20, she found herself "lackinge in performing my dutie" in "priuat praier and examination"; on August 26 she reports, "this day, as euer, the diuell laboreth to hinder my profittable hearinge of the word and callinge vpon god"; and on September 14, she prays, "Lord, for Christs sack, pardone my drousenes which, with a neclegent mind, caused me to ommitt that medetation of that I had hard, which I ought to haue had."

But beyond these comments on the quality of her meditations, particularly marked in the early months, Margaret Hoby provides almost no information about its content. Her extensive reading in scripture and religious texts is notably interactive, accompanied by a good deal of writing, not only in the diary itself, but apparently also in the margins of scripture, as we see in the frequent comment, "[I] went to praier and to writ som notes in my testament" (Aug. 10, 1599), or "I wrett notes into my bible" (Aug. 12, 1599; the terms "bible" and "testament" are used nearly interchangeably here). Hoby's "testament" has not survived, but these references convey the sense of her reading as a form of dialogue, as she recalls and summarizes, notes particular passages, and responds. Hoby uses the familiar formulas of the Church and the *Book of Common Prayer* in her self-examination.[14] She records that after reading from the Bible "I returned in to my hart, examenid my selfe, and Craued pardon for my severall ommitions and Comitions" (Oct. 7, 1599). And like others of her generation she considers both bodily illness and spiritual weakness as the consequence of a spiritual fault: "I . . . neclected my custom of praier, for which, as for many other sinnes, it pleased the Lord to punishe me with an Inward assalte" (Sept. 10, 1599); "I went to priuat praier : and, hauinge supped, I was at publeck praers very sicke : the Lord pardon the sinne for which I was so punished, it beinge the will of god often to punishe one sinne with another, for I had Litle proffet by that praier, by reasone of my sicknes" (Sept. 19, 1599).

Although Hoby may well have begun her diary as an aid to self-examination, this model accurately describes only part of the existing text. For while the initial impulse was clearly to compile a spiritual record as part of an exercise of devotion, the latter sections of the diary are almost entirely a listing of events. In contrast to the entries of the early years, which record the minutiae of daily existence, the occasions if not the content of spiritual observance, the later entries record the noteworthy or extraordinary events of secular life:

On February 2, 1602:

this day I made a dinner for some of our neighbours : and my Mother, w^t Mr Mills and his wiffe, was there Likewise, who Came the night before to my Mother.

Or March 26, 1603:

this day, beinge the Lordes day, was the death of the Quene published, and our now kinge Iames of Scotland proclaimd kinge to sucseede hir : god semd him a long and Hapie Raing, amen.

Whereas earlier sections of the diary painstakingly record the perform-ance of daily spiritual exercises, later sections resort to a shorthand summary, as for example on August 8, 1602, " *The Lordes day the :8: day.* This day, I praise god, I hard all the exercises w^t good health" (in contrast to a previous Sunday, which reads, "I praise god I hard all the exercises, although I was not verie well"). In this time of scanty notation, the latter part of 1602, which includes only fifteen entries for the last four months of the year, still reflects a strong interest in the quality of her spiritual experience.[15] On October 31 (the eve of All Saints' Day and a Sunday), she records, "thIs day I hard the exercises, not so affected as I ought, and at night went to priuatt praier : some new quickeninge." By contrast the whole of November receives only one entry: "all this moneth, I praied [praise?] god, I haue had my health, and inioyed much Quiatt"; and the month of December only two – one recording a marriage and the other, an acquittal for coining and a hanging for the same offense.

How then to characterize this text? Is there a genre into which it fits, and to what extent is such a genre adequate or helpful? From what I have said above, it seems clear that this is neither simply a spiritual diary nor a record of events, but two kinds of diary conjoined, with one fading imperceptibly, if unevenly, into the other. Neither category will provide a sufficient model for what we find, nor do we have any definitive explanation for the change in type, despite the sensible statement of Joanna Moody: "We can never really know what it was that prompted her enthusiasm for the daily reckoning which begins in August 1599, nor can we know if this was the only diary Lady Hoby kept. However, the fact that the emphasis shifts over time to a simple record of routine existence hints at a private inner life conflicting with, and finally giving in to, the demands of household and of a wider world."[16] But as with most issues concerning the diary, we have too little evidence to assert such a conflict – beyond the commonly felt tension between public and private, inner and outer, active and contemplative life. In fact, as Elspeth Graham suggests, in the diary of Margaret Hoby the movement from spiritual to secular activities may be the less significant because "there is no absolute difference between spiritual and social aspects of virtuous femininity."[17] Indeed, as Graham further argues, the "juxtaposition of references to her religious duties with the details of secular aspects of her life implies an integration of the spiritual into a daily routine" (226).

Yet while the shift in emphasis over the course of the diary is clear, my present concern is less with the reasons for the change than with a way to read this text, a method that informs us without distorting the original, a mode of inquiry that allows for its genre without answering all questions about it in terms of genre. But there is a second question: what is the value of an elliptical, terse, repetitive, and generally unexceptional account of the daily life of a woman who lived four hundred years ago? To be sure, Hoby's diary provides a good deal of information on her skills and responsibilities, her degree of independent action, her religious attitudes, her use of time: all of these are of particular interest to the social historian.[18] But to press a little further, what is the appeal of this text as text; why, beyond its historical interest, would anyone read it? Or, to put it another way, why should I be drawn to Margaret Hoby's diary while the second volume of the Countess of Montgomerie's *Urania* remains on the shelf? It seems to me that part of the fascination of Hoby's text is not just what it reveals, but what it hides. It offers two quite contradictory pleasures, that of transparency and that of concealment.[19]

First, the matter of transparency: Hoby's diary is documentary evidence of daily life at the transition from Elizabethan to Jacobean England. Although limited to the life of a single individual, it gives a great deal of information about habits and types of reading, religious attitudes and frequency of worship, agriculture, housekeeping duties and practices, responsibilities on the estate, social encounters and relationships, law suits, travel, health and treatment of diseases, and many other areas of life. We learn how long it took to get to London; how often Margaret Hoby visited her mother or her physician; how often she went to church and sometimes what she thought of the sermon; how late the roses bloomed in Yorkshire in 1603; and that the lady of the manor assisted in the preserving of quinces and sweet meats, and in the making of rush lights; that she collected rents, paid wages, helped her husband determine the location of cottages, tended to the sick in her vicinity, assisted at childbirth, oversaw workmen, made sure the granary was ready to receive the harvest, gathered apples, worked in her garden; that she spent, like others of her generation, countless hours in needlework; but also that she enjoyed walking, bowling, fishing, and even the odd picnic in the fields.

Still, perhaps as intriguing as the information Margaret Hoby's diary conveys is the information it seems to withhold, or the questions it leaves us with. Somehow the very (apparent) completeness of the account must leave us puzzled. How in a typical day, so filled with prayer, worship, and the reading of religious texts, did she get anything *done?*[20] What in fact is the distribution of time between work and prayer? Why, in a text that records so much, is there so very little evidence of an interior life? Did Margaret Hoby ever feel anything? Did anything ever disturb the regular exercises she set herself or the relative equanimity that results?[21] For Friday, December 28, 1599, Hoby records:

After priuat praers I did eate my breakfast, then I went to church : after I Came home I was busie tell dinner time, then I tooke the Aire abroad, and, after my Cominge home, I went about the house, talked a whill, and then I examened my selfe and praied : then I went to supper : after, to the publece praers and examenation of the Morninge sarmon : after, I wrett to my mother, then I praied, and so went to bed:

Or Monday, October 29, 1599:

After priuat praier I did eate my breakfast, then I did go about the house tell allmost diner time, then I praied and then dined : after I had rested a while, I wrett my sermone, and then took a Lector, and, after, I hard praier and a Lecttor, because, in regard of mens dullnes after meat and being winter, it was thought more conuenient to be before supper : after, I praied priuatly and then of the testement and so went to bed:

Reading this text forces a confrontation between Margaret Hoby's practices and expectations and ours. Her daily life (need I say it?) involved private prayer before breakfast, reading of scripture, frequent reading of sermons or other religious material, public prayer and self-examination. She attended two formal services of worship on Sundays, and occasionally on other weekdays; she recorded the essence of those sermons and wrote responses to her reading of biblical passages. Precisely because these are not part of the experience of most of her present readers, we are more likely to be struck, possibly even thunderstruck, by the repetition of these events and practices. In no other text am I so often tempted to speak of "an example chosen at random," since a hasty glance suggests a kind of numbing uniformity in the entries. Expecting from a diary the unusual, the personal, the event or emotion that sets one day apart from the next, we are the more impressed by what seems an endless repetition of the mundane and trivial. Here, of course, the generic expectation can help us – the reminder that the diary is an aid to spiritual discipline rather than an end in itself, that it records the performance of duty rather than reflecting the experience that resulted. What may strike the modern reader as excessive, useless, tedious, repetitious, or perverse is in fact a sign of order, stability, and meaning in Margaret Hoby's life, yet it may even, paradoxically, be a source of strength for her and an attraction for us.[22] Trying to place the function, if not the significance, of this careful record-keeping, we might look for analogous models in our own lives: the daily newspapers that record, besides more variable events, the rising and setting of the sun and the phases of the moon (even though these repeat yearly and monthly); the tide tables; the daily horoscope; or perhaps closer to the personal experience of some, the weight-watcher's diary, recording the number of points or calories for a given day, or the weblog, containing minutiae of scant interest to other readers. All these are contemporary forms of monitoring, contributing in varying degrees to an awareness of one's environment or to a sense of control of one's life.[23] And of course the order here is that of spiritual discipline, a form of observance analogous to the monastic life, practiced by the administrator of a large household.

Margaret Hoby's diary exists not to record her emotions but rather the way in which she spends her time, and our sense that she has filled her diary, and her life, with an endless round of prayer and work means that she has succeeded: she attempts to give a faithful accounting of her time, to show that no moment was wasted, that it was spent either in work or in devotion.[24] The entry for December 28, 1599, cited above, in which she was "busie tell dinner time" suggests the norm of useful household activity, in contrast to the rare moments, duly recorded, in which she felt she had wasted time.[25] The very sequential listing of activities, as well as the relative balance of work and devotion in this entry, is both typical and exemplary:

After I was redie I betooke my selfe to priuat praier, wherin it pleased the Lord to Deall mercifully: after, I went about the house, and instructed Tomson wiffe in som principles of relegion, and then eate my breakfast, and then walked abroad tell all most :11: of the Clock : and after I had read :2: chapters of the bible, I went to diner : after dinner I went to worke, at which [*page torn*] Contenewed tell :4:, then I took order for supper [*page torn*] went to praier and to writ som notes in my testament, from which I was Called to walk with Mr Hoby, talkinge of sundrie busines, and so to supper : imediately after praer and Lector, for the diligent attencion of which the Lord did heare my praier by remouing all wanderinges which vse to hvrt me so that I receiued much Comfort, I went to bed. (Aug. 10, 1599)

Where we might find an imbalance of the sacred and the secular, Margaret Hoby's attitude, as conveyed by the sequential listing of prayer, church, prayer, meals, work, reading, etc. – the unbroken round of activities – suggests that the two are coequal aspects of her existence, dual forms of devotion and service.[26] If Margaret Hoby had lived a century earlier, the ordering of her life might have been more obviously external; had she been a member of a sequestered religious community, the hours of prayer and of work (*ora et labora*) would have been strictly prescribed and jointly observed.[27] Her attempts to create such a structure while managing a large household and engaging in the affairs of the world are perhaps in some sense the more striking and the more strenuous. And indeed the relatively few personal comments in her diary often deal precisely with the balance of work and prayer, the quality of her devotional life, as she records the conversations that, though pleasant, were useless; the illness that kept her from the usual time of prayer; the generic description of something as "nesesarie busenes" (Mar. 29, 1600); her decision (May 4, 1600) to "eate som thinge before supper beinge verie emptie, which, of purpos, I vse to doe, that I may be the fitter to heare [prayers and meditation]"; or her resolve after an afternoon of "idle conversation": "both my selfe did talk and heare of more worldly mattres then, by godes assistance, I will here after willingly doe" (Aug. 19, 1599).

In this as in all other texts, syntax creates meaning and strongly influences our perceptions. In the life of Margaret Hoby no event is unconnected with any other event. In the act of recording, through a series of *afters* and *thens*, she places all experience under the examining eye of spiritual discipline. From her rising in the morning to her going to bed, each of her actions is scrutinized, placed in daily accounting, linked to the next. And while the reader searches for a moment of time not taken up with work or prayer, Margaret Hoby works to construct a record and indeed a life that includes *no* moment *not* taken up with work or prayer. Hoby's diary is in the plainest of styles; it appears direct, unmediated, and unpremeditated. It is strangely devoid of emotion or personal revelation. It has little to recommend it as a literary text. And yet, I submit, there is something intriguing about it. For although the individual entries are strikingly similar, clearly members of the same species, they are nevertheless varied, reflecting Hoby's attempts to shape her life after a pattern, after a series of questions like those offered by Featley. In fact, the organization of the entries, the plain, unelaborated, sequential style, has the quality of a litany itself, making the daily entries sound like a series of only slightly varied petitions in a very long prayer.

> In the morninge, after priuat praier, I Reed of the bible, and then wrought tell 8: a clock, and then I eate my breakfast : after which done, I walked in to the feeldes tell: 10 a clock, then I praied, and, not long after, I went to dinner; and about one a clock I geathered my Apeles tell :4:, then I Cam home, and wrought tell almost :6:, and then I went to priuat praier and examenation, in which it pleased the lord to blesse me : and besiech the lord, for christ his sack, to increase the power of this spirite in me daly Amen Amen : tell supper time I hard Mr Rhodes read of Cartwright, and, sonne after supper, I went to prairs, after which I wrett to Mr Hoby, and so to bed. (Aug. 28, 1599)

Although this text seems light years away from Donne's intensely personal, rhetorically sophisticated, and elaborate self-analysis in the *Devotions upon Emergent Occasions*, both share the notion that the daily activities of the subject are worth recording. Donne recounts his experience with a host of questions and a wealth of biblical quotations and literary context; Margaret Hoby simply records her daily life; but for both writers the subject's life in this world merits close attention. In contrast to the kind of spiritual autobiography shaped by a dramatic experience or a distant goal, Hoby's diary is concerned with and faithful to the moment.[28]

Why read this diary? Is there anything remotely pleasurable about the experience? And is there anything remotely literary about this text? I can only attest to my own encounter with this material: for purposes of illustration, any entry will do; on first glance they are all alike. But some are more heavily devotional than others, some days more filled with domestic labor, others with social or devotional work. And although the series of events is regular, it is by no means identical from day to day; the very attempt to find the pattern reveals the variations; the search for variations documents the pattern. Part of what I take to be the pleasure in reading this text may result from the slight variations, in the rhythms of the litany, in the kind of seamless linking of events that implies a thread of meaning and intent running through them. Paradoxically, then, in an account that is in some ways maddeningly incomplete, one of the pleasures may be completeness: the sense that every moment is, according to the writer's view of things, accounted for; the sense of the rhythm of a life that begins and ends with prayer.

In one sense Hoby tells all, in that she leaves no moment unrecorded. But in a life in which so little seems to vary – since the daily routine of religious devotion underlies all – minute deviations assume greater importance. For while Margaret Hoby emphasizes one kind of activity – private prayer, public prayer, listening to, recording, rethinking sermons or other religious texts, instructing the members of her household – the curious modern reader is particularly eager to note other aspects of her life – her duties on the estate; the extent of her responsibilities; her relations with her husband, her mother, her neighbors; the degree of her personal freedom of thought and action. And so, oddly, the pleasure of reading Hoby also consists in ferreting out the little bits of information that give a sense of her larger life. At first these are few and far between: days seem to pass with almost no variation. But this is hardly the case: a list of Lady Hoby's activities soon gives a lively sense of the breadth of her work. Within the first month we hear that she was "busie in the graniry," gathered apples, wound yarn, assisted in childbirth, dispatched a messenger to Linton (her mother's residence), and consulted with her husband about "the best places where Cotiges might be builded" (Aug. 20, 1599).

In contrast to Lady Anne Clifford, whose diary I shall consider next, Margaret Hoby lived in a manor house given to her and her first husband on their marriage;[29] although Sir Thomas Hoby outlived his wife, she had survived her first two husbands and hence was the most permanent administrator of the estate. Many of her duties are supervisory – making sure that all is ready for the harvest, overseeing those she describes as "my workmen," as well as "Mr Hobes workmen" (June 3, 1600); measuring "some Corne to know what prouision we had" (Aug. 1, 1600). She consults with the new miller, supervises haymakers, plowmen, woodcutters, and her maids; she frequently pays bills and receives rents and tithes. In London, it is she who lays in a supply of wood in late October. She also joins in the domestic and agricultural labors of the estate – preserving quinces, damson plums, and sweetmeats; distilling rose water and aqua vitae; making candles; dyeing cloth; she sows (or supervises the sowing of) wheat and rye; works in the garden; and sees to her honey and bees. Other entries are more general, signifying multiple supervisory activities: frequently she "went about the house" (presumably to oversee and give orders), or "tooke order for diuers thinges touchinge the house" (Aug. 14, 1599). Like all women of her generation she spent a good deal of time in needlework, the activity so common that it was simply called "work," frequently accompanied by other activities such as conversation or reading aloud.

Besides such general managerial tasks Margaret Hoby bore a large share of responsibility for the well-being – physical and spiritual – of the members of the household and neighborhood. While she could travel to York to consult a physician, she herself seems to have been the most sought-after and experienced medical practitioner around: she assists at childbirth, dresses the wounds of a seriously injured workman, prepares purges and herbal treatments, and in a sadly hopeless case is called to try to save an infant "who had no fundement, and had no passage for excrementes but att the Mouth" (August 26, 1601). Such medical skill was not unusual among women of her time and station, as the work of Lady Grace Mildmay and Lady Anne Halkett attests,[30] but these activities as healer are also intimately connected with her devotional life. In fact one wonders whether the sudden increase in medical ministrations in February of 1600 is the result of an epidemic of wounds and sores at Hackness, or of Margaret Hoby's heightened sense of such service as a form of devotion. On January 30, 1599/1600, she records:

After I had praied priuatly I dressed apoore boies legge that Came to me, and then brake my fast wth Mr Hoby : after, I dressed the hand of one of our seruants that was verie sore Cutt, and after I wrett in my testement notes Vpon James : then I went about the doinge of some thinges in the house, paiynge of billes, and, after I had talked with Mr Hoby, I went to examenation and praier, after to supper, then to the lector : after that I dressed one of the mens handes that was hurt, lastly praied, and so to bed:

The biblical epistle of James, mentioned in this entry, is concerned particularly with the charitable duties of the Christian, with emphasis on help for the unfortunate: "Pure religion and undefiled before God and the Father is this, To visit the fatherless and widows in their affliction, and to keep himself unspotted from the world" (James 1:27). This epistle also stresses the importance of good works as a defining quality of faith:

What doth it profit, my brethren, though a man say he hath faith, and have not works? Can faith save him? If a brother or sister be naked, and destitute of daily food, And one of you say unto them, Depart in peace, be ye warmed and filled; notwithstanding ye give them not those things which are needful to the body; what doth it profit? Even so faith, if it hath not works, is dead, being alone. Yea, a man may say, Thou hast faith, and I have works: shew me thy faith without thy works, and I will shew thee my faith by my works . . . For as the body without the spirit is dead, so faith without works is dead also. (James 2:14–18, 26)

It may of course be a coincidence, or an awareness of her duty prompted by the injury of one of the estate's more important servants (Moody, 58n

114), but for three weeks Margaret Hoby lists the dressing of wounds among her daily activities. On February 11, 1600, she adds to these activities the preparation of food ("meate") for Mr. Procter, who is ill, and on February 20 she visits him; both these benevolent acts are in accord with Christ's instructions to his disciples in Matthew 25:35–45 to visit those who are sick and in prison.

Clearly Margaret Hoby's life as mistress of the estate involved a good deal of labor and responsibility. The same may be said of her religious experience. While Lady Hoby's devotional life might be regarded as evidence of conformity to a presumably patriarchal system, it is in fact a realm in which she shows considerable freedom and independence.[31] Her own devotion is supported by the frequent attention of her chaplain Richard Rhodes. He prays with her at times privately, and presumably officiates at the household's daily public prayers (June 7, 1600); he reads, either from scripture or books of sermons or theology (Grenham, Perkins, Cartwright, Babington, etc., even "of the princples of poperie out of one of their owne bookes"; May 16, 1600).[32] There are far more references to solitary conversations with Mr. Rhodes than to those with him and her husband, a fact that suggests a relatively independent intellectual and spiritual life: "After priuat praier I talked a while with Mr. Rhodes, then I did eate my breakfast," she records on November 1, 1599; or "after the Lector I hard Helurn read of the Book of marters, and taked with Mr Rhodes, and so went to bed" (Oct. 1, 1599); "I sawe some thinges done in the house : after, I wret notes in my bible, then I praied with Mr Rhodes" (Sept. 29, 1599). It may be that the cessation of the diary is connected with Mr. Rhodes' departure from the household.[33]

This change in the diary's emphasis and the frequent mention of Rhodes as a partner in reading or conversation have led some critics to speculate about the intimacy of the relationship between Margaret Hoby and Richard Rhodes. Diane Willen describes Hoby as "emotionally dependent on her chaplain" and "perhaps [seeking] to compensate for a less than satisfactory marriage" (571); she cites Patrick Collinson's reference to "the spiritually intimate dealings – one is tempted to call them affairs – between women of the leisured classes and certain popular and pastorally gifted divines."[34] In such a case one form of domination or dependence might replace another. Even the usually cautious Dorothy Meads wonders whether the "vague but oft-mentioned 'temptation'" of the diary "materialized for Margaret, not yet thirty, in the form of Richard Rhodes and young William Eure" (267). We shall of course never know the answer to this question. To her credit, Lamb considers the evidence but refrains from concluding more than it allows, noting that if Margaret Hoby "felt sexual tension with Mr. Rhodes, his presence did not seem to cause marital strain" (84). Yet Lamb does find competition of a different sort: "in her diary as a whole, Hoby defined her Self – her inner truth – through religious discourses much more than through her marriage relationship." Her "collaborative enterprise of discerning her election [undertaken with Rhodes] was more absorbing, and more ultimately meaningful, than marriage" (85).

This speculation, though understandable in a text that yields so little information about the writer's emotional and psychological state, also points to the difficulty we face in applying twenty-first-century categories to seventeenth-century experience. Our privileging of the sexual and psychological is likely to distort texts whose primary emphasis is on the spiritual and factual. For example, Lamb's gloss on the entry of September 1, 1599 ("I praied priuat with Mr Rhodes, wherin I had more comfort then ever I receiued in my Life before, I praise god") – "This spiritual intimacy provided her immense gratification" – may attribute an erotic content to what was in fact spiritual comfort, a category more easily grasped by Hoby's contemporaries than by us.[35] In fact this instance of the difficulty of interpretation – and the temptation of over-interpretation – is a problem with the diary more generally, a point I'll have more to say about later.

In her pious household, Margaret Hoby also assumed primary responsibility for the religious instruction of her servants.[36] The first complete entry in the diary records that she "instructed Tomson wiffe in som principles of relegion." And two weeks later, "Mr Rhodes and my selfe had som speach with the poore and Ignorant of the som princeples of religion" (Aug. 22, 1599). She listens to him catechize or takes a more active role, as when she talks "with a yonge papest maide" (Feb. 24, 1600), presumably with the intention of conversion, or reads "till church time, to a sicke maid in my house" (May 24, 1601); she talks with a woman who has lived incestuously with her husband, prays with a neighbor, offers John Brown the best counsel that she can, and visits Mrs. Munkman "who was sore aflicted in minde" (Jan. 20, 1604). Both publicly and privately she fosters the spiritual life of the household – taking notes on the sermon, reading scriptures, writing in her sermon book and in her testament, hearing "the Lector" (presumably the reading of either scriptural passages or such texts as Foxe's *Book of Martyrs* or Gifford on the Song of Solomon). In their strongly Protestant household in a Catholic district, Margaret and Thomas Hoby further the public and domestic aspects of Protestantism: while he goes to search out recusants, she maintains daily worship, reading of appropriate texts, and suitable conversation and instruction at home.

Margaret Hoby was not only mistress of her household but also of her spiritual life. The texts she chose to hear are intellectually challenging, and her preference for them, presumably the result of her upbringing in the household of the Countess of Huntingdon, reflects her own attitudes. While she regularly attended two worship services on Sunday, her several visits to London allowed her to enrich her daily devotions with a choice of preachers. She went, for example, to Westminster Abbey in the morning and, when the weather and her health allowed it, by boat to Black Friars (the parish of her mother-in-law, the formidable Lady Russell) to hear Mr. Egerton preach.[37] We also see her forming independent judgments of what she hears, finding "nothinge worth the notinge" in a sermon at Westminster Abbey (Oct. 28, 1600) and discerning a "faulse possion" [position] in one at York Minster (Apr. 13, 1600); she preferred instead the "godly preacher, Mr wilson," whom she heard at York Minster on April 16, 1600.[38] There are indications of individual struggles of conscience. On May 6, 1600, she expresses her reluctance to be a witness at baptism, even as a courtesy to a friend, and three days later, she records, "I walked with Mr Hoby and Mr Rhodes, and talked touchinge baptismie," presumably trying to make up her mind on this theological point.[39]

If the diary raises questions for some about Margaret Hoby's feelings for her chaplain, it also supplies no definitive picture of the relationship between Margaret Hoby and her husband. We know that she was originally far from enthusiastic about the match: Thomas Hoby had pursued Margaret when she was the widow of Walter Devereux, but was beaten out by the agility of the Sidneys and their powerful allies the Huntingdons.[40] And she appears to have married him in part as a way to resolve financial difficulties remaining from her second marriage.[41] Yet much in the diary suggests a good working relationship, with frequent consultations between two people who are in effect partners in the family business. We find such entries as "after I had talked a good time with Mr Hoby of Husbandrie and Houshoulde matters, we went to bed" (May 13, 1600) or "After priuat praier I went [or walked] abroad with Mr Hoby" (May 9, 1600; May 10, 1600); or "after supper I examened papers, when lector was done, with Mr Hoby" (Sept. 15, 1599).

In addition to the diary's innate taciturnity, one's curiosity about the degree of intimacy or affection arises in part from the relative inconsistency of the references. During some periods Thomas Hoby appears frequently in the diary, usually in a burst of references; then he disappears altogether for days or weeks at a time. Thomas Hoby is frequently absent from home, on short and long stays, often associated with his office as Justice of the Peace and representative of Parliament.[42] On one occasion Margaret Hoby notes that he has gone out at night in pursuit of recusants and apparently does not return home until the next morning,[43] but mostly his presence – or absence – goes unremarked. Thomas and Margaret Hoby certainly do not always take meals together, even when he is at home. And Margaret Hoby's diary consists almost entirely of references in the first person: "After priuat praier I reed" (July 27); "I was busie about the house" (July 28); "I was busie with Roses" (July 22); "I went about and wrought tell dinner time" (July 21), and so on are typical of the references for July 1600. Only twice in the entire diary does she refer to him as "my husband" (Aug. 6, and Aug. 9, 1600), though her habitual way of referring to a spouse ("Mr Hoby") is not unusual for the time.[44]

Since this diary clearly focuses on Margaret Hoby's actions, her use of her time and her devotional life, rather than her personal relationships, one cannot infer too much from the absence of references to Sir Thomas Hoby. Sometimes she records a journey, such as a visit to her mother in Linton, and then to York, where she suddenly mentions conversing with her husband after dinner (Sept. 23, 1599). In this instance it appears that she returns home alone (on Sept. 27, 1599) and that her husband stays on in York; he perhaps preceded her on the journey as well.[45] But the references are so spotty and so brief that it's impossible to know whether their encounters were relatively few, or whether they simply are not usually mentioned. Sometimes when he is about to leave, or when he has just returned, there is a series of encounters, but we do not always even know when he departs. After her return to Hackness, she writes to him and to her mother on September 29, 1599; he does not return until October 5: "then Mr Hoby Came home, with whom I talked tell diner time"; she then pursues her household duties. Sir Thomas Hoby is mentioned again on October 6: "then I went abroad with Mr Hoby" and on October 9 when she ate breakfast but not supper with him: "I went to supper and, sonne after, went to bed, Mr Hoby Cominge home late." On October 11, she "walked with Mr Hoby," and then on October 15 "did take my leave of Mr Hoby," shortly before going to church; he then disappears from the record until December 12. There follow a number of references (Dec. 12: "I talked with Mr Hoby"; Dec. 13: "I walked abroad with Mr Hoby"; Dec. 15: "walked and Conferred of diuers thinges with Mr Hoby"); he does not reappear until December 27 and 30.

From these references it would seem that however good – or distant – her relationship with her husband may have been, Margaret Hoby also carried on a largely independent existence, a life with its own routine, social encounters, religious duties and experience. In general the relationship between the two seems amicable and certainly not emotionally charged;[46] there is evidence that he consulted her about business affairs and left much of the management of the estate in her hands. But a couple of instances complicate this picture. In July of 1600, Margaret Hoby "wrett an answer to a demand Mr Hoby had giuen me ouer night," and then later that day "returned vnto my Clossitt and altered that a litle which before I had wretten"; on the next day, after supper she gave "Mr Hoby that that I had wretten"; the following day, she was unwell. In her usual taciturn fashion Margaret Hoby gives no indication of the nature of the demand or her reply; it may – or may not – be connected with the sale of Linton, her mother's estate, which is referred to on July 23. In the days thereafter there are several references to their encounters: on July 25 "after Priuat praier I brak my fast with Mr Hoby" – a rarity; on July 28 "I walked with Mr Hoby"; and on July 29 "I wrought, walked about with Mr Hoby amonge workmen . . . then I talked with Mr Hoby of sunderie thinges." On August 1, "I dined with Mr Hoby and so kept him Companie all the day"; again after supper "I walked with Mr Hoby, and, after, I went to priuat praier and so to bed." In the days that follow there are frequent outings (August 3 and 4) culminating in that of August 5 – "I walked abroad with Mr Hoby and was allmost all the after none in the feld with him" – that suggest a return to the usual tenor of their relationship, or perhaps a better understanding, prompting the two exceptional references to him as "my husband" on August 6 and 9.

But how to interpret this evidence? In a document with so few emotional clues, it's difficult to know what these markers mean, if markers they be. The psychological content, as well as the degree of explicitness in the record, is very different from that of the diary of Lady Anne Clifford, which represents a tense emotional battleground. As a reader, one wants to note the unusual in the record, yet not to engage in over-interpretation. That the diary is not a place to record personal crises is equally evident in the case of a group of drunken neighbors who imposed themselves on the Puritan Hobys. The references to this encounter are extremely brief: on August 26, 1600, Lady Hoby "made prouision for som strangers that Came: after I went to priuat examenation and praier, then I went to priuat, supper, and after to bed." On the following day, "after I was readie [i.e., dressed] I spake with Mr Ewrie, who was so drunke that I sone made an end of that I had no reasen to stay for : and, after, praied, brake my fast, praied, and then dined." But the incident, which involved a shouting match, rocks being thrown at the house, and final insults, led the Hobys to file a law suit that ended in the Star Chamber and to persist, despite the urgings of Burghley himself, until damages were awarded them the following summer.[47] In the face of this disturbing encounter Lady Hoby records only that "hauinge talked with Mr Hoby about the abuse offered by Mr Ewere and his Companie, I went to priuat praier and so to bed" (Aug. 28, 1600). Further instances of emotional distress are found by Dorothy Meads in the size of the handwriting (272, n 369) and by Joanna Moody, who notes the misdating of the entry for August 29 (108, n 187), but the clues are circumstantial rather than explicit.

Two points emerge: first, even in this very unpleasant and upsetting situation, Margaret Hoby permits herself only the briefest of references: she records her actions and her devotional exercises, but not the substance of her conversations or the nature of her feelings. Second, if there had been marital tension in mid-July, it seems likely that this incident, which pitted the Hobys against their neighbors, drew them closer together. Whereas Margaret Hoby had earlier visited and corresponded with Lady Eure,[48] the new year finds them deciding together to avoid an encounter with the offending son: on January 25, 1601: "Came in Mr Ewry, so that we Came a way, rather giuinge place to him then our affections whic might haue bin prouoked."

These two instances in the diary – the one concerning an undisclosed message on paper, to which we are tempted to give some importance, and the other a near brawl in the house, recorded in the most understated of ways – surely indicate the author's restraint and suggest something of the limits of our ability to interpret this material. Because the clues are so few, we are likely to seize on anything: Joanna Moody, for example, sees significance in Margaret Hoby's fatigue after returning from attendance at childbirth, as evidence of her desire for children, a point supported, she thinks, by the reference (Oct. 7, 1603) to that blessing which she does not have.[49] But we do not know: attendance at childbirth may well be tiring whether or not one wishes for children. And if Margaret Hoby is so very close-mouthed about the intrusion of young Mr. Eure and his friends, we should be doubly cautious about assigning too much meaning to her taciturnity about her relationship with her husband.

In fact, the taciturnity, and even the heavily repetitious pattern, may be one of the pleasures, as well as one of the qualities, of this text. In Margaret Hoby's decision to keep a record of her spiritual exercises she exercised a measure of self-determination and self-control that are significant in themselves. If the diary is deficient in emotional expression it is perhaps precisely because the emotion was poured out in the devotions and prayers themselves.[50] Margaret Hoby's diary is primarily a tool for self-monitoring, rather than a means of self-expression. Yet we as readers, while acknowledging the former, also seek and find the latter. The shaping of her life, which depends so heavily on prayer, reading of scripture, and devotion, emerges less as a monotonous pattern or an image of subjection to a pattern than as a matter of choice and control, an elusive record of an ongoing interaction with a model of life. Margaret Hoby has chosen her model, and however foreign it may be to our own existence, it enables a succession of individual actions with their own determination of time, place, and action: "After I was readie I praied priuatly."[51] And in the opening and closing, in the rhythm of her daily life and in the syntax in which she expresses it, we may also sense a degree of agency and confidence, marked by the ever-present and powerful first person of this text. For the religious and domestic life here recorded, however constrained by routine and location, is represented by a subject who chooses to engage in these activities and to record them. It is the first, but not therefore the least, in this series of self-representations.

CHAPTER 2

The construction of a life: the diaries of Anne Clifford

The diaries and personal records of Anne Clifford are not only more extensive than those of Margaret Hoby, covering over thirty years of her life, but also more varied in genre, style, and approach, and far more deliberately constructed. Taken together they constitute a remarkable account of a life lived, observed, and carefully presented in written form; they manifest strong and characteristic themes and an often painful tension between personal relationships and dynastic claims. I want to consider how Anne Clifford understood what she was doing, what purpose she intended these records to serve, and what the limits of interpretation might be. While these texts of course supply information about Clifford's life, the conclusions about her character and intentions that have been drawn from them vary widely. But as before I am less concerned with information per se than with more formal aspects of the text as they create meaning, and with the experience of reading, an experience that is considerably more complex and nuanced than any summary might suggest.

Anne Clifford, daughter of George Clifford, third Earl of Cumberland, one of Queen Elizabeth's most flamboyant courtiers, and his wife Margaret Russell, youngest daughter of the Earl of Bedford, was born in Skipton Castle in 1590. She was married twice, first in 1609 to Richard Sackville, grandson of Elizabeth's Lord Treasurer, just days before he became the third Earl of Dorset. She bore him five children, only two of whom survived. In 1630, six years after Dorset's death at the age of thirty-four, Anne Clifford became the second wife of Philip Herbert, fourth Earl of Pembroke and Montgomery.[1] Both marriages placed her in the highest ranks of courtly society, but neither was particularly happy.[2] Anne Clifford and Philip Herbert, remarkably ill-suited to one another, separated in 1634, perhaps over his attempts to arrange a marriage between her daughter Isabella and his son. One of the chief struggles of Clifford's life was her attempt to gain control of the family property, which had

34

been willed by George Clifford to his brother Francis, and which Anne finally inherited in 1643. Widowed for a second time in 1650, Anne Clifford spent her remaining years until her death in 1676 in the north of England, rebuilding and maintaining her castles and engaging in other public works – the restoration of churches and the founding of an almshouse.

Throughout her long life, Anne Clifford showed a strong interest in keeping personal and family records. One of her earliest purchases, when she was ten, was an account book; she spent her mature years assembling the Great Books of the Clifford Family, and kept records until the day she died.[3] Although often linked together, the several forms of Clifford's life writings have their own distinct character; they differ in scope and style, and very likely in presumed audience and intention.[4] The earliest text (1603), which recounts the events of Anne Clifford's fourteenth year, has a strong narrative thread, but also contains a good deal of tangential material. The 1616–19 diary is closer to what we would call a journal – consisting of entries for particular days (though by no means for every day), giving a strong but complex sense of immediate reaction to events. The last twenty-five years of Anne Clifford's life are covered by annual summaries that, according to contemporary suggestion, are based on the diaries, which were then "laid aside."[5] Finally, we have a journal of the last months of Clifford's life, a more detailed record that resembles the 1616–19 text. Presumably this too would have become an annual summary if she had lived to compile it. Different from all these is Clifford's brief account of her life from her conception until 1650; written in 1652–63, it covers a period for which no other records exist; whether it too was based on more detailed journals is unknown. I shall look at each of these texts in turn, considering its particular character, the kind of self that emerges from it, and its place in the larger whole of Anne Clifford's work.

When she composed the first narrative section, Anne Clifford was barely thirteen, the only daughter and, as she reminds us, the only living child of George Clifford, Earl of Cumberland, and his wife Margaret. At the time of this account, two years before George Clifford's death, Anne's parents were already estranged, and the tensions that emerge from this youthful account anticipate those in Anne Clifford's own marriage, as recorded in her journal of 1616–19. The 1603 narrative, which begins *in medias res*, represents a young girl enjoying the connections of the court provided by her parents and her mother's sister the Countess of Warwick.[6] It's not clear whether this is the first of Anne's diaries, nor just why she chooses to begin at this point, though this is certainly a most eventful year in the kingdom, and she is of an age to be fully conscious of it. Partly because Clifford provides no background or introductory statement, her narrative has a remarkable freshness and immediacy, and the lack of subordination or obvious organizing principle – the fact that events of national consequence and merely personal interest are described in the same paragraph – conveys at once naiveté and credibility. She does not attempt to separate the great occasion from her own feelings and experiences but rather joins the two with simple directness, representing the momentous yet peaceful transfer of power from Elizabeth to James through the eyes of a young but well-positioned observer. We sense her frustration at not being a full participant in the events she describes:

A little after this Q. E.'s Corps came by night in a Barge from Richmond to Whitehall, my Mother & a great Company of Ladies attending it where it continued a great while standing in the Drawing Chamber, where it was watched all night by several Lords & Ladies. My Mother sitting up with it two or three nights, but my Lady would not give me leave to watch by reason I was held too young.[7]

Again, when the formal burial takes place in Westminster, "My Mother & my Aunt Warwick being Mourners, . . . I was not allowed to be one because I was not high enough, which did much trouble me then, but yet I stood in the Church at Westminster to see the Solemnities performed" (D. J. H. Clifford, ed., 22).

This brief narrative ingenuously combines the normal concerns of an emerging adolescent with larger familial and political issues. Frequently, the young Anne Clifford seems to have nothing more on her mind than sociability: she details time happily spent with friends and cousins: "All this time we were merry at North Hall. My Coz. Frances Bourchier & my Coz. Francis Russell & I did use to walk much in the Garden & were great one with another" (27). She also recounts how her mother, presumably trying to instill appropriate manners and mores in her daughter, "being extreme angry with me for riding before with Mr Mene, . . . commanded that I should lie in a Chamber alone, which I could not endure" (25).[8]

But Anne Clifford also describes the jockeying for power among the powerful nobles of the kingdom, in their attempt to determine whether the great under Elizabeth would be the great under James: "At this time we used very much to go to Whitehall and walked much in the Garden which was frequented by Lords & Ladies. My Mother being all full of hopes every Man expecting Mountains & finding Molehills, excepting

Sir R. Cecil and the House of the Howards who hated my Mother & did not much love my Aunt Warwick" (22). Though not yet a combatant, Anne Clifford conveys a clear sense of the high stakes and the battle lines: there is, for example, the "strife between my Father & Lord Burleigh, who was the President and who should carry the Sword" (22) as well as the rather desperate attempts to be among the first to meet Queen Anne on her journey from Scotland. Anne's mother hoped to join her sister Warwick in going to attend on the Queen, but was prevented because "her Horse . . . were not ready"; in their great haste to overtake those who had gone before, they "killed three Horses that day with extremities of heat" (23). Besides rivalry and ambition, there are sharp reminders of material reality ranging from the merely unpleasant to the mortally dangerous: on the one hand "we all saw a great change between the fashion of the Court as it is now and that in the Queen's time, for we were all lousy by sitting in the chamber of Sir Thomas Erskine" (22); on the other, near their lodgings at Hampton Court "were Tents where they died 2 or 3 in a day of the Plague" (25).

Anne is also keenly aware of the tensions between her father and mother as they are played out against the backdrop of the court. She records, for example, that "My Father used to come to us sometimes at Clerkenwell but not often, for he had at this time as it were wholly left my Mother, yet the House was kept still at her charge" (22). And while her father, like her husband-to-be, played a prominent role at court, her mother was sometimes left in an embarrassingly exposed position: "the Court . . . were banqueted with great Royalty by my Father at Grafton where the King & Queen were entertained with Speeches and delicate presents . . . [M]y Mother was there, but not held as Mistress of the House by reason of the Difference between my Lord & her which was grown to a great height" (24). Anne Clifford records her father's perform-ance of his paternal duty as well as his evident lack of enthusiasm: "sometimes My Mother & he did meet, when their countenance did shew the dislike they had one of the other, yet he would speak to me in a slight fashion & give me his Blessing" (26). Characteristically, Anne does not take sides in this debate, merely noting its effects, though other passages indicate her emulation of her father as well as her love and admiration for her mother.[9]

The brief narrative of this year includes so many different facets of life, often jumbled together, that one could conclude that no planning or organization was involved, that the text merely projects youthful first impressions. Yet the passages I've cited, like many others in this apparently randomly structured narrative, articulate the themes that dominate the accounts to come: ambition, inheritance, kinship, and courtship. The illness of the Queen may be the starting point of Anne's diary because it is then that she realizes the fragility of court hopes and the tenuousness of influence: she notes her special closeness to her maternal Aunt Anne Dudley, Countess of Warwick, Queen Elizabeth's Lady of the Bedchamber, "to whom I was much bound for her continual care & love of mee, in so much as if Queen Elizabeth had lived she intended to prefer me to be of the Privy Chamber for at that time there was much hope and expectation of me as of any other young Ladie whatsoever" (21). The struggle between her father and Burleigh over the ceremonial bearing of the sword is interesting not only in itself, but also for its implications for the writer: "it was adjudged on my Father's side because it was an office by inheritance, *and so is lineally descended to me*" [emphasis mine] (22). And the diary itself is anchored in space and time by a series of marginal notes that establish far-reaching connections: for example, Clifford records of the death of the Queen, "This Message was delivered to my Mother & me in the same chamber where afterwards I was married"; and then by a marginal note, "I was at Q. Elizabeth's death 13 yrs & 2 months old, & Mr R. Sackville was 14 yrs old, he being then at Dorset House with his Grandfather & that great family. At the death of this worthy Queen my Mother & I lay at Austin Friars in the same chamber."[10] In short, while the apparently haphazard chronological narrative is the more credible and appealing for its lack of an obvious agenda, it clearly anticipates the concerns of her later life, and these links emerge as Anne Clifford annotates what she herself has written.

The second distinct section, which begins in 1616 as a day-by-day book, lacks the narrative connections of 1603, yet its telegraphic style manifests far more strongly than the earlier record the drama of Anne Clifford's own life. One wonders whether journal or narrative material from the intervening years has been lost, since it is hard to imagine the observant and engaged writer of the extant texts keeping no records for thirteen years. But it may also be that Anne Clifford took up her diary in 1616 just as her relationship with her husband of seven years became somewhat contentious. The conflict between them is a major theme of this document, as is Clifford's sense of herself and her creation of a self to present to the world.

Recent readers of the 1616–19 diary have seen quite deliberate patterns in her self-presentation, raising questions about how we should approach this text. Richard T. Spence, who suggests 1615 as the date for the beginning of marital tension, also raises the important question of the diary's function and the degree to which it is constructed, even fabricated.[11] Beginning from the assumption that a diary ought to be a factual account, Spence finds this one lacking for his purposes: "A major obstacle to any assessment of the Dorset marriage is that virtually everything known about it comes from Anne herself. . . . There are grounds for regarding the *Diaries* as a partial, even prejudiced, source which has to be assessed cautiously and critically like any historical document" (59–60). Spence suggests (62–63), that Anne's version of events is quite different from what actually happened, and before long undertakes a defense of her husband: "It is partly because of the *Diaries* that Dorset has suffered so much adverse comment by Anne's biographers. He had shortcomings aplenty, shown in his extravagance, gambling, infidelity and wasting of his huge landed inheritance in a manner recalling Earl George's [Anne's father], though without the latter's redeeming feature of outstanding service to the realm. Anne was all too conscious of the parallel and her reaction to it is reminiscent of her mother's" (60).[12] Likewise, Barbara Lewalski, though she displays no particular desire to see Dorset vindicated, suggests another antecedent for the *Diary:* "John Foxe's female martyrs supply the paradigm for Anne Clifford's self-portrait in her *Diary* as a loving wife who patiently endures great suffering at the hand of her husband and much of society."[13]

Both these comments raise the question, not only of the accuracy of the diary, but also of its purpose and the degree to which it shapes and interprets events. To be sure, there is something about the day-by-day account that leads one to expect a faithful record, if not of events, at least of the author's perception of them. Yet Spence's protest seems to misread the personal interest of the author: why keep a diary to record someone else's point of view? While it is useful to call attention to the deliberate shaping of the text, simply regarding it as biased limits our understanding in other ways.[14] Lewalski's comment also seems to overstate the case, to give too little attention to the subtlety and complexity of Anne Clifford's self-construction.

Real questions remain about Clifford's purpose in writing, about the extent to which this is a personal, private account, to what extent written for others to see.[15] Anne Clifford writes, I am persuaded, in the deepest possible sense for herself. She writes to construct her life, to understand it, to place herself in relation to her husband, his servants, the court, and her mother; and she writes to justify her actions to herself. As Katherine Acheson remarks, "The diary of 1616 to 1619 is a work by which she remembered herself, rather than one by which she wished to be remembered" (36). In some sense the diary seems to be what Anne Clifford says to herself in preparation for presenting herself to the world, writing "to prepare a face to meet the faces that you meet," as T. S. Eliot put it.[16] In the 1616–19 diaries in particular, we see the tensions to which she is subject and her reaction to them. Sometimes her response is extraordinarily tight-lipped and restrained; at other times she writes more explicitly about her feelings. But never does the diary become confessional in the way modern readers might expect. There is a great deal that she need not say because, as author and subject, she knows it already; and there is a great deal she omits, perhaps because she foresees readers other than herself. That one of the four years (1618) is entirely missing may suggest that some readers – very likely members of her family – nevertheless found her account too explicit.[17]

If one were to read the diaries in a formalist way, looking for shapes and connections as one might in any other text, a number of features would be immediately obvious. First is the physical layout of the text, made easily evident in Acheson's critical edition: on the right hand are the daily references to the author's own activities, on the left, marginal notes, sometimes material that appears to have been added later or references to contemporary events outside her immediate household (e.g., "Upon the 24th [March 1616] my Lady Somerset was sent from black fryars by water as prisoner to the Tower"). Some notes supply information that Clifford could not have had at the time, such as the apparent cause of the death of her mother, noted three weeks before the illness itself is described in the daily record, or the reference to the birthday of her future son-in-law, age eight in December 1616, to be married to her daughter Margaret, not yet two years old. This method of marginal notation has the advantage of allowing later additions by juxtaposition; it also links Clifford's own experience to the larger world, and the present to the past and the future. The layout of the text gives it the quality of dialogue, whether between Clifford's initial observations and her later notations, or between the life in which she is fully present and the life to which she is connected, in time or space. Clearly, this is not simply the record of Anne Clifford's experiences, but rather a deliberate construction of herself, subject to later revision, within a larger realm.

Second, although the diary at first looks like a day-by-day account, clearly much has been omitted: there are only six references for the month of January 1616 and ten specific references for February; evidently a good bit of selection has taken place. Unlike Margaret Hoby, who (at least in the early stages of her diary) resolutely records each day, Anne Clifford records only the notable occurrences. But as with the prose narrative of the year 1603, the *principle* of selection is not immediately made clear. That principle of inclusion or omission, in fact, is one of the intriguing aspects of the diary: it comes across as a direct record, yet one from which we know details are being withheld, leading us to probe for further information.[18]

If, as has been suggested, the diary was intended not as an end in itself but as material for a narrative summary, such as we have for the years 1650–75, its form might not be so crucial. But we have no summary for the period 1616–19. Moreover, as with the diary of Hoby and the other texts that are the subject of this study, I'm concerned with the effect on us and with the experience of reading. In reading the diary one has a steadily growing sense of the degree to which it is coded, to which it represents a complex and ardent struggle, and in which events that seem trivial or unrelated are in fact part of a tightly woven whole. Thus on the one hand the diary strikes us as forthright and unpremeditated, and yet as we read, we find strong thematic currents, rare self-disclosure, and a good deal of tight-lipped determination.[19] Reading it is like being let in, gradually, on a family secret in the course of a dinner party: over the hors d'oeuvres one notices little; by the end of the evening the tensions are wrenchingly apparent.

The construction of the diary is at once seemingly haphazard and yet deliberate. It lacks the obvious shape of art, in which passages are carefully selected to create a definite, if complex, pattern. Rather, we experience the immediacy of life, its apparently random vicissitudes: just when things are going well, they may take a sudden turn for the worse: Anne Clifford's relief that her mother is not so ill as she has feared is quickly followed by word of her death (May 22 and 29, 1616). Or contrarily, just as she is reconciled to spending a gloomy winter alone in the north of England, her husband sends word that she is to depart for London within a few days (Nov. 19, 1616).

It is not only the reader who seeks patterns in these entries, but also Clifford herself, as she looks for the resolution of her dispute with her husband, gaining the legal title to her land, or the return of her child to health. With its dual system of entries, the diary gives us in full measure the suspendedness of daily life, as well as the interconnections of events, established in such marginal notes as this: "Upon the 24th [of May 1616] being friday between the hours of six & 7 at night died my deare Mother at Broome in the same chamber where my father was borne; thirteen years & two months after the death of Q. Eliz. & 10 years & 4 months after the death of my father, I being then 26 years old & 4 months & the Childe two years old wanting a month." As she records events, she also strives to see their connections to other events, holding her life together by a series of happenings that to her are far more than coincidences. After her mother's death, when she and her husband are for a time reconciled, she notes: "Upon the 24th [August 1616] in the afternoone I drest the Chamber where my Lady died & set up the Green Velvet bed where the same night we went to lye there."[20] In the later summaries (1650–75) such connections become more formalized, but at this point they are only some of the stuff – or perhaps the whalebone ribs – of the account.[21]

Anne Clifford's diary is multi-functional. Most simply, of course, it records the events that Clifford considers important as a way of remembering. But in the process of recording, Clifford also interprets. As Spence complains, the picture that emerges of the Dorset marriage is hardly an unbiased one; Richard Sackville, had he kept a diary, might have recorded other events and other readings of them. But Clifford interprets in a way – recording her public statements and at times her private reactions – that contributes to self-understanding and self-presentation. Justified in her own eyes, she can present a carefully considered image to the outside world: "I beseech'd His Majesty to pardon me for that I wou'd never part with Westmorland while I lived upon any Condition Whatsoever. sometimes he used fair means & perswasions, & sometimes fowle means but I was resolved before so as nothing wou'd move me" (Jan. 18, 1617). The diary also serves as a convenient memorandum and in some instances as a legal document, to record her actions and intentions in the event of later challenge or question. For example, a notation in April 1616 gives her interpretation of an action she is forced to take: having been instructed not to go to London as she had expected, along with Dorset's horses and men, she writes: "there being a paper drawne to shew that their going was by my Lords direction contrary to my Will" (44).[22]

Although the diary enables Clifford to present and justify her actions, this important function is performed without a great deal of self-revelation, or perhaps better, explicit confession. There are, to be sure, comments about her feelings, like the opening of February 1616: "All the tyme

I stay'd in the Country I was sometimes merry & sometimes sad, as I heard news from London"; or the note after her successful resistance against the King in February 1616: "Next day was a marvellous day to me through the Mercy of God for it [was] generally thought that I must either have sealed to the agreement or else to have parted with my Lord" (42). But the diary is the more intriguing because these comments are relatively rare. This is not a vehicle for the outpouring of emotion; rather, the emotion is more often conveyed in the significance of the recorded events. Since the feelings that the events engender are well known to the writer, there is no need to articulate them. Yet once the reader understands the importance of these events, no further commentary is required to convey emotion. Indeed, the very taciturnity of the account, its restraint, is an important source of its power, as events are listed without commentary, creating a mosaic of favorable or unfavorable circumstances.

The diary begins at the beginning of the year 1616, a time of celebration, as subsequent references to New Year's gifts and masques at court make clear. But it also begins with an image of confinement: "Upon new years day I kept my Chamber all the day" (Acheson, 39). It is also noteworthy that, as so often in the diary, Anne Clifford and her husband are engaged in separate activities: "my Lady Rich & my sister Sackville supping with me, but my Lord & all the company at Dorset House went to see the maske at the Court." As is characteristic of Clifford, we hear of no particular reason why she kept to her chamber all day on New Year's Day, nor why she was accompanied by her friend and her sister-in-law rather than her husband. We simply see what quickly becomes a pattern in the account, that of separate activity. She does attend the masque at court five days later, in the company of Lady Arundel and in the context of a lavish supper for the Florentine ambassador, so that her life in this season is hardly devoid of entertainment and in particular of female companionship. Nevertheless, the diary also underscores the relative power of these two spheres: in the margin opposite the entries for January 4 and 6, Clifford writes: "Upon the 5th being twelfth Eve my Lord play'd at Dice in the Court & won nine hundred twenty shilling pieces and gave me but twenty."

The issue that runs like a leitmotif through the diary is of course Anne Clifford's inheritance – the property that was entailed on the heir, whether male or female, but that George Clifford, shortly before his death, willed to his brother Francis. Margaret, as dowager Countess of

Cumberland, and, after her death, Anne, undertook a long legal battle to regain the property, arguing that the Earl of Cumberland had no legal right to alter the original provision.[23] Both before and after her mother's death, Anne was subject to enormous pressure to agree to a monetary settlement – a solution favored by a husband whose life at court and gambling debts required constant funding. The diary records attempts at influence from many sources: the Archbishop of Canterbury, her husband's uncle Lord William Howard, her brother-in-law Edward Sackville, her cousin Francis Russell, Lord Roos, the son of William Cecil, the King himself, and a group of distinguished judges – the Attorney General, the Solicitor General, and the Lord Chief Justices of Common Pleas and of the King's Bench.

In the period of 1616–17, nearly every conversation takes place against the backdrop of this suit. On January 16, 1616, Clifford writes:

my Lady Grantham told me the Archbishop of Canterbury wou'd come to me the next day & she perswaded me very earnestly to agree to this business which I took as a great argument of her love. also my Coz. Russel came to see me the same day & chid me & told me of all my faults & errors in this business & he made me weep bitterly, then I . . . went to see my Lady Wotton at Whitehall where we walked 5 or 6 turns but spoke nothing of this business though her heart and mine were both full of it.

Anne Clifford here subjects events to powerful interpretation. It's not clear why Lady Grantham's persuasion to do what Clifford was resisting is "a great argument of her love" – unless it is because it is coupled with her warning about the Archbishop of Canterbury's impending visit. Nor can we judge the accuracy of Clifford's statement that both Lady Wotton and she were thinking only of "this business" though as her first cousin Margaret Wotton was very likely disposed to sympathy.[24] But the very assertion clearly indicates the extent to which Clifford's own life is pervaded by this concern. In this situation her mother was her strongest ally, although "in all this time of my troubles my Coz. Russel was exceedinge Carefull & kind to me" (Jan. 20, 1616); and interestingly, while King James was pressuring her to agree, Queen Anne "gave me warning to take heed of putting my matters absolutely to the King lest he shou'd deceive me" (marginal note Jan. 18, 1617).

The day-by-day events of the diary, in which each encounter is read against the background of this struggle over money and legal rights, portray a situation in which Anne can seldom initiate action: she can only resist, steadfastly refusing to agree to the settlement advocated by her uncle, her husband, and the King. And resist she does, over the course of several years. Yet the picture of her that emerges is neither one of simple stubbornness nor passivity, but rather of considerable strength of character, resilience, endurance, and ingenuity. Moreover, the diaries convey extraordinary depth of feeling, not by expressing but by re-straining emotion, by telling more often of events and actions than of feelings.

Since the effect of the diaries of 1616–19 is so powerful and so intricately constructed, I want to consider some of the often quite subtle ways in which the drama of Clifford's life emerges, by looking at passages, sometimes miscellaneous but also strongly coded, that represent the tensions in her life. In this situation a picture emerges, if not resembling one of Foxe's martyrs, certainly of a woman strongly withstanding a variety of pressures. In the taciturn record negative events have the impact of artillery shells and positive ones of a breath of fresh air. By way of example I take May 1616, which shows particularly well this interplay of forces.

This month provides a quite complete record – with separate entries for twenty-two of the thirty-one days. And it is a month full of action: Clifford's husband urges her to surrender all claims to the northern property; her only child is removed from her at her husband's insistence; and her mother, her chief ally in the fight for her land, dies. Particularly striking in this account are two possibly contradictory qualities: on the one hand the concentration on certain themes and ongoing events creates a dominant concern, something tending toward a sort of unified text; on the other hand, the reader, like the writer, is constantly buffeted by changing circumstances, either a series of negative events or a reversal of expectations. The month begins with the loss of a secure and agreeable place to live: "Upon the 1st Rivers came from London in the afternoon, & brought me word that I should neither live at Knoll nor Bollbroke" (46). This news is immediately followed by pressure from her husband, the threat that "my Lord wou'd come down & see me once more which wou'd be the last time that I shou'd see him again." The stakes are raised by the removal of her daughter (not yet two years of age): "Upon the 3d came Basket down from London & brought me a letter from my Lord by which I might see that it was his pleasure that the Childe shou'd go the next day to London." Less than a week later comes the news that her mother is gravely ill.

Margaret Clifford's illness, death, and burial are major concerns of this section of the journal, and Anne Clifford herself was subject to extended uncertainty and false report. First came the warning on May 9: "I received a letter from Mr Bellasis how extream ill my mother had been . . . & as they thought in some danger of Death." The next day there was a false reprieve: "Rivers brought me word . . . that she was not in such danger as I feard"; on the 13th she realizes "how very sicke & full of greivous paine my dear Mother was so as she was not able to write herself to me"; on May 22 "Mr Davys came down from London & brought me word that my mother was very well recovered of her dangerous sickness." Exactly a week after this reassurance, she receives "the heavy news of my mothers death . . . the greatest & most lamentable cross that could befall me." In fact the text gives us a dual perspective – the false reassurance of May 22 in the body of the text is juxtaposed with the marginal note: "Upon the 24th being friday between the hours of six & 7 at night died my deare Mother at Broome in the same chamber where my father was borne." Although the journal has none of the sense of control of an artistically constructed narrative, of an end that we might foresee, it does have some of the power of one. Death or the fear of death pervades the month: when not present in the text, it is present in the margin, in anticipation of an event that the writer was still unaware of.

The style in which the entries are written also contributes strongly to our view of Clifford as the vulnerable recipient of events and news reports: by beginning each entry with the date – a natural enough approach – she conveys the sense, altogether justified in this month, that almost every day brings some new cause for alarm. The rhetorical technique is *anaphora*, conveying a series of hammer blows from without. Isolated at Knole, Clifford receives messages from a variety of couriers – Rivers, Basket, Grovenor, Richard Jones, Thomas Petty, Mr Davys, and Kendall.[25] Besides being the bearers of (usually) bad news, the messengers themselves are not always friendly, most notably Mathew Caldicott who, as on May 14, is frequently a cause of discord between Clifford and her husband. In addition to the anxiety about her mother's health, Clifford is subject to constant pressure from Dorset – so that the messages from London are a series of threats – this is the last time she will see him, her child will be removed, she will no longer be able to reside at Knole or Bolebrook. The threats are also intermixed with persuasion: "The 14th Richard Jones came from London to see me & brought a letter with him from Mathew the Effect whereof was to perswade me to yeild to my Lords desire in this business at this time or else I was undone for ever."

The month includes a number of references to condemnation or approval. Although no explicit connection is made, the reference to the arraignment of Frances Howard Carr for murder contributes to the sense of female vulnerability: "Upon the 24th my Lady Somerset was arraign'd & condemn'd at Westminster Hall where she confess'd her fault & ask'd the King's mercy & was much pity'd of all the beholders." In contrast to Lady Somerset's confession, however, Anne Clifford does not give up her own earnest attempts at persuasion: "Upon the 10th early in the morning I writte a very earnest letter to my Lord to beseech him." And she clearly values any sign of success or approval from the outside world, as in her attempt to justify herself to her husband's steward: "Upon the 11th . . . before Mr Legg went away I talked with him an hour or two about all the business & matters between me & my Lord, so as I gave him better satisfaction & made him conceive a better opinion of me than ever he did."[26] Moreover she is clearly grateful for the visit on May 28 of "my Lady Selby" who "told me that she had heard some folks say that I have done well in not Consenting to the Composition" and for the visit of the Bishop of St. David's, following the news of her mother's death, "to comfort me in these my afflictions."

Earlier I described the diary as a kind of coded message – not because it is intentionally deceptive but because Clifford simply expresses a number of things elliptically. But the May diary contains a larger than usual number of explicit expressions of feeling: when Clifford hears that her child will indeed be taken from her she "wept bitterly" (May 3); she speaks of "being in the midst of all my misery" (May 4) and of "a grievous & sorrowfull day to me"(May 9); she says she has "many times a sorrowfull & heavy heart" (May 12). But more powerful and characteristic than these statements is the juxtaposing of events or references that intensify the effect of the text without calling attention to the process, perhaps even without Clifford's being fully conscious of it, creating a mode or theme to which the reader is increasingly sensitized. For example, while the entries throughout May contrast her husband's freedom and her own imprisonment, his gaiety of life and her desolation, they also focus on mothers and daughters. The most obvious part of this struggle is Dorset's removal of their daughter Margaret from her mother's residence: child custody is clearly one of his weapons in the attempt to gain her consent to a monetary settlement rather than title to her northern castles. Anne Clifford decides on the most rational course: although "at the first [it] was somewhat grievous to me but when I consider'd that it would both make my Lord more angry with me & be worse for the Child, I resolved to let her goe" (46). But after this decision the marginal notes continue the references to children: "about this time I heard my sister Beauchamp [her husband's sister Anne Sackville] was with Childe" (juxtaposed with May 1); on May 10 she petitions her husband and tries to enlist the support of "my sister Beauchamps."

We can sense the depth of Clifford's feeling in the alternatives she suggests – "Upon the 10th early in the morning I writte a very earnest letter to my Lord to beseech him that I might not go to the little house [Little Dorset House] which was appointed for me, but that I might go to Horsly & sojourne there with my Childe & to the same effect I writ to my sister Beauchamps." The message is full of intensifiers: written *early in the morning, a very earnest letter,* written to *beseech* Dorset, and followed up with a similar letter to his sister, Anne (Lady Beauchamps). Anne Clifford's request was not granted, but there is perhaps a self-consoling note ten days later, when she recalls that "my Brother Compton & his wife kept the house at West Horsely & my brother Beauchamp & my sister his wife sojourn'd with them, so as the Child was with both her aunts" (50). There is a sign of partial reconciliation on May 11 when Mathew arrives from London: "my Lord sending me by him the Wedding ring that my Lord Treasurer & my Old Lady [her husband's grandfather and grandmother] were married withall, & a message that my Lord wou'd be here the next week, & that the Childe wou'd not as yet go downe to Horsly." In response to this token from her husband, Clifford offers one of her own: "I sent my Lord the wedding ring that my Lord & I was married with." There is of course an implicit reason for these apparently conciliatory gestures from Dorset: "the same day came Mr Marsh from London & perswaded me much to consent to this agreement" (48).

In this situation Anne Clifford is both mother and daughter, and her grief over her mother's death is not only a matter of personal emotion but also a realization of her weakened position. Moreover, in recording the time and place of her mother's death, she also connects it with her own age and the age of her daughter: "I being then 26 years old & 4 months & the Childe two years old wanting a month." In marginal notes, Clifford documents just when her husband learns of the event – perhaps to distinguish his unrelenting attempts to persuade her to give up her claims from cruelty in her bereavement.[27] While he was exerting so much pressure on her, he did not know of her mother's death, but shortly thereafter, they make common cause to secure the northern property, and a brief reconciliation ensues. In this sequence of good and bad news,

The construction of a life: Anne Clifford   49

her mother's will is seen as having particular significance: "wherin she appointed her body shou'd be buried in the Parish Church of Anwick [Alnwick] which was a double grief to me when I consider'd her body shou'd be carry'd away, & not be interred at Skipton [Clifford's own birthplace], so I took that as a sign that I should be disinherited of the Inheritance of my forefathers" (May 29; 51). Two days later "Mr Jones brought me a letter . . . wherein it seem'd that it was my mothers pleasure her body shou'd be conveyed to what place I appointed & which was some contentment to my agrieved soul" (52). Margaret Clifford's death then means loss of support in Anne Clifford's dynastic claims, and the terms of the will seem an omen that Anne will lose her inheritance. To lose Margaret Clifford is, as Hamlet might say, to lose father and mother at once.

Anne Clifford's sustained struggle for her inheritance, as seen in the diary of May 1616 and elsewhere, was immensely complicated by the fact that her husband, for whom she clearly cared, was usually on the opposing side: "I came to my Lodging with a heavy heart considering how things stood between my Lord & I" (Feb. 26, 1616). Unlike Margaret Hoby, who uses the "I" whether her husband is in residence or not, Clifford clearly feels her isolation, as seen in her complaint that she is "like an owl in the Desert."[28] All too often her husband is at court and she is in the country, and she keenly feels her lack of freedom: on October 11, 1616 "I sent a very earnest Letter to my Lord that I might come up to London." The answer, returned eleven days later, is "that I could not goe to London *all this winter*" (emphasis mine).[29] Even movement within the countryside is restricted, as when on August 4, 1617, Dorset "went to Penshurst but wou'd not suffer me to go with him, although my Lord & my Lady Lisle sent a man on purpose to desire me to come[.] he hunted & lay there all night." Clearly Clifford is subject to a kind of emotional blackmail – imprisoned in one of the greatest houses in England, deprived of her child, of the companionship of her husband, and, according to some indications, of sexual relations: as she records for April 23, 1617: "this night my Lord shou'd have layen with me in my Chamber, but he & I fell out about Mathew."

In the relatively spare record of Anne Clifford's diary, not only particular events but also apparently trivial activities serve as markers of her psychic state – matters such as reading and sewing, household tableaux, references to clothing, and exchange of gifts. Anne Clifford's diary is neither so complete, in the sense of accounting for each moment of the day, as Margaret Hoby's, nor so likely to include mention of household activities. Lady Margaret Hoby seems to have spent much more time supervising the household than the Countess of Dorset, but when circumstances are particularly tense between Clifford and her husband, her account of her daily activities begins to resemble Hoby's, as she turns to traditional female occupations. Having been sent down to Knole on half an hour's notice after refusing Dorset's proposal to "pass my right of the lands in Westmorland to him & my Child," she writes, "at this time I wrought very hard & made an end of one of my cushions of Irish stitch work" (June 8 and 15, 1616). Later that year, expecting to be confined to Brougham Castle for the winter, she writes, "Upon the 4th [of November] I sat in the drawing Chamber all the day at my work," and a week later, "Upon the 12th I made an end of the long cushion of Irish stitch which my Coz. Cecily Nevil began when she went with me to the Bath, it being my Chief help to pass away the time to worke."[30] But whereas Hoby's sewing is simply recorded as a daily activity, a useful occupation, for Clifford it is associated with tedium or respite in despair: "I went in the afternoon & said my prayers in the standing in the Garden & spent my time in reading & working as I used to do. the time grew tedious so as I used to go to bed about 8 o'clock and lye abed till 8 the next morning" (Mar. 11, 1617).[31] Yet needlework can also be a sign of (short-lived) domestic accord, as when in August 1616, "in the afternoon I wrought Irish stitch & my Lord sat & read by me."[32]

The references to reading in Anne Clifford's diary suggest a range of interests both broader and more secular than Margaret Hoby's. Her favorites are evident in the Great Picture, which she commissioned to represent herself and her family.[33] There are also mentions in the diary of Montaigne's *Essays*, *The Faerie Queene*, *The Arcadia*, Chaucer, and Ovid; and there is a good deal of secular nonfiction: Leicester's *Common Wealth*, Josephus, Richard Knolles's *Generall Historie of the Turks*. Like Hoby, Clifford records a course of reading undertaken with her chaplain: in February and March of 1617, perhaps in observance of Lent, they seem to have reached Deuteronomy in the reading of the Old Testament. But whereas Hoby's religious activity, in particular her reading of (or listening to) religious texts, is a sphere of self-determination, even this activity of Clifford's is strongly influenced by her husband, who objects because "it wou'd hinder his Study very much" (76), and hence broken off.[34]

For Anne Clifford, no less devout a Christian than Margaret Hoby, religion is very clearly a source of refuge and strength, rather than a prompting to self-examination and penitence.[35] On March 16, 1617, she writes: "this day I spent walking in the Park with Judith & carrying my Bible with me thinking on my present fortunes & what troubles I have pass'd through"; in the marginal note for March 14, she records that when her uncle, cousin, and husband "did what they could to cut me off from my Right, . . . I reffer'd my Cause to God" (74). Anne Clifford, seeing herself as she hopes others will see her, calls upon God as an arbiter, even a champion in her legal struggle: "about this time I used to rise early in the morning & go to the standing in the garden, & taking my prayer book with me beseech God to be mercifull towards me in this & to help me in this as he hath always done" (April 1616; 45). And when she feels she has triumphed, she renders appropriate thanks for a surprising delivery: "Next day was a marvellous day to me through the Mercy of God for it [was] generally thought that I must either have sealed to the agreement or else to have parted with my Lord" (Feb. 18, 1616; 42).

Although Margaret Hoby's diary includes a good deal of information about daily life in the manor house, it nowhere records what she wore; by contrast, Clifford's diary contains repeated references to clothing, references that are to some extent a barometer of her inner state. A number of these relate to her wearing mourning for her mother, as on October 17, 1616: "the 17th was the first day that I put on my black silk grogram gowne"; and December 23, 1616, "I had a new black wrought Taffety gown which my Lady Sr Johns taylor made." At the same time, in her husband's absence, she seems to have dressed informally, and not necessarily in black: "all this time since my Lord went away I wore my black Taffety nightgown & a yellow Taffety waistcoat" (Nov. 20, 1616). The end of her mourning for her mother comes with the visit of the tailor to take measurements for a new gown, and on June 13, 1617, she tried on "my sea water Green Sattin Gown & my Damask Embroidered with gold, both which gowns the taylor which was sent down from London made fit for me to weare with open Ruffs after the french fashion" (85). Twenty-two months later she returns to mourning for the death of Queen Anne (Apr. 18, 1619), enriched by the addition on April 27 of "my new black mourning night gown & those white things which Nane horne made for me" (108). Even such somber clothing is a matter of interest and display, as in May, having been one of the mourners at the Queen's funeral, she goes afterwards "to my sister Beauchamp to shew her my mourning attire" (111).

Clothing also seems closely connected with Anne Clifford's attempts to remain on good terms with her husband. The marginal note for March

15–16, 1617, indicates dissatisfaction with her mode of dress; although it doesn't specify from what sector, her husband seems the likeliest source: "This day I put on my Grogram mourning gown & intend to wear it till my mourning time come out because I was found fault with withall for wearing such ill Cloaths." Spence (69) sees this as a kind of riposte, an act of defiance, but as with much in Clifford's diary, it's not clear just how to read it. Later that spring she writes, "still I strived as much as I cou'd to settle a good opinion in him towards me" (Apr. 16, 1617), and when Dorset seems to have given in she notes, "all this time I wore my white satten gown & my white waistcoat" (80) – perhaps in celebration of Easter, perhaps as a means of preserving self-respect or continuing to be attractive to a husband with a mistress in London. After a difficult summer between her and her husband (1617), she describes her apparel at court: "all this time I was at the Court I wore my green Damask gown imbroidered, without a farthingale" (93). And toward the end of the year, eight months pregnant, she musters a quite splendid display: "Upon the 28th [December] I went to Church in my rich night gown & Petticoat both my Women waiting upon me in their Liveries but my Lord stay'd at home." The mention of her handsome dress and her husband's absence in one sentence may convey a certain disappointment.

Throughout Anne Clifford's life, clothing seems to have been a marker: the plainness of her dress in later life was noted in her funeral sermon as a sign of her valuing the soul over the body: "her dress, not disliked of any, [was] yet imitated by none."[36] John Donne, in a tribute to the ease and breadth of her knowledge, said, "She could discourse of all things, from Predestination to Slea silk."[37] Although Clifford's diary offers no explanatory comments on clothing, it details variations in her dress that reflect many aspects of her situation – formal mourning, pregnancy, despondency, and celebration – vivid reflections of her state of mind and being.

The diary, as I have been suggesting, is neither an altogether ordered and patterned whole nor a merely random collection of facts and dates. The record for 1616, filled with the struggle for Clifford's land and the custody of her child, and marked by anxiety over her gravely ill mother, is a powerfully dramatic whole. But even the diary of 1619, which Martin Holmes describes as somewhat fragmented, repays careful attention.[38] Though less consistent in its theme than the month of May 1616, for example, in its incompleteness and mixture of events, it vividly represents the quality of Anne Clifford's life. Clifford has compiled a record that, because it is in the main so very taciturn, cries out for interpretation; yet precisely because it withholds so much, such interpretation must be cautiously undertaken. For example, Clifford need not tell her original audience – if we assume that to be herself, members of her family, or of her social circle – of her husband's quite open affair with Lady Penistone.[39] But one watches with wonder, and probably with dismay, as she recounts in the margin of August 1619: "all this summer L^{dy} Penniston was at the Wells near Eridge drinking the water," and then notes in the parallel right-hand column, "the 24th after supper came Sr Thos Penniston & his Lady Sr Maxmilian Dallison & his Lady. the 25th they stay'd here all day there being great Entertainment & much stir about them."

There was apparently no outcry from Anne Clifford, either in life or in the diary, at being asked to entertain her husband's mistress in her own home, but such relatively detailed notice of this visit carries a good deal of emotion as its subtext. And in this one instance, she allows her social circle to do the commenting for her: the next marginal note reads: "This coming hither of my Lady Pennistons was much talked of abroad in the world & my Lo. Was much Condemn'd for it."[40] Not only comment but juxtaposition is important, enabling us to observe a meaningful sequence of events:

the 26th they all went away
the 27th my Lo. rid abroad betymes in the morning & came not in till night.

Anne Clifford has presented in sequence Lady Penistone's summerlong sojourn only a few miles from the Dorsets' home, her visit to Knole, her departure, and her husband's subsequent day-long absence. Although there is no explicit statement, the next entry may well be Clifford's response, a refusal to take part in a situation so humiliating: "this night the two green beds in my Chamber were removed." As in the case of the riotous neighbors recorded in Margaret Hoby's diary, much that is felt is not expressed here, and a great more is implied. Moreover, Anne Clifford's situation, of a piece with much that is detailed in her account, is far more personally painful. She is pitted against her husband and humiliated before a larger social circle, whereas the insult faced by the Hobys actually seems to bring them together.

Anne Clifford's very failure to express outrage transmits some of those feelings to the reader, giving us the sense of a powerful drama under the surface. But partly because this is a diary rather than an autobiography or novel, and partly because of its fragmentary state, the reader may well overlook other aspects of Clifford's situation – not only sexual jealousy but also the hopes for pregnancy and children. The several visits Dorset paid to Knole in June of 1619 (he was in residence from June 18 to 23 and returned again on June 26) were fruitful. On October 2 Clifford notes, "upon the 2^d I began to think I was quick with Child, soe as I told it to my Lo. my Sister Sackville & my Sister Compton." That this is a marginal note suggests that it may have been added later, when the suspicion was confirmed; however, there is no confirmation in the text itself, only a few clues: "about this tyme [October 15] I kept my Chamber & stirr'd not out of it till the latter end of March so as most of my friends thought I wou'd not have escaped it." The knowledge of her early pregnancy may be one more factor in the suppressed distress of the late August entries. In the autumn, what might have been only ill health is clearly something more, possibly a difficult pregnancy – she records a fainting fit on November 8: "I was so ill that I fell into a swoon which was the first time that I ever swoonded" – and a general malaise: "Upon the 29th [Nov.] all the Ladies & gentlewomen hereabout being very kinde to me all this tyme of me not being well" (119). It is a sign of the subtlety of this record that some commentators have apparently missed the clues and seen here only an instance of Lady Anne's obstinacy – not stirring from her chamber to see her guests – "my Lord Russel and my Coz. Sr Edward Gorge" – and declaring on October 29: "after this I never stirr'd out of my own bedchamber till the 23^d of March" (118).[41]

This section of the diary continues tense and unresolved to the very end, suggesting a tug of war in the Dorset marriage. On the one hand, there are some signs of victory – or at least a gain of ground – in the marginal note: "the 29th of Nov^{ber} was the last tyme my Lord saw my Lady Penistone at her mothers Lodging in the Strand." Like other marginal notes it must have been composed somewhat after the fact, but how does Anne Clifford know that this is the last meeting? By her husband's assuring her that it was to be the last time that he saw his mistress? Or by her own subsequent observation? Some further ambiguity clings to the phrasing: were there other places, public or private, at which Dorset saw Lady Penistone, or does this mark the end of this particular liaison? In the weeks that follow, the signals of amity are somewhat mixed: Dorset gives Anne "three of his Shirts to make Clouts of" (presumably in anticipation of the birth of their child),[42] but two days later "my Lord & I had a great fallen out" – on the usual topic – "he saying that if ever my Land came to me, I should assure it as he would have me." Yet it looks as if Lady Anne may have won this round; keeping to her chamber, she gets her husband to come to her: "upon the 18th my Lo. came & supped with me in my Chamber which he had not done before since his coming from London for I determined to keep my Chamber & did not so much as go over the threshold of the door."

The tension between Anne Clifford and her husband and the dialogue between the daily records and the marginal notes in 1619 are complicated, suggesting an ongoing struggle, perhaps an inner debate, over the issues of self-determination and independence. Confined to her chamber by ill health and perhaps her own resolution (she had after all participated freely in life at court during her previous pregnancy in 1617), Clifford records two other instances of liberty and imprisonment, extremes that help define her own position. The sentencing of Lord and Lady Suffolk (Thomas Howard and Catherine Knyvet) to a fine of £15,000 and imprisonment in the Tower "during the Kings pleasure" (marginal note and entry for Nov. 20) is balanced by her husband's license: "all the tyme of my Lords being at London he kept a great table having a great company of Lords & Gentlemen that used to come & dine with him" (119). In between these two extremes of liberty and confinement Clifford defines her own sphere: although she cannot go to court, she is also not imprisoned in the Tower; and just as she notes these two points of the compass, Anne Clifford finds a kind of liberation in hearing of her father's exploits as a naval adventurer: "Upon the 24th Sr Francis Slingsby came hither to me & Read to me in the sea papers upon my fathers Voyages."[43] Her chamber becomes in this instance a destination, a space in which to contemplate (and perhaps join in imagination) the freedom and prowess of her father. Moreover, in the next entry she explicitly defines her activities and this space as positive: "Upon the 28th though I kept my chamber altogether, yet methinks the time is not so tedious to me as when I used to be abroad" (119). Although it may be easier to find this setting pleasurable since she receives news of "how ill things were likely to go in Westmorland" (119), her state of wellbeing is not merely dependent on external affairs as it had been earlier.[44] These entries late in 1619 suggest a new and striking determination on the part of the woman who in October 1616 "sent a very earnest Letter to my Lord that I might come up to London" (59) and in March 1617 "wrote a letter to my Lord to beseech him that he wou'd take Knoll in his way as he goes to London" (73). Clifford's firmness of purpose is perhaps rewarded by her husband's sending her he pedigree of the Sackvilles (Dec. 26), presumably a contribution to her writing of the family history, in a sense providing a matching piece to the Clifford pedigree that she is compiling, and a recognition of the two genealogies being of equal interest.

As I hope the above discussion makes clear, Anne Clifford's diary amply repays close attention: the more one looks, the more fully it reveals itself as a source of information and dramatic tension. This final year, much like earlier sections of the diary, is a shaped record: it not only allows us to see general tendencies but also suggests Anne Clifford's own efforts to understand and to mold her life.[45] Although it takes some time to learn the players, the plot, and the rules, Anne Clifford's diary is an absorbing representation. Yet precisely what kind of attention is appropriate? Much in this text makes us want to look for the shaping patterns, for definitive markers and directions, even as we as readers may be inclined to seek (or find) them. But the very episodic quality of the whole, the quick oscillation between moments of joy or triumph to moments of disappointment or near despair, also makes that a risky undertaking. One must read, then, alert to connections of fact and feeling, to emotions not expressed yet strongly present, without imposing on the whole the expectations we would have of a fully wrought literary text.

The final sections of Anne Clifford's life records, for the years 1650–75, return to the narrative mode, giving a summary of each year's events, apparently compiled from more detailed records, but the voice is much older and the approach more systematic than in 1603. This section of the text, while in some ways more formulaic than that of 1616–19, gives us an even stronger sense of Anne Clifford's remarkable character and the extent to which she herself constructs both her life and the record of it. And it gives us insight into the relationship between the narrative and diary forms that Clifford used.

The year 1650 opens with the account of the death of Clifford's second husband, Philip Herbert, Earl of Pembroke and Montgomery, and a summing up of his life, character, and accomplishments. Given the very difficult relations between the two, Clifford's summary seems quite generous: "He was no scholler at all to speak of . . . Yet he was of a verie quick apprehension, a sharp understanding, verie craftie withall, and of a discerning spiritt," and "generallie throughout the Realme very well beloved."[46] Clifford, who here puts "the best possible construction" on Pembroke's behavior, uses biblical references to place her own experience in that framework of meaning: the death of her husband occasions the reflection "Is there not an appointed time to man upon earth?" from Job 7.1, and a reference to Job 8 on God's justice.

But the narrative also strikes an important new note, as Anne Clifford takes charge of her life with vigor, determination, and pleasure. Interestingly, Edward Rainbow notes that Clifford began to keep "the exact Annals of divers passages, which were most remarkable in her own Life, ever since it was wholly at her own disposal, that is, since the Death of her last Lord and Husband, *Philip* Earl of *Pembroke*" (51). Her account of Pembroke's death is followed by an account of herself: she moves from one of her northern castles to another; and in so doing she closes the circle of her life: "that was the first time I came to Skipton where I was borne." Her carefully retrospective comments define who she is – "(I being then Countesse Dowager of Pembroke and Montgomerie) as well as Countesse Dowager of Dorset" – and where she is – "this was the first time that I lay for a twelve monthe together in anie of my owne Howses" (106). Resident in the north of England, she not only experiences the pleasure of the retired life (a conception shaped and expressed by numerous references to Ecclesiastes and Psalms) but also engages in an even more characteristic activity: "this time of my stayeing there I employed my selfe in Building and Reparacons at Skipton and Barden Tower, and in Causeing the Boundaries to be ridden."[47] The first-person pronoun, so common in the writing of Margaret Hoby, now becomes more prominent. Clearly this is the time in which Anne Clifford truly comes into her own – she is at last heir to her father's property, which she had so long sought, and perhaps even more important, she is independent, self-determining, a builder and restorer as well as landowner.

A reader of the 1650–76 records will understand why this section has received less attention than the diary of 1616–19. Although Anne Clifford remains the chief character, the intense struggle with her husband over her inheritance is gone, replaced by a broader concern with her extended family and more frequent mention of national affairs. Much of this record is, at first glance, repetitive and formulaic, providing information that might have been gleaned from the family history or the castle guest book. Indeed, precisely which castle Clifford occupied during what period seems to have become an overriding concern. For example, in 1667 she writes:

The 10th day of Januarie in this year (after I had layen in Skipton Castle in that chamber within the walles of it wherein I was borne into the world, ever since the 9th day of August last) did I remove from thence with my family, and so went through the Haw Parke and by Skibden and Halton and those waies, I in my Hors Litter and some of my Cheife women in my Coach, into my House or Towre of Barden in Craven, where I had not bin since the 6th day of May in

1663, till now. And where I now continued to lye (in the same chamber I formerly used to lye in) till the 29th day of Julye following that I removed from hence with my familie towards Pendraggon and Appleby Castles in Westmerland. (184)

Anne Clifford frequently records, as here, the route she traveled (sometimes with great difficulty over extremely rugged terrain in the depths of winter), and which chamber she occupied.

But as with so much else in these diaries, these facts acquire weight and significance in the telling. Like Margaret Hoby trying to render a complete accounting of her time, Anne Clifford seems anxious to verify her occupation of space: she is concerned to be in residence, always to tell where she was, always to be somewhere that belonged to her, and by being there to assure its belonging to her. Part of the reason may well be the struggle for the land itself and the fact that possession of the property was a strong point in one's favor in a lawsuit. Part of it may also be the quite practical need to maintain oversight of properties at some distance from one another. But Anne Clifford's account also gives the sense of beating the bounds, the ritual walking of the perimeter of a parish to insure that fences were in order and that tithes would be forthcoming.[48]

The very syntactic structure of Clifford's prose and the cross-referencing of these accounts suggest that she is reluctant to let go of one location until she has secured another, as if this were a game of musical chairs that might leave her without a place to settle. This presumably subconscious concern actually makes the deciphering of the account, or the envisioning of her location, more difficult than it need be. The narrative above might read more simply "from August 9, 1666 until January 10, 1667, I resided at Skipton Castle (my birthplace). On January 10, I went to Barden Tower, where I remained until July 29, at which time I moved to Pendragon and Appleby Castles." This is clear enough, but it misses the sense, pronounced in Clifford's own narrative, of one place of residence and one stay linking hands with those that go before and come after. Each arrival looks back to the previous departure from that place, and each departure looks to the next destination. In fact the only time the next destination is not given, but left blank in the manuscript, is in the last year of her life, when she departed Brougham Castle for the grave.[49]

Moreover, the places that Anne Clifford occupies are for her and her reader richly endowed with ancestral or historical connections: she comments repeatedly that at Skipton Castle she lies "in that chamber within the walles of it wherein I was borne into the world." And about Brougham

Castle she repeatedly states, "where my Noble Father was borne and my Blessed Mother dyed."[50] Her being able to occupy these places is the result of her own restoration: in 1663 she mentions that she came "to Skipton Castle into the now repayred Old Buildings there, to ly now for a time in the Chamber wherein myself was borne. For though thatt and the cheife partes of the Castle were pulled down by the demmaunds of Cromwell in 1648, yet did I cause it to be rebuilt as it now is in the yeares 1657, 1658 and 1659" (162). Lady Anne has outlasted not only the competing heirs but also Oliver Cromwell himself, and she sees her restoration of and to this property as a sign of God's providence, as she carefully, sometimes laboriously, states the significance of her return: "I did not come to ly in this Old part of the Castle wherein I was borne, since I was carryed out of it when I was about eight weeks old, [with] my Father and Mother and my Brother Robert, Lord Clifford from thence towards London, till this sixth day of May. And it is to be accounted a great and wonderfull providence of God that now, in the 73rd yeare of my age I shold ly againe in thatt Chamber wherein I was borne into the World" (164). Each place that Anne Clifford visits or stays is touched with the memory not only of her own previous sojourns, but also of her parents – the previous residence with her family, the last visit with her mother. This tendency to connect a particular place with events that had occurred there, which is a feature of the 1616–19 diaries, becomes one of the most pronounced characteristics of these later years. It is one of the chief ways in which she creates order and structure in a life that otherwise might seem a mere sequence of events.

Not only does Anne Clifford herself maintain a controlling presence in her northern territories, she also celebrates each visit of each member of the family as a kind of triumphal journey: the more Sackvilles, Tuftons, and Comptons that occupy these spaces, the more secure the family inheritance; and the recording of them has the quality of a litany. The reference for the year 1663 will stand as the example of many:

And the third day of August this Summre being Munday did my Daughtre the Countesse of Thanet with four of her younger Sonnes – Richard, Thomas, Sackville and George Tufton, and her Daughtre Ladie Frances Tufton come hither from their journie from Yorke and from London hither into Skipton Castle in Craven to mee about 8 a clock at night, into the chamber where I then lay, and wherein I was borne into the world; and I then kiss'd them all with much joy and comfort. It being the first time that I saw my Daughtre of Thanet or these four younger Sonnes of hers in Skipton Castle or in Craven, for it was the first time that my Daughtre of Thanet or these her four younger Sonnes ever came into Craven. (165)

The paragraph continues until Lady Anne has recorded her most recent contact with each of the family members mentioned. As with the diary of Margaret Hoby, although the syntax here is literally paratactic, the effect is oddly hypotactic – suspending the reader in an endless chain of comings and goings. We might describe this simply as the musings of an elderly woman (she was seventy-three at the time) reluctant to yield to another speaker and recalling with matriarchal intensity each visit of her family. Any veteran of contemporary family life might imagine her meeting them at the door with the joyful – or possibly guilt-inducing – reminder that she hasn't seen them for *five years*. But whatever relations in Anne Clifford's family may have been, the rhetoric here exerts a remarkable control: the boundaries of Anne Clifford's sentences embrace not only her property but also the lives of her family. In some sense, so long as they are preserved in these records, they cannot cease to exist. And indeed, these annual records are a kind of parallel project to the family genealogies that she so carefully maintained and that constitute a remarkably complete family history.

The accounts of these family visits are not only an obvious source of satisfaction, pleasure, and pride (like the note that the visit of Nicholas Tufton was "the first time I saw any Grandchild of mine that was an Earle"; 172), but also for Clifford a confirmation of Divine Providence, which she articulates with the help of scripture: "Soe this twenty sixte day was the first tyme that I ever saw my Daughter of Northampton or her Lord or their Child here att Skipton. And the first time that I ever saw this younger daughter of myne or any Childe of hers in any of the lands of myne Inheritance. Which gave me reason to apply to my selfe that saying of Israel unto Joseph: Gen. 48.11 – for I never saw any Child of hers till now" (121). The passage in Genesis – "I had not thought to see thy face; and lo, God hath shewed me also thy seed" – reveals the extent to which Anne Clifford, very much like Margaret Hoby, sees herself living out a scriptural pattern, finding her models for success or failure in biblical language and texts. Remarking on her return to Brougham Castle in 1653, she writes:

And I had not layne in this Brougham Castle in Thirty Seaven yeares till now. For ye month of December in One Thousand six hundred and sixtene (when I was married to Richard, Earle of Dorset) I went out of itt upp towards London to him, and never lay in itt till this night. In which long time I past through many strange and hard fortunes in the Sea of this World. Soe as I may well apply that Saying to myself: Ps. 107 & Ps. 109.27 (120)

The passages in Psalms to which Clifford refers celebrate deliverance from a time of travail; images of the Israelites wandering in the wilderness or enduring the Babylonian captivity seem to strike Anne Clifford as just right for the occasion. And however much such references may seem to a modern reader self-righteous or overstated, inhabiting her property is for Clifford a clear reason for jubilation and a clear sign of vindication. The earlier pleas for divine help, expressed in 1616–19, "beseech[ing] God to be mercifull towards me & to help me in this as he hath always done" (Apr. 1616; 45) are here, in Clifford's eyes, answered:

They wandered in the wilderness in a solitary way; they found no city to dwell in. Hungry and thirsty, their soul fainted in them. Then they cried unto the Lord in their trouble, and he delivered them out of their distresses. And he led them forth by the right way, that they might go to a city of habitation . . . so he bringeth them unto their desired haven . . . that they may know that this is thy hand; that thou, Lord, hast done it. (Ps. 107:4–7, 30; Ps. 109:27)

As a matter of personal piety, Anne Clifford constructs a kind of numerology of blessings, finding arithmetical verification of her favored state: "And I saw her not since the twenty eight of July 1656 till this Twentyeight of this month [August 1658] that she now came hither to mee, where shee and her three Sonnes now lay for nyne nights together. Soe as I have now seen Nyne of my said Daughter's Children here in Westmerland which I account a great and singular Blessinge and Goodnesse of God towards mee" (138). In addition to the formulaic account of visits paid and received, Anne Clifford carefully records the births of her daughters' children and her great-grandchildren, conveying a strong sense of her interest in the family line and a picture of considerable tenderness.[51] She gives particular attention to the lives and childbirth experiences of her granddaughters, thus emphasizing a line of inheritance from one woman to another, a pattern that begins with her initial concern in 1617 that a legal reversal for herself is also a reversal for her daughter Margaret.[52]

Typically for this period of the summaries, significant events such as births and deaths are recorded both at the beginning of the annual account and at the appropriate place in the year's chronology, thus intensifying the emotional impact through repetition. For example, the opening paragraph for 1665 records both the marriage of Clifford's granddaughter Frances Tufton on February 23 and her death on November 22 in childbirth. The first is celebratory: "Which Grandchild of mine had bin once or twice in the Low Countries for the cure of Ricketts. But thanks be to God she came now to be well married" (176). The second is more detailed, and in its sequential, nonhierarchical organization, movingly conveys Clifford's own sense of loss:

The 22nd of the said November, about one a clock in the afternoon, (to my unspeakable greife), dyed my dear Grandchild the Ladie Frances Drax who was my Daughter of Thanets third Daughter but sixth Child, and was borne in her Fathers House in Aldersgate Streete in London Towne the 23rd of March in 1642, as the yeare begines on New yeares Day. . . . And she was married in the same Thanett House the 23rd of Februarie last to Mr Henrie Drax. And she dyed, (as aforesaid), the 22nd of November in a hyred house at Buckwell in Kent nere Hothfeild being then in labour of her first Childe which was a Sonne of whom she could not be delivered, for the Childe was dead within her a few houres before her owne death. (178)

As with other sections of Clifford's late diaries, much here is formulaic and factual: there is a great concern, even obsession, with getting the facts right, noting the time of births and deaths, the place, those in attendance, etc. Many of these could have been copied from the family Bible or the family chronology, and we know that Clifford was at great pains to keep such a record. But interestingly, the style of composition, the unwillingness or inability to let go of the subject, conveys as much feeling as the explicit yet dignified acknowledgment – "to my unspeakable greife." Clifford moves beyond the genealogy of her granddaughter – her place in the family ranking, place of birth, married name, the name of her husband, place of death, its occurrence in a hired house – to more intimate and painful details. She also gives a little vignette of her daughter Margaret's attempt to attend her daughter's first childbirth, abandoned when she learned of her death: "And whilst she was in labour did my Daughter of Thanet her Mother, beginne her journie from Bolebrooke in Sussex toward Buckwell aforesaid to see her. But hearing of her death before she came hither, she returned immediately back to Bolebrooke again where she lay when her sayd Daughter was buryed, which was on the 1st of December. . ." The record for the year concludes with an account of the writer's own activities which in context is elegiac: "And both when she dyed and was burried did I lye in my owne Chamber in Cliffords Tower in Brough Castle where I heard first of all the sad news of her death, the 6th day of the said December" (179; 1665). In other words, Lady Frances had been brought to bed, died, and been buried before the news reached her grandmother. The report of the marriage begins the year; the account of the death ends it; there is nothing more to say.

There is also a kind of balancing of good and ill fortune, a sort of spiritual ledger, created in the very syntax and rhythm of Clifford's sentences, as in this juxtaposition of times and places of life and death: "And whilst I now lay here in Brougham Castle in my owne Chamber, where my father was borne, and my Mother died, I had the joyfull newes howe that on the second day of this September (being a Saturday) my Grandchilde ye Lady Margarett Coventry, wife of Mr George Coventry, was delivered of her first Childe" (123). The method by which Clifford recounts the birth of her granddaughter and the death of her daughter Isabella has an analogous symmetry, balancing gain and loss: "The 14th day of March in this yeare [1661] was my Daughter of Northampton delivered of her third Daughter and sixth Childe, the Ladie Alethea Compton – in her Lordes House in Lincolnes Inne feilds at London . . . . And the 14th daie of October following dyed her Mother, my Daughter of Northampton in the said House in Lincolnes Inne feilds after she had but a while before come up thither to take phisick"(150). The death of the daughter is repeated in greater detail later in the year, but this time the lag between the death and her learning of it is the occasion for meditation: "the same 14th day of this October about 9 a clock in the morning, after she was dead (though I then knew it not) did I remove out of Appleby Castle in Westmerland into Pendraggon Castle in the same Countie, where I now lay in the second Storie that looks East and South" (154).

In this recollection Clifford's concerns are dynastic, familial, and maternal: while the connection is not made explicit, in looking east and south, she would have looked toward London, where the family drama was playing out. In noting with satisfaction that "This [was] the first time I lay in the said Pendraggon Castle since it was lately repaired and made habitable by mee to my great costs and charges after it had layen desolate ever since the 15th yeare of Edward the third in 1341, which is 320 yeares agoe," she appears to change the subject. But in fact the two points are related. This castle "was the cheife and beloved habitation of Idonea the younger Daughter and Coheire of Robert de Viteriponte my Auncestor, she dying without issue . . . and then all her Inheritance in Westmerland came to her eldest Sister Isabella's Grandchild Robert, Lord Clifford and his posteritie to whom I am heire by a lineal descent" (154). Anne's daughter Isabella must have been named, if not for this early ancestor, then for her successors: the names Isabella and Margaret are prominent in the Clifford genealogy. Isabella bore six children, only two of whom survived her, and only one – Alethea, who was born shortly before her mother's death – was to live out the following year. Isabella was survived by her elder sister, Margaret, Countess of Thanet; and it is Margaret's child and grandchildren who became the heirs of Anne Clifford. Clifford's sorrow for her daughter's death is thus mingled, in the reporting of it, with the thoughts of her distant ancestors and the way the line was preserved – through its women as well as its men – to her own day, just as her grief over her mother's death in 1616 is linked with her sense of her own threatened inheritance and her anxiety for her own daughter Margaret.[53]

Although the activities of her family dominate the annual reports of 1650–75, Anne Clifford also notes significant public events, including the restoration and coronation of Charles II, the Fire of London, the Peace Treaty of Breda, the visits of the Prince of Tuscany and Queen Henrietta Maria (and the latter's subsequent death), the election of the Pope, the visit of William of Orange, the death of Anne Hyde, Duchess of York, the Duke's marriage to Mary of Modena. Yet sometimes these references also have a particular connection with the family: Clifford reports that the Great Fire had consumed "not only Baynards Castle, but Great Dorsett House and Little Dorsett House (in which place I had spent much of my time when I was Wife to my first and second Husbands), but also did consume that ancient and Noble Church of St Paules in London, and the whole streets of Cheapside, Blackfryers and Whitefryers and all the Houses between that and ye River of Thames." And then, characteristically finding providential mercies amid losses, she notes, "But in all this desolation Thanet House in Aldersgate, my Daughter of Thanets Jointure House was then preserved" (183).

While these later records give greater space to national events than the 1616–19 diary does, Anne Clifford often recounts her family's activities with an equal sense of drama: for example, the visit of one of her grandchildren receives as much attention and anticipation as that of the Queen of France. And in later years in particular, Anne Clifford's own movements come to resemble royal progresses, reported in detail suitable to that rank:

For on this 19th of Aprill 1672 (as aforesaid) being Friday, about 10 a clock in the fornoone after I had layen in my Chamber in Pendragon Castle in Westmerland ever since the 17th of November last, did I remove out of it, and came through the great chamber downe the staires into the Court, where at the Hall doore I went into my Horslitter in which I rid through the Gatehouse there and through the River of Eden, and over part of Ashfield and through Wharton Park and in sight of that Hall, and through Kirkby Stephen and Brough Sowerby to my Castle of Brough in the same County, my Gentlewomen and Maidservants attending me in my Coach drawn with 6 Horses and my Menservants on Horsback and a great many of my Tenants and Neighbours of Mallerstang, Kirkby Stephen, Brough and Appleby and other places in the County comeing along with me. And so we came to my said Castle of Brough about 1 a clock in the afternoon, where in the Court of it I allighted out of my litter, and came upstairs into ye Hall where all ye strangers that accompanied mee took their leaves of mee and went away to their severall Homes, . . . (212)

The movement here is a little stiff and ponderous, and probably excessively detailed. In earlier years, when she could walk beyond the Hall door and could ride on horseback (as she did in 1616–17), there was no need or inclination to record the stages of the journey so minutely.[54] If Clifford's record-keeping here seems mechanical, her residence in these castles, her maintaining of sovereignty over them, is what keeps her going, both physically and psychically. The unbroken syntactic links – the *ands* and *wheres* that keep their hold on the reader – are also the stages by which Anne Clifford retains her hold on life and action. The story told in her funeral sermon of her persisting in a similar journey in January, even though she fainted three times on the way, is an instance of her remarkable resolve. According to Bishop Rainbow:

She having before fixed on that day, and so much company being come purposely to wait on her, *she would* go; and although assoon as she came to her Horse-litter, she swooned again, and was carried into a Chamber, as before, yet assoon as that Fit was over, she went; and . . . when some of her servants, and others represented to her, with repining, her undertaking such a Journey, foretold by divers to be so extremely hazardous to her life; she replied, *she knew she must die, and it was the same thing to Her to die in the way, as in her House; in her Litter, as in her Bed;* declaring a courage no less than the great *Roman* General – *Necesse est ut eam, non ut vivam;* She would not acknowledge any necessity why she should Live, but believed it necessary to keep firm her Resolution. (Rainbow, 46)

Even when some of Anne Clifford's earlier vigor is gone, the pattern of her life and syntax remains, demonstrating her persistence as head of the household (and as it were lord of the castle) to the end.

Whereas the 1616–19 diaries have a kind of dramatic tension, and the narrative summaries of 1650 and the years following offer more succinct but less emotional accounts, the summaries of the later years are laced with considerable detail. This suggests that the earlier summaries were compiled primarily from other records, perhaps from the diaries themselves, while for the later years Clifford drew on more recent memories. We learn for example that the father of one of her grandsons-in-law died of gangrene of the toes (154), that her daughter and granddaughter nursed most of their own children (123), that her grandson's wife was on one occasion a little indisposed (173); such details might not have survived in earlier, briefer, annual summaries. But in the final months of Clifford's life, from January through March of 1676, the text reverts to the form of 1616–19, with individual daily entries. Because death prevented her from turning this daily account into summary form, we have a far more direct view of Clifford's character in a diary that in some respects returns to those early years.

Perhaps most striking is Clifford's remarkable vigor and clarity of mind: until a few days before her death she carried on a lively correspondence with family and friends, dictating several letters in a day in response to the post from London (which appears to have arrived once a week).[55] Trivial daily events that would perhaps be noted in an account book but omitted from the annual summary are still here; they give a sense of the extent to which her life, after all, resembled the domestic responsibilities of Margaret Hoby. She maintained strict supervision of the affairs of her estates – regularly recording, for example, the payment for twelve bushels of malt for beer for the household, and a corresponding supply of sack, white wine, and claret; she arranged payment for the transport and cutting of wood, for a new garden and garden wall at Brough Castle, and for "mending the Fences, scaling the Molehills & dressing the Middows at Southfield and Rampkin Close."[56]

There are also some amusing glimpses of Lady Anne's never-failing concern for finances: on February 7, 1676, six weeks before her death, she duly paid "the Deafe woman of my Almeshouse at Appleby . . . for 5 dozen yards of Bonlace."[57] Clifford herself had set up the almshouse as a charitable establishment to house twelve widows, yet in this instance, she was "very angry" with this particular widow "for bringing so much and told her I would have no more of her" (249). Two days later (Feb. 9), she similarly complains to her wine dealer, and later to his wife, that he has overcharged her. Perhaps this is the querulousness of an infirm elderly woman. Yet Clifford's interest in life in general persists, as she records in February 1676 the birth of four stillborn puppies in her chamber, assists a neighbor with a badly broken leg by lending him her horse litter (251), and stays current with the news, noting not only "that the Danes had taken Wismar from the Swedes" (under Gustavus Adolphus) but also that the King "doth forbid all coffee houses or the selling of coffee publickly" (Jan. 4, 1676; 232).

In returning to the daybook format of 1616–19, the journal of the last months of Clifford's life gives us an apparently less structured, less edited text than that of the intervening years. But like that earlier section, it has a marked thematic unity, and makes explicit connections with that earlier period. Like many in old age whose memories of the distant past are sharper than those of more recent occurrence, Anne Clifford recalls in the last months of her life significant events and occasions. But in this written text, as in her life, these recollections create a remarkable degree of symmetry and unity. One suspects that Anne Clifford had an excellent memory, but also that she was assisted by the records that she had done so much to compile. She deliberately cultivates these memories, as each day that passes becomes the occasion to recall an earlier day: on January 6, "Being Twelfth day, I remembered how this day was 54 yeares since, at night, [that] at a Mask performed in the King's Banqueting house at Whitehall & in the Privy Galleryes there, did I see King James the Scotchman, and it was the last time I ever saw him or Hee mee" (233). She remembers a number of significant events of fifty-nine years back, suggesting that she had looked specifically at that record, detailing in particular the struggle for her land:

The 18th day I remembered how this day was 59 years (since) I went with my first Lord, Richard Earle of Dorset, before King James, into his Inner Drawing Chamber at Whitehall where ye King earnestly desired mee to subscribe to an award which hee intended to make betwixt mee & my said Lord on the one part, & my Uncle of Cumberland & his Son Henry Lord Clifford on the other part, concerning the lands of my antient Inheritance in Craven & Westmorland. But (by God's Grace) I began to deny it, it being the first time I was ever before that King (239).

She recalls as well Queen Anne's contrary counsel, "to persist in my denyall of trusting my cause concerning my lands of Inheritance to her husband King James' award" (240). Competing with this memory, reflecting the complex reality of 1616, is the memory of returning from court to her daughter Margaret, who was "ill with her long Ague" at Knole.

January 30, 1676, is the occasion of a double remembrance – the day of her own birth in 1590 and the beheading of King Charles I in 1649. "The 30th Day being Sunday, I considered how this day was 86 years & then Fryday about 7 a clock in the evening was my blessed Mother with very hard labor brought to bed of mee in hier owne chamber in Skipton Castle in Craven, where she then lay" (244). The word "considered" suggests that the events of previous years are the subject of meditation as well as memory. Often these meditations are supported by biblical references: January 30 brings to mind Psalm 1 – perhaps an appropriation of its text to her own life, or that of Charles: "Blessed is the man that walketh not in the counsel of the ungodly, nor standeth in the way of sinners, nor sitteth in the seat of the scornful. But his delight is in the law of the Lord; and in his law doth he meditate day and night." There are also frequent references to Psalm 121: "I will lift up mine eyes unto the hills, from whence cometh my help. My help cometh from the Lord, which made heaven and earth . . . The Lord shall preserve thy going out and thy coming in from this time forth, and even for evermore" (Ps. 121:1–2, 8); and to passages in Ecclesiastes that reflect on the transience of human life, whose length is known only to God.

These references suggest that Anne Clifford kept regular diaries at least into the mid-1620s, and they allow us to fill in information otherwise missing from her record. We learn of the birth of her son, Thomas, Lord Buckhurst, on February 2, 1620 (confirming the sense that something more than obstinacy kept her in her chamber late in 1619) and the death of that infant son the following July. The memory of so brief a life calls again for the familiar passage from Ecclesiastes, which begins, "To every thing there is a season," and continues, "All are of the dust, and all turn to dust again" (Eccles. 3:1, 20). There are indications that the keeping of diaries was a family practice, since Clifford recalls not only the day, time, and circumstances of her own birth but also the fact that on February 6 it was "86 years [since] the good news *was brought to my father and my Aunt of Warwick and her husband* [emphasis mine], to Bedford House in the Strand, both by letter and word of mouth, that my Mother was brought a bed of mee the 30th of the month before in Skipton Castle in Craven with very hard labour" (248), strongly implying that her mother or her father kept similar kinds of records.[58]

Marked as the intervening years have been with the deaths of grand-children and children (intermingled with births and family visits), this time of year, appropriately at the beginning of Lent, is particularly full of recollected farewells: "the 9th day being Ash Wednesday, I remembered how this day was 72 years [ago] dyed in North hall house . . . my worthy Aunt Anne Russell, Countesse Dowager of Warwick.[59] It is also the occasion, not of the death of her first husband, but of their last leave-taking: "And I remembered how this day was 52 yeares [since] my first Lord Richard, Earle of Dorset, came into the Tower chamber in Knowl house in Kent where I then lay, and there he kiss'd mee and my two daughters, which I had by him, & that was the last time hee lay in Knowl house, for that day hee went up to Great Dorset House in London Towne & . . . continued to lye there . . . till his death happened the 29th of March following" (250). Had Anne Clifford lived until March 29, she would doubtless have marked Dorset's death as well, for she marks all significant dates and looks for significance in each date. In this period she typically begins each day's entry with a remembrance of the past (whenever there is a significant anniversary) before going on to the events of the present. In his funeral sermon, Bishop Rainbow associates these acts of remembering with a sense of accountability akin to Margaret Hoby's: "Diligence was a noted Virtue in her; her active Soul filling up all the Gaps of Time, with something useful or delightful to her self or others . . . But she had such a desire to know, review, and reflect, upon all the occurrences, passages, and actions of her Life, as thinking it an especial mean *to apply her heart to Wisdom, by so numbering her days*, that none of them might be wholly lost" (50). Although Clifford still lives in the present – paying her servants, listening to the service of worship, making decisions about her household, and writing to her granddaughter Alethea just a week before her own death – one also senses that it is the past that gives the present meaning, that each day is the occasion for a memory of a prior event, and that these memories lead to religious meditations, informed by the ongoing biblical references.

While these connections between past and present are a strong structural element in the diaries, some of Clifford's less elegiac memories provide a somewhat more detailed version of events recorded earlier: she recounts, for example, her journey northward with her husband in February 1616, recalling the stages of travel, the inns at which they stayed, the sights they took in on the way (Warwick Castle and Church, Guy's Cliff, Killingworth Castle),[60] and the notable places of Litchfield. She remembers her marriage, February 25, sixty-seven years before, and her attending church with her husband in Litchfield on that anniversary seven years later (257–58), as well as the date (Mar. 6, 1609) when she was brought by "my blessed Mother with many in our company . . . from her house in Austin Fryers to the Court of little Dorset House . . . to lye there with my first Lorde" little more than a week after her marriage. The significance to her, both early and late, of this anniversary may be seen in the reference February 1619, "my Lord shou'd have gone to London the 24th of this month but I entreated him to stay here the 25th, because on that day 10 years I was married, which I kept as a day of Jubile to me" (Acheson, 100–1), suggesting that such an occasion was of greater importance to her than to her husband.

The daily record of these last months (in contrast to the more selective record of 1616–19) contains items that, as in the diary of Margaret Hoby, create almost a sense of litany, of a repeated series of events that give life its structure if not its meaning. Throughout this three-month period, and absent from the previous year's record, comes the notation, "I went not out of the house nor out of my chamber today" (231). This statement from January 1, 1676, creates a perhaps accidental, yet nonetheless striking, connection with the entry for January 1, 1616: "Upon new years day I kept my Chamber all the day." Because Anne Clifford is unable to go abroad, her chamber becomes the focal center of activity: she recounts again in highly formulaic fashion how her servants attended public worship, the parson came to her, what the dining arrangements were, and more. The resemblances from one entry to another are so strong that one suspects that the secretaries who recorded Lady Anne's diary entries in these last months must have used certain formulas:

The 2nd day being Sunday, yet I went not out of the house nor out of my chamber today. But my 2 gentlewomen Mrs Pate and Mrs Susan (Machell) and Mr Tho. Gabetis my Shiriff and his wife, and 3 of my Laundry maids and most of my chiefe Servants went to Ninekirkes, where Mr Grasty the Parson preached a Sermon to them and the Congregation.

And today there dined without with my folks in the Painted Room, and with the Sherriff and his wife, Mr Grasty the parson, my two farmers here – William Spedding and his wife, & Jeffrey Bleamire and his son, so after dinner I had them into my Room and kist the women and took the Men by the hand. And a little after Mr Grasty the parson said Common Prayers and read a Chapter and sang a Psalm as usuall to mee and them and my family, and when prayers were done they went away. (January 1676, 231–32)

Sunday after Sunday, Lady Anne monitors the church attendance of her household, and Sunday after Sunday, she "kist the women and took the Men by the hand." Always they dine without and then attend her in her chamber. Sometimes the sermon is designated a "good" or "very good" one; once she is so struck by the sermon that she feels it has been directed only at her; sometimes those who come to her chamber are rewarded with a gift, most often of buckskin gloves, a ring, or a sum of money. The same procedure was repeated each Wednesday, though less elaborately, when her chaplain regularly "said Prayers [using the *Book of Common Prayer*] and read a Chapter" (233).[61]

While Anne Clifford recalls and relives the events of the past, she also documents the progress of her last illness. She was clearly subject to abdominal distress, described as "Extream ill fitt of the wind," and loose stools that sometimes led to fainting fits. Nevertheless, these notations are usually paired with a reason for thankfulness – a good, or relatively good, night's sleep, often accompanied by a reference to Ps. 23:4: "Yea, though I walk through the valley of the shadow of death, I will fear no evil: for thou art with me; thy rod and thy staff they comfort me." Clifford is clearly aware of the seriousness of her physical situation: on March 12 she writes "tho' this day I had an Extream ill fit of the wind in the afternoon, so that I was in great danger (and yet in no danger) of Death, and yet I slept well in ye night I thank God, notwithstanding" (265). In other words, for the faithful and composed Christian, death itself is not a danger, except as a form of speech. Part of her confidence lay in her knowledge of scripture and her application of it to her life: as Edward Rainbow records in his funeral sermon, she had "by heart" the entire eighth chapter of Romans, which speaks of the movement from death to life, and from corruption to incorruption (Rainbow, 62).

Appropriately, Anne Clifford's last recorded memories of the past are of her mother, a woman who was both mentor and model. On March 15, 1676, Clifford recalls their last time together, a visit that lasted until April 2, 1616, and on March 20, two days before Clifford's own death, she dictates: "I remembered how this day was 60 years [since] I and my blessed Mother in Brougham Castle in Westmorland, where wee then lay, give in our answer in writing that we would not stand to the Award the then four cheif Judges meant to make concerning the lands of mine Inheritance, which did spin out a great deal of trouble to us, yet God turned it for the best." Clifford couples this memory with a closing reference to Deuteronomy 23:5: "the Lord thy God turned the curse into a blessing unto thee, because the Lord thy God loved thee."

In meditation, memory, and the composition of the text of her diary until the day before her death, Anne Clifford creates a consistency of theme and of vision – the value of her mother's strong will and influence, and the value that they shared most intensely – Anne Clifford's right to inherit her father's land. It is a story of remarkable persistence, but no more so than the diary record that Clifford herself so carefully maintained. In its syntax and in its structure, Anne Clifford's final diary reflects the circumstances in which she finds herself and, even in her last extremity, strives to control. It also shows her growth as a person, from a young woman of notable steadfastness yet little authority to someone who, as Bishop Rainbow recounts, exercised dominance over herself and those around her.[62] Even though this final record does not have the kind of polish we would expect of a public document, it is clearly shaped, with and against life itself, to reflect Anne Clifford's understanding of herself and her place in the world. In reading it and noting its remembering of the past, one may recall the words of the poet with whom she had dined nearly sixty years before: "Thy firmness makes my circle just, / And makes me end where I begun."[63]

CHAPTER 3

Pygmalion's image: the lives of Lucy Hutchinson

In moving from the diaries and annual records of Margaret Hoby and Anne Clifford to the autobiographies of Lucy Hutchinson, Ann Fanshawe, Anne Halkett, and Margaret Cavendish, we turn again to generic questions. A diary may constitute the final form intended by the writer – as in the diary of Margaret Hoby, which is a fairly immediate and unrevised recording of events – or it may serve as basis for a more coherent narrative form, like the summaries of Anne Clifford's later years. But the life records to which we turn next – those of Hutchinson, Halkett, Fanshawe, and Cavendish – raise much more substantial questions about narrative form and principles. Whereas diaries by their very nature are often concerned with discrete events, a memoir or autobiography forges connections between the disparate occurrences of daily life to construct a narrative line. Although we found in the diaries of Hoby and Clifford considerable purposefulness – in the case of Hoby the accounting for time, in the case of Clifford the justification of herself and her position – an autobiography is much more likely than a diary to articulate the writer's intentions. And whereas a diary or journal might be written to oneself, an autobiography, even if not intended for print publication, presupposes an audience beyond the self.[1] In autobiography we would expect to find a more fully developed and coherent narrative, a more explicitly directed account, a stronger sense of self and of audience.

At first glance it appears that Lucy Hutchinson and Margaret Cavendish contented themselves with very brief accounts of their own lives in contrast to more ambitious and extended accounts of their husbands' lives.[2] Given the scope of Lucy Hutchinson's *Life of John Hutchinson of Owthorpe*, which runs to nearly three hundred pages in the Oxford edition, and the *Life of Mrs Lucy Hutchinson, Written by Herself: A Fragment*, a mere twelve pages, it may seem peculiar to give much attention to the latter. The relative length of the two texts suggests that Lucy Hutchinson was interested chiefly in her husband and appears, in her words, as a shadow, a mirror image of him. The history of publication – the frequent linking of Lucy Hutchinson's autobiographical fragment with the completed life of her husband and the tendency to place hers first – contributes to this view, and seems to imply that she abandoned the account of her life for his.[3] But Lucy Hutchinson's account of her life was not merely abandoned by its author but also cropped, truncated by her own or someone else's censoring hand; hence it is quite possible that this mere fragment was originally considerably longer.[4] Moreover, despite the way in which these texts usually appear, it is not at all clear that the narrative of her life preceded his in composition; rather the way in which these texts have been published has determined and perhaps distorted our reading of them. David Norbrook, for example, argues for a reverse chronology, pointing to internal evidence for the composition of her own life between 1664–72. Even if inconclusive, this consideration should lead us to question the assumption that Lucy Hutchinson's *Life of Colonel Hutchinson* is her "last best work."[5] The apparently dependent and subordinate status of Lucy Hutchinson's *Life* and its fragmented form connect it with the autobiographical writing of Ann Fanshawe, Anne Halkett, and Margaret Cavendish. But rather than being determinative, these qualities demand exploration. At least in the case of Lucy Hutchinson, I shall argue, the author is by no means so dependent or so ancillary as she at first appears but has in fact a quite prominent role, both as shaper of and as a character in these two lives.

Like her future husband, Lucy Apsley came from a well-positioned and strongly royalist family. Born January 29, 1620, she was the daughter of Sir Allen Apsley, Lieutenant of the Tower of London. At age eighteen she married John Hutchinson, a committed Puritan who became military governor of Nottingham during the Civil War and who was a signatory of the order for the execution of Charles I. Although not one of those exempted from the Act of Oblivion, and hence supposedly not subject to legal proceedings after the Restoration, John Hutchinson was nevertheless arrested and died in 1664 while imprisoned in Sandowne Castle. In the years after his death, Lucy Hutchinson composed a life of her husband that constructs him as a model of virtue and accomplishment, a project she represents as undertaken for her consolation and for the edification of her children.[6] In the introductory section Hutchinson suggests, using a familiar trope, that her subject needs no hyperbole: "A naked, undressed narrative, speaking the simple truth of him, will deck him with more substantial glory, than all the panegyrics that the best pens could ever consecrate to the virtues of the best men."[7] But of course the narrative is far from simple, and every inch a panegyric. I want to consider more closely how it achieves its effects and how Lucy Hutchinson depicts not only her husband but also herself within this text.

As Estelle Jelinek points out, a common fallacy regarding autobiographical writing is that it is confessional.[8] We have seen how little of the confessional mode is found in the diaries of Margaret Hoby and Anne Clifford; this is equally the case with the autobiographical fragment of Lucy Hutchinson, which includes a relatively small proportion of personal detail. Like Halkett and Clifford, both of whom were eager to place themselves in the context of their ancestors and immediate forebears, Lucy Hutchinson also seeks a larger context for her life. But hers is not merely familial (though she gives careful attention to her parentage and ancestry) but notably historical, national, and devotional. As she traces her line back to Saxon and Norman England, she finds evidence of particular blessings in both the place and the time of her birth. In constructing the life of her husband and herself within it, Lucy Hutchinson forcefully employs the tropes of romance and of psychological journey to depict a pair of lovers, not star-crossed but rather particularly favored by Providence. In dealing with Hutchinson's self-representation, I shall look first at her own memoir, and then, because it also significantly represents her, at her *Life of John Hutchinson of Owthorpe*.

Lucy Hutchinson undertook her brief autobiography, she tells us, in order to "stir up my thankfulness for things past, and to encourage my faith for the future."[9] By enumerating instances of good fortune that range from her parentage to the place of her birth to its timing, she seeks evidence of providential care in her own life. But although this effort has a personal application, it is also related to a much larger project, the placing of her life in all of history. Perhaps appropriately, Lucy Hutchinson's prose – and her conception of her task – rather startlingly recall Richard Hooker's celebration of the laws of God manifest in creation:[10]

The Almighty Author of all beings in his various providences, whereby he conducts the lives of men from the cradle to the tomb, exercises no less wisdom and goodness than he manifests power and greatness in their creation; but such is the stupidity of blind mortals that, instead of employing their studies in these admirable books of providence wherein God daily exhibits to us glorious characters of his love, kindness, wisdom and justice, they ungratefully regard them not, and call the most wonderful operations of the great God the common accidents of human life, especially if they be such as are usual, and exercised towards them in ages wherein they are not very capable of observation, and whereon they seldom employ any reflection. (3)

Although the style here is more paratactic than the grandest of Hooker's periodic sentences and the diction more uneven, Hutchinson does use hypotaxis for dramatic effect as she sets the wisdom and generosity of God against the limited perceptions of human beings. The opening, with its carefully wrought syntax and its broad reference, clearly signals the importance of Hutchinson's task. Her particular devotional exercise, articulated in the second paragraph, is then set against this very large background. She undertakes the story of her own life both as an expression of gratitude to her creator and as a means to inspire that attitude, attempting to recollect "as much as I have heard or can remember of the passages of my youth and the general and particular providences exercised to me, both in the entrance and progress of my life. Herein I meet with so many special indulgences as require a distinct consideration, they being all of them to be regarded as talents entrusted to my improvement for God's glory" (3).

In this striking passage, which is far from personal, confessional, or idiosyncratic, Lucy Hutchinson sets her experience *sub specie aeternitatis.* Her language – the reference to "talents entrusted to my improvement" – recalls the biblical parable of the talents, with its strict scrutiny of the use each servant has made of the sum entrusted to him (Matt. 25: 14–30), and marks her life itself as a religious exercise, just as her earlier statement recalls other biblical language: "for in things great and extraordinary, some, perhaps, will take notice of God's working who either forget or believe not that he takes as well a care and account of their smallest concernments, even the hairs of their heads" (3).[11] The writing of her life story, then, is not in the first instance intended to inform the reader, but as an act of devotion, a memorandum to herself, to awaken her faith and gratitude and to set her experience in a providential context.[12]

After this prologue, Hutchinson turns toward a conventional but dramatically phrased account of her birth and parentage: "It was on the 29th day of January, in the year of our Lord 1619/20, that in the Tower of London, the principal city of the English Isle, I was, about four of the clock in the morning, brought forth to behold the ensuing light. My father was Sir Allen Apsley, lieutenant of the Tower of London; my mother, his third wife, was Lucy, the youngest daughter of Sir John St. John . . . ." (4). In addition to the carefully climactic phrasing, in which Lucy Apsley emerges to the roll of timpani and the clash of cymbals, there is a nice play on notions of light – the light of dawn, the light of her own life, associated with her name, Lucy (from *lux*). But rather than continuing with a recital of God's mercies in her own life, in the sense we might anticipate, she instead begins at the beginning – with the history of the British Isles from the Romans to the present:

> Whoever considers England will find it no small favour of God to have been made one of its natives, both upon spiritual and outward accounts. The happiness of the soil and air contribute all things that are necessary to the use or delight of man's life. The celebrated glory of this isle's inhabitants, ever since they received a mention in history, confers some honour upon every one of her children, and with it an obligation to continue in that magnanimity and virtue which hath famed this island and raised her head in glory higher than the great kingdoms of the neighbouring continent. (4)

Hutchinson's style here seems grandiose indeed for an autobiography. If she were a present-day undergraduate, one might consider this an instance of an "as the ages roll" paragraph, in which the writer fast-forwards through history to arrive at the topic for the present six-page essay.[13] Or one might suspect that the writer, lacking confidence in the importance of her own corner of her subject, wants to start with the big picture. A contemporary reader of autobiography, eager to learn details of Lucy Hutchinson's life (and aware that this is a fragment, a document deliberately truncated), may well be frustrated by such a beginning, and anxious to have her get on with more personal details. Such cultural conditioning, the divergence between Hutchinson's expectations and ours, probably leads us to misunderstanding. But for Hutchinson, God's mercy to her in particular is only part of a grand design that includes all of England and all of history.[14] Even in giving the place and time of her birth she employs a balanced style and level of diction that convey both the significance of these points and the judiciousness of the observer: "Nor is the place only, but the time of my coming into the world, a considerable mercy to me. It was not in the midnight of popery, nor in the dawn of the gospel's restored day, when light and shades were blended and almost undistinguished, but when the Sun of truth was exalted in his progress and hastening towards a meridian glory" (7). The level of generality of the opening pages and a syntax that anticipates Dr. Johnson's deliberative prose seem chosen as markers of rational and trustworthy discourse. In constructing a story of herself, she places her life within a far larger context; her particular existence is part of a divine plan.

But judicious deliberation is by no means the only mode of Hutchinson's self-representation. Into this narrative of probity – the record of her "pious and virtuous" parents, of her paternal grandfather, who was "a gentleman of a competent estate, about £700 or £800 a year, in Sussex" (8) – intrudes a sequence of romance episodes that lead to her parents' marriage and that prepare for the romance of her own life. After the death of his first two wives, her father's "friends . . . had procured him a match of a very rich widow, who was a lady of as much discretion as wealth; but while he was upon this design he chanced to see my mother, . . . and though he went on his journey, yet something in her person and behaviour he carried along with him, which would not let him accomplish it, but brought him back to my mother" (10).

Hutchinson, as if aware of the shift in style and focus, and of the extent to which her characters assume the strongly delineated qualities of fairy tale, describes her orphaned mother's upbringing in the house of her uncle, whose wife was "so jealous of him, and so ill-natured in her jealous fits to anything that was related to him, that her *cruelties to my mother exceeded the stories of stepmothers*" (10; emphasis mine). True to generic pattern, her mother "was by the most judgments preferred before all her elder sisters, who, sometimes envious at it, used her unkindly" (10). And like Cinderella winning the attention of the Prince, Lucy St. John receives the attentions of "one of greater name, estate and reputation than the rest [who] happened to fall deeply in love with her" (10). But the movement toward this happy ending is thwarted by an equally melodramatic development, for "the gentleman who had professed so much love to her, in her absence had been, by most vile practices and treacheries, drawn out of his senses, and into the marriage of a person, whom, when he recovered his reason, he hated" (10–11). Although the plot, as briefly outlined, would support an extended treatment, Hutchinson firmly pushes it aside: "the circumstances of that story not being necessary to be here inserted . . ." (11).

She chooses instead the quick strokes of melodrama: her mother's first suitor is led astray "by most vile practices and treacheries"; her uncle's benevolent wife is also beset by "subtle wicked persons"; her mother responds by "endeavouring to vindicate injured innocence." Into this distressing situation steps her father: "While she was deliberating . . . my father accidentally came in there, and fell so heartily in love with her that he persuaded her to marry him, which she did" (11). We cannot know which details of this story are original with Lucy, or the extent to which it reflects the telling of the story within her family, though the strongly drawn happy ending certainly suggests the latter. Her mother, who had been contemplating withdrawing "to wear out her life in the service of

God" (11), is providentially rescued by the sudden appearance of her future spouse and preserved to be the mother of his children, of whom the author is one. The disparity in age, which in some accounts might be a significant difficulty, is only the last bit to be grateful for: "her melancholy made her conform cheerfully to that gravity of habit and conversation, which was becoming the wife of such a person, who was then forty-eight years of age, and she not above sixteen" (11).[15] In this family narrative then Hutchinson draws on a surprising variety of rhetorical and narrative techniques, using a prose style that might be appropriate to the story of a nation and creating accounts of human relationships suited to romantic fiction.

Hutchinson next offers companion portraits of her parents, presenting them as examples of ideal virtue and excellence. In prose shaped by such rhetorical devices as *anaphora* and *isocolon*, Hutchinson lists her father's qualities: "He had great natural parts, but was too active in his youth to stay the heightening of them by study of dead writings; but in the living books of men's conversations he soon became so skilful that he was never mistaken, but where his own good would not let him give credit to the evil he discerned in others. He was a most indulgent husband, and no less kind to his children; a most noble master . . . He was a father to all his prisoners" (12). Hutchinson's mother is a thoroughly suitable companion for her father – "Never did any two better agree in magnanimity and bounty than he and my mother, who seemed to be actuated by the same soul" – right down to her tolerance for aristocratic prisoners performing chemical experiments in the Tower of London. As he was "a father to all his prisoners," so was she "to all the . . . prisoners that came into the Tower, as a mother" (13).

Those who find the opening section of the fragmentary autobiography audacious will be even more struck by the more specific account of the birth of the author, virtuous daughter of virtuous parents. The story that moves purposefully through British history to the birth of Lucy Apsley Hutchinson also moves from dreams and predestinations, signs of a significant event, to their fulfillment. Indeed, her parents' joy at her birth takes the quasi-mythic form of a star to portray a particularly blessed individual: "My mother, while she was with child of me, dreamed that she was walking in the garden with my father and that a star came down into her hand, with other circumstances, which, though I have often heard, I minded not enough to remember perfectly" (14). Whatever Lucy Hutchinson's mother may have experienced, the terms of this representation awaken associations that range from the poetry of George Herbert, in which "Me thoughts a starre did shoot into my lap" ("Artillerie"), taken as a clear sign of the presence of God "whose ministers / The starres and all things are"); to the sign of divine favor in the *Aeneid*, in which "a star fell out of the sky" as Aeneas prepares to leave Troy.[16] While Hutchinson discounts these as "vain prophecies," and cannily notes that the extra attention she received produced its own results,[17] her narrative strategy in recounting them – like her placing herself in the context of British history – is an act of considerable audacity. In the process of awakening her own gratitude, she marks herself as someone particularly singled out for favor.

Lucy's blessings were, in fact, many: her parents celebrated rather than regretted the birth of a daughter after three sons; her mother's joyful anticipation was reinforced by her father, who "told her, her dream signified she should have a daughter of some extraordinary eminency"(14). Not only did Lucy have unusual abilities – "By the time I was four years old I read English perfectly, and [had] a great memory" – but she was also given an education denied to most girls of her time: by age seven she had "eight tutors in several qualities, languages, music, dancing, writing and needlework" (14). In contrast to Anne Clifford, whose father would not permit her to learn languages,[18] Lucy Hutchinson says, "My father would have me learn Latin, and I was so apt I outstripped my brothers who were at school" (14–15). Her precocious abilities make her sound like something of a trial: she despised playing with other children and went out of her way to be disagreeable to visitors of her own age, "tir[ing] them with more grave instructions than their mothers, and pluck[ing] their babies to pieces" (15). Although she hated needlework and refused to practice musical instruments "but [except] when my masters were with me," adults seem to have found her excellent company. While Lucy maintains a certain healthy skepticism about the approbation she received, noting the "great admiration of many that took my memory and imitation for wit" (15), recalling such acclaim does not seem disagreeable to her.

On the one hand Lucy Hutchinson presents herself as a paragon who "was convinced that the knowledge of God was the most excellent study, and accordingly applied myself to it . . . . I used to exhort my mother's maid much, and to turn their idle discourses to good subjects" (15). But despite the tendency to priggishness this might imply, she shows somewhat more liberal (or perhaps rationalizing) qualities as well, for she believed that "when I had done this on the Lord's day, and every day performed my due tasks of reading and praying, that then I was free to anything that was not sin; for I was not at that time convinced of the vanity of conversation which was not scandalously wicked" (15). Indeed, she seems to have occupied a rather privileged position between classes and generations: "I thought it no sin to learn or hear witty songs and amorous sonnets or poems, and twenty things of that kind, wherein I was so apt that I became the confidante in all the loves that were managed among my mother's young women" (15). It's not clear from this passage whether Lucy later changed her mind about the nature of sinful conversation, becoming stricter in her views as she grew older, or whether she simply had fewer opportunities. But whereas Anne Halkett rather tartly remarks that she "need nott give account of" "my childish actions . . . , for I hope none will thinke they could bee either vicious or scandalous,"[19] Lucy Hutchinson's fragmentary phrases suggest the contrary: "any one mentioned him to me, I told them that I had forgotten those extravagancies of my infancy" (15).

We have no information on the identity of "him"; the reference, tantalizingly, follows the excision of many leaves.[20] Clearly some sort of relationship or inclination is suggested, something that she now claims to have left behind: in her newfound wisdom she "knew now that he and I were not equal; but I could not for many years hear his name without several inward emotions"(15). But unfortunately for the reader, at just this promising moment the memoir breaks off, and we are left with a sequence of distressing endnotes: according to Hutchinson's first editor, the Rev. Julius Hutchinson, "Many leaves were at this point torn from the ms," and a few lines later, "Here the story of herself abruptly ends."[21]

As in the autobiography of Anne Halkett, just as the narrator begins to satisfy our curiosity about "what really happened," the narrative is interrupted – not by the writer, or at least not in the act of writing, but rather by a later reader, quite possibly a family member, who presumably found the account detrimental to the reputation of the writer or those associated with her.[22] Julius Hutchinson's endnotes speculate that this is a reference to "some amour in which Mrs H. was disappointed,"[23] and indeed, as with Halkett, it is precisely as the narrator appears in a vulnerable position, in particular with regard to romantic interest or sexual mores, that the account is interrupted. In these instances then – and we should add also the experience of Elizabeth Pepys, whose husband instructed her to destroy her diary after she had read an unflattering portion of it to him[24] – it is not only that women exercised self-censorship, but that on those apparently rare occasions when they revealed their more intimate thoughts, such writing was deliberately removed.

*

But if Lucy Hutchinson chooses not to tell her story in the first person, or possibly breaks it off herself at this point, she offers a second, equally interesting version of herself within the life of her husband. As one might expect, in this second narrative her activities play a much smaller part than his. As N. H. Keeble remarks, "Colonel Hutchinson is . . . the unchallenged protagonist of the *Memoirs*. It is his spiritual progress which is traced, his character and behaviour which are vindicated. Lucy Hutchinson herself, 'the faithfull depository of all his secrets' . . . plays a very slight part in his history,"[25] becoming in effect his subordinate and dependent. But as Keeble notes, Lucy's strategy is deeply paradoxical: "The text denies Lucy Hutchinson any being apart from John Hutchinson even as, without him, it confers on her an enduring identity; it characterizes her as his shadow when his surviving image is hers; it presents him as her author when he is her literary creation" (235). Keeble sees as one of the chief advantages of Hutchinson's narrative strategy a freedom "from subjectivism" (237), giving her a kind of authority she would not otherwise have: "The Colonel's wife, then, could not write his *Life*, but 'I' can. This separate 'I' is not, however, merely writer and historian: she is an independent intelligence, capable of adopting a point of view on both the Colonel and his wife, a satirist and polemicist of acerbic acuity, and a person wholly committed to a particular interpretation of the events narrated."[26]

Yet while the events of Lucy's own life occupy relatively little space in the work she entitled the *Life of John Hutchinson*, the apparently impersonal narrative allows her to play a quite central and dramatic role in the scenes in which she does appear, a role that, described in the first person, might well appear immodest. And, as I shall suggest below, modesty gives way to a sense of destiny. This section of the narrative takes as its focus the coming together of John Hutchinson, represented as a most remarkable man, and Lucy Apsley, who by the very act of his choosing becomes remarkable as well. Moreover, the quite romantic story reenacts in a number of ways the plots laid out in the far briefer narrative of the lives of her parents and herself cited above.

John Hutchinson, by any measure the hero of this story, is not only morally exemplary but also an extremely attractive figure. In the prefatory sections directed to her children Hutchinson writes:

He was of a middle stature, of a slender and exactly well-proportioned shape in all parts; his complexion fair; his hair of light brown, very thick set in his youth, softer than the finest silk, curling into loose great rings at the ends; his eyes of a lively grey; well-shaped and full of life and vigour graced with many becoming motions; his visage thin, his mouth well made, and his lips very ruddy and graceful, although the nether chap shut over the upper, yet it was in such a manner as was not unbecoming; his teeth were even and white as the purest ivory; his chin was something long, and the mould of his face; his forehead was not very high; his nose was raised and sharp; but withal he had a most amiable countenance, which carried in it something of magnanimity and majesty mixed with sweetness, that at the same time bespoke love and awe in all that saw him. (18–19)

This description, full of praise of the physical, intellectual, and spiritual qualities of John Hutchinson, as well as explanations of qualities – like the underbite, the low forehead, or the sharp nose – that might be seen as less desirable, continues for two full pages.[27] As Keeble notes, "John Hutchinson is the complete gentleman"; and in fact, "Lucy Hutchinson has stolen the Royalists' clothes: John Hutchinson excels in precisely those accomplishments upon which Royalists prided themselves, which, indeed, they supposed distinguished their Cavalier culture from the vulgarity of all rebels and fanatics" (Keeble, ed., xxii).

Lucy Hutchinson's narrative mixes a number of genres and styles. Hers is a panegyric of her husband, a history with attention to the events of the Civil War,[28] an account filled with detail to support its veracity, and a spiritual biography that records her husband's progress from youth to maturity, past the pitfalls of temptation and idleness. Early in the narrative, John Hutchinson is the protagonist in a scheme that in its way anticipates Bunyan's *Pilgrim's Progress*: "God began early to exercise him with affliction and temptation" (39) as he encounters "continual solicitations to sin and lewdness," which Hutchinson "by the grace of God resisted"(41).[29] This paragon of virtue is much admired and pursued by women; yet, guided by an unknown destiny, he resists all blandishments: "In the house with Mr Hutchinson there was a young gentlewoman of such admirable tempting beauty, and such excellent good nature, as would have thawed a rock of ice, yet even she could never get an acquaintance with him. Wealth and beauty thus in vain tempted him, for it was not yet his time of love; but it was not far off" (44).

The brief section depicting the early life of John Hutchinson and his courtship of Lucy Apsley is also filled with motifs common in romantic fiction: the prophetic warning; the parallel situation; the refusal to apply that warning to oneself; the ironic reversal. Although Lucy Hutchinson calls attention to her own supposed rejection of romance, and although her protagonist ridicules it, its devices play an important role in the construction of her story. Indeed, Hutchinson uses the conventions of romance to trump the genre, to assert the greater significance and veracity of her own tale, at the same time that she takes full advantage of its tropes:

"I shall pass by all the little amorous relations which, if I would take the pains to relate, would make a true history of a more handsome management of love than the best romances describe; for these are to be forgotten as the vanities of youth, not worthy of mention among the greater transactions of his life" (51). There are teasing anticipations of developments to come, such as the warning before John Hutchinson goes to Richmond to "take heed of the place, for it was so fatal for love that never any young disengaged person went thither who returned again free" (45). Moreover, although "Mr Hutchinson laughed at him" (45), rejecting the analogy, there is a further anticipation of his own fate in the "very true story of a gentleman who not long before had come . . . to lodge there" and, hearing of a recently deceased gentlewoman, "grew so in love with the description that no other discourse could at first please him . . . [and] grew desperately melancholy" (45). In due course John Hutchinson himself, having been intrigued by the sight of Lucy Apsley's books, falls in love with the image he constructs of her. Fortunately, she, unlike the aforementioned gentlewoman, is not dead, and not even (as he fears) promised to another in marriage:

Then he grew to love to hear mention of her, and the other gentlewomen who had been her companions used to talk much to him of her, telling how reserved and studious she was, and other things which they esteemed no advantage. But it so much inflamed Mr Hutchinson's desire of seeing her that he began to wonder at himself, that his heart, which had ever had so much indifferency for the most excellent of woman kind, should have so strong impulses towards a stranger he never saw. (47)

Just as John Hutchinson appears as the world's most eligible bachelor, much courted by parents for their daughters, Lucy Apsley appears as the cruel Petrarchan lady. By no means to be approached, she is said to be "of an humour she will not be acquainted with any of mankind . . . ; she shuns the converse of men as the plague, she only lives in the enjoyment of herself, and hath not the humanity to communicate that happiness to any of our sex" (48). When he thinks, mistakenly, that she is already married, John Hutchinson behaves in a way that would not surprise us in Dante or Petrarch: "Mr Hutchinson immediately turned pale as ashes and felt a fainting to seize his spirits in that extraordinary manner that, finding himself ready to sink at table, he was fain to pretend something had offended his stomach and to retire from the table into the garden."[30] And although she is no beauty ("in a careless riding-habit she had a melancholy negligence both of herself and others," 49), Lucy Apsley has a lack of concern with her appearance that gives her an air of sovereignty ("as if she neither affected to please others, nor took notice of anything before her," 49). Moreover, as in the best of fantasies, this young woman who cares for no man has, quite remarkably, another admirer besides John Hutchinson: the source of his information is "a man of good understanding and expression, and inspired with some passion for her himself" (47). Lucy Hutchinson describes a highly romantic circumstance – John Hutchinson is initially intrigued when he hears a poem of hers set to music – yet what attracts him is "something of rationality in the sonnet beyond the customary reach of a she-wit" (47).

In using such familiar motifs (the unconcerned maiden, the rival admirers), as well as others less familiar (the lady noted for her learning rather than her beauty), Hutchinson works to make her story both romantic and credible, as she asserts not the ways of the fiction writer but of Providence itself, and indeed uses our usual attitudes to the one to set off the greater credibility of the other. In this narrative Lucy Hutchinson combines the motifs of providential guidance (which leads ultimately to a companionate marriage) with those of Petrarchan courtship: John Hutchinson, whose "desire of seeing her" is "so much inflamed" that "he began to wonder at himself," does not yet understand what the narrator affirms is the controlling force here: "certainly it was of the Lord, though he perceived it not, who had ordained him, through so many various providences, to be yoked with her in whom he found so much satisfaction" (47). Whereas Hutchinson himself is inclined to believe the mystifying story and think that "there was some magic in the place which enchanted men out of their right senses," the narrator is wiser: "it was the effect of a miraculous power of Providence, leading him to her that was destined to make his future joy" (49). That the influence of Providence in bringing about this match is foremost among Lucy Hutchinson's concerns is further emphasized in a section of the manuscript omitted from the published version: John Hutchinson "often recounting gods mercies" "would sett this in the first ranke" – "to be yoked with her whom the Lord had chosen for him."[31]

What first appears a conventional courtly dance is altered in the sequel, for the lady, despite her reputation, proves both sensible and agreeable: "He found withal that though she was modest she was accostable and willing to entertain his acquaintance, which soon passed into a mutual friendship between them, and though she innocently thought nothing of love, yet was she glad to have acquired such a friend, who had wisdom and virtue enough to be trusted with her councils" (50). The relationship that then emerges fulfills the requirements of romance in the familiar pattern of resistance to a convenient marriage proposed by her family: "Her mother and friends had a great desire she should marry, and were displeased that she refused many offers which they thought advantageous enough; she was obedient, loth to displease them, but more herself, in marrying such as she could find no inclination to" (50). The conclusion intensifies and combines the romance narrative and the spiritual biography. It balances a full measure of passion with religion, maintaining what Lucy Hutchinson considers appropriate priorities:

> never was there a passion more ardent and less idolatrous; he loved her better than his life, with inexpressible tenderness and kindness, had a most high obliging esteem of her, yet still considered honour, religion and duty above her, nor ever suffered the intrusion of such a dotage as should blind him from marking her imperfections, which he looked upon with such an indulgent eye as did not abate his love and esteem of her, while it augmented his care to blot out all those spots which might make her appear less worthy of that respect he paid her. (51)

This narrative then is very far from simple biography, or even simple panegyric. It incorporates a number of strategies and perspectives into Hutchinson's strongly shaped account. While the text elsewhere asserts John Hutchinson's political and moral principles, it here concentrates on familiar motifs, enlisting the hyperbolic, absolutist tropes of courtly poetry and romance to present the ideal Puritan marriage, in which the lady is subordinate to her husband yet remains his "meet help," in which the opposites of passion and reason are held in dynamic equilibrium, and in which the love of God dominates the love of human beings. In the introductory summary addressed to her children, Hutchinson writes:

> Never man had a greater passion for a woman, nor a more honourable esteem of a wife; yet he was not uxorious, nor remitted not that just rule which it was her honour to obey, but managed the reins of government with such prudence and affection that she who would not delight in such an honourable and advantageable subjection, must have wanted a reasonable soul. He governed by persuasion, which he never employed but to things honorable and profitable for herself. He loved her soul and her honour more than her outside, and yet he had even for her person a constant indulgence, exceeding the common temporary passions of the most uxorious fools . . . Yet even this, which was the highest love he or any man could have, was yet bounded by a superior: he loved her in the Lord as his fellow-creature, not his idol, but in such a manner as showed that an affection, bounded in the just rules of duty, far exceeds every way all the irregular passions in the world. (26)

While this description of the marital state is a far cry from John Hutchinson's turning pale as ashes at the thought that the woman whom he has heard about but not yet met is already married, and while it rather conforms more closely to the hierarchical notions of marriage of Hutchinson's day, and to the religious principle that love of God is to be valued higher than the love of any created being, it is nevertheless strong in its conviction that this relationship, like that of Adam and Eve in Paradise, is to be preferred to all other models. Hutchinson combines the ardor of the romance narrative with the idealization of the hero and the appropriate hierarchies of secular and sacred, Platonic and erotic love.[32]

To illustrate her assertion that "'Twas not her face he loved," Lucy Hutchinson tells of falling ill with smallpox on the day appointed for her wedding. Although the disease "made her the most deformed person that could be seen for a great while after she recovered. Yet he was nothing troubled at it, but married her as soon as she was able to quit the chamber, when the priest and all that saw her were affrighted to look on her" (52). Throughout this narrative of courtship and marriage, Lucy Hutchinson has it both ways: John Hutchinson loves her rather than her face; he is therefore undeterred by her disfiguring attack of smallpox; God rewards him by restoring her former good looks. She has no regard for men, yet has two suitors; though modest and retiring (yet witty and accomplished), she writes a poem that captures her future husband's fancy. Unable or unwilling to tell the story of her life in an independent text, she nevertheless co-stars in a romantic drama directed by Providence.

To the other tropes we've been considering, Lucy Hutchinson adds that of Pygmalion, fashioning a woman in the image he would have her: "'Twas not her face he loved, her honour and her virtue were his mistresses; and these (like Pygmalion's) images of his own making" (52). Although, as Keeble observes, it is Lucy Hutchinson who fashions our picture of John Hutchinson, she depicts herself as his creation: "for he polished and gave form to what he found with all the roughness of the quarry about it" (52). On the one hand she represents herself as existing only in his presence: "for she was a very faithful mirror, reflecting truly, though but dimly, his own glories upon him, so long as he was present; but she, that was nothing before his inspection gave her a fair figure, when he was removed, was only filled with a dark mist, and never could again take in any delightful object, nor return any shining representation" (51). Nevertheless, despite this image of extreme subordination and dependency, she also depicts herself as an altogether satisfactory creation and a fully adequate partner: "meeting with a compliant subject to his own wise government, he found as much satisfaction as he gave, and never had occasion to number his marriage among his infelicities" (52).[33]

In "'The Colonel's Shadow': Lucy Hutchinson, Women's Writing and the Civil War," N. H. Keeble sees a paradox in Lucy Hutchinson's conservative ideas about the appropriateness of female subordination and the nature of her narrative, arguing that "Every page . . . constitutes an implicitly ironic and assertive gloss on the text's explicitly deferential submissiveness" (235) and that "for all her disavowals and self-effacement, she is his author, he her creation; though she marginalizes her own participation, she remains much the most forceful and decisive character in the action. She, not he, animates a text devoted to him" (244).[34] I agree that in this text Lucy Hutchinson is the shaper both of her husband's image and our understanding of his life, but where Keeble sees her striving to de-emphasize her artistic presence, I see her taking a central role. Her skill seems to me to reside not only in a quasi-objective stance but also in a persuasive narration. In the passages we've been considering, Lucy Hutchinson strongly defends her husband's principles and actions, but she also represents herself as his fit and willing partner. While she verbally articulates her subordinate position, she also places herself centrally and dramatically in the narrative.

That Lucy Hutchinson had very strong views about her importance in this relationship is perhaps nowhere more evident than in her most famous act of disobedience, her writing, under John Hutchinson's name, a "petition of submission and repentance" to the Speaker of the House of Commons, an action that she must then defend. She depicts both her intentions and her husband's chagrined response, emphasizing her concern for his welfare and his (in her view) excessive inclination toward self-sacrifice:

. . . his wife, who thought she had never deserved so well of him as in the endeavours and labours she exercised to bring him off, never displeased him more in her life, and had much ado to persuade him to be contented with his deliverance; which, as it was eminently wrought by God, he acknowledged it with thankfulness. But while he saw others suffer, he suffered with them in his mind and, had not his wife persuaded him, had offered himself a voluntary sacrifice. (286)

In describing this incident, which transpired very much against John Hutchinson's wishes,[35] Lucy places her husband's integrity and sympathy on one side, and her own good intentions and the will of God on the other. Faced with this unequal balance, what could John Hutchinson do but surrender: "being by her convinced that God's eminent appearance seemed to have singled him out for preservation, he with thanks acquiesced in that thing" (286). Lucy Hutchinson here not only saves her husband (as she thinks) from sure destruction, and depicts that salvation in her narrative; she also discerns yet again the hand of Providence in this deliverance, even as she forcefully articulates that interpretation of events.

Susan Cook has suggested that Lucy Hutchinson abandoned her own independent narrative of herself because her writing "does not go as planned," that "it is clear that she has deviated from her prescribed form of strict spiritual autobiography, which should be concerned with relating God's dealings with her, and not with profane episodes in her life."[36] But although she breaks off the account of her own life, Lucy Hutchinson emerges even more strongly in her account of her husband. Moreover, she characteristically mixes genres for her own purposes rather than conforming to a single model. In the *Life of John Hutchinson*, Lucy Hutchinson manages to combine spiritual autobiography and romance, and while maintaining a strong sense of hierarchy – as a married woman she (usually) defers to her husband, as a married man he loves her faithfully, yet not so much as he loves God – she also depicts herself as a most desirable object for a most desirable man, and their coming together as the creation not of a writer of fictions but of Divine Providence itself. Whether in her autobiographical fragment, in which she arrives at a climactic moment in the providential scheme of things, or in her biography of her husband, as both narrator and actor, Lucy Hutchinson takes upon herself the role of discerner and articulator of the divine will. A powerful narrative strategist who uses a rich array of models and motifs, she is perhaps the true Pygmalion of these texts.

CHAPTER 4

Ann Fanshawe: private historian

Like Lucy Hutchinson and Margaret Cavendish, who wrote full-length biographies of their husbands, Ann Fanshawe constructs an account that focuses on the achievements of Sir Richard Fanshawe, and on their material and symbolic vicissitudes and successes. Writing to her son Richard (the only surviving male child), Ann Fanshawe promises "the most remarkable actions and accidents of your family, as well as those of more eminent ones of your father and my life."[1] As family historian, Fanshawe adopts one of the forms acceptable to women of her time, and so commits herself to a purpose that helps shape her presentation. Untitled, and not intended for publication, the text was copied by an amanuensis, corrected, and handsomely bound with "red leather, gilt tooled, in the centre of both covers a device of arms, Fanshawe impaling Harrison."[2]

Ann Harrison Fanshawe, the daughter of John Harrison and his wife Margaret, was born in 1625. She met her future husband Richard Fanshawe at Oxford, where he, like her father, had gone to support King Charles; the two were married in 1644, shortly after Fanshawe was appointed Secretary for War to the Prince of Wales; he was thirty-six; she was nineteen. Their life thereafter was a series of extensive travels and adventures caused by the Civil War and their loyalty to the King. In twenty years Ann Fanshawe bore six sons and eight daughters, only five of whom survived infancy. Besides being a diplomat, Richard Fanshawe was an accomplished scholar of classics and Hispanic languages, best known for his translation of Camoëns's epic *The Lusiads*. After the Restoration, he served Charles II as ambassador to Portugal and Spain. He died abroad in 1665, shortly after having been recalled as ambassador. Ann Fanshawe survived her husband by fifteen years, and wrote her narrative in 1676.

Ann Fanshawe's decision to write a family rather than a personal history lays her work open to later misunderstanding or criticism: although her editor John Loftis finds the redeeming value of the memoir in its providing "a human dimension to generalized interpretations of the

Wars' impact on the gentry and aristocracy" (xv), he also comments, "The passages devoted to family history are often tedious," and "Lady Fanshawe . . . occasionally writes as though she is transcribing household records" (ix). But such a judgment gives insufficient weight to Ann Fanshawe's original audience, her purpose in writing, and the extent to which those purposes dictate the kind of information she chooses to include and the style in which she writes.[3] The style of Fanshawe's narrative, though more utilitarian and less emotionally intimate than what we shall see in Lady Anne Halkett's, is nevertheless an essential and revealing element of her self-representation.

As Paul Delany asserts, the function of style can "best be understood by examining each autobiographer's relation to his audience – the way in which he presents himself to them, and the devices he uses to create the particular image he desires. An autobiography can scarcely be composed without assuming a role; the author 'plays his part' by selecting certain of his past actions for emphasis and omitting others, by manipulating his presentation of past episodes so as to show himself in a particular light, and by the overall tone of his narrative."[4] As chronicler of her family's history and as the preserver of a legacy for her husband's heir, Ann Fanshawe in effect solves a problem raised by Delany, the issue of the significance of content, "a sense of one's importance as an individual" (108). In writing her account, Ann Fanshawe does not claim personal significance, nor even present herself as a witness to particular great events of history. Although she necessarily places her strongly royalist family against the backdrop of the Civil War and Interregnum as she recounts their fortunes, her purpose in writing – to record the family history for the family – determines her emphasis.

Ann Fanshawe's choice of genre raises another issue for contemporary readers – the lack of personal revelation, the sense, as articulated by Mary Beth Rose, of something lost or repressed, the belief that, had Lady Fanshawe lived in a less restricted social structure, her life and her memoirs would have reflected greater independence and achievement.[5] As Delany points out, "Seventeenth-century autobiography in Britain, far from being a lyrical expression of 'renaissance individualism,' was the servant of didactic, historical, or controversial purposes. Its practitioners devoted relatively little effort to establishing autobiography as a literary genre: caught up in the turmoil of contemporary religious and social struggles, they cared more for the content than for the style of their works, and aimed at functional cogency rather than aesthetic perfection" (174). Yet Ann Fanshawe's narrative does not fit neatly into the category of any one set of expectations: assuredly not confessional or testimonial, nor primarily aesthetic in intention, this family history employs a range of literary styles and conceptions as Fanshawe's material or her attitude toward it alters with time.[6] Like the work of Lucy Hutchinson, it does not demonstrate a single conception or master narrative form, but rather embodies a series of identifiable approaches, ranging from vivid anecdotes to catalogues of fabrics, equipage, and men. I shall consider these approaches in sequence, seeking to discover their place in the whole and the reasons for such variations of conception.

Like Anne Halkett, whose memoirs were also written in the late 1670s (though not published until later), Ann Fanshawe begins with a devotional invocation – "Lord prosper Thou the works of our hands upon us, prosper thou our handy works" – and with advice to her son that mixes piety and prudence, seamlessly combining the language of the Bible – "Indeavour to be innocent as a dove but as wise as a serpent" – with the canny approach of Polonius: "Unnecessarily deliver not your opinion but when you doe let it be just, and considered, and plaine" (101). She also urges her son (in echo of St. Paul) to adopt a principle – indeed a survival mechanism – that informs a good deal of the subsequent narrative: "Indeavour always to be content in that estate of life which it hath pleased God to call you to" (101). She concludes with the notion of a Deity to whom one is answerable – "forget not that you must give God an account here after, and upon all occasions" (102), an image that flows easily into the invocation of the primary authority in the family, in language that again has biblical overtones: "Remember your father, whose true image though I can never draw to the life unless God will grant me that blessing in you. . . ." (102).[7] The life of Richard Fanshawe then is intended to be not merely interesting but also exemplary for his son and heir.

The account that follows is part family history, part gallery of patron saints – the host of witnesses assembled to guide the young Richard Fanshawe on his way. Ann Fanshawe divides the family into two branches, her husband's and her own, and, as befits her announced purposes, gives priority to the former. Sir Richard Fanshawe himself is presented as a man without fault, an example of moderation, temperance, and self-control. The few individualizing features merge into a cameo of the perfectly distinguished gentleman:

He was of the highest sise of men, strong, and of the best proportion, his complexion sanguin, his skinne exceeding fair, his hair dark brown, and very curling, but not very long, his eyes gray and penetrating, his nose high, his countenance gracious and wise, his motion good, his speech cleare and distinct. He never used exercise but walking, and that generally with some book in his hand, which often-times was poetry, in which he spent his idle houres. Sometimes he would ride out to take the air, but his most delight was to goe only with me in a coach some miles, and there discourse of those things which then most pleased him of what nature soever. He was very obliging to all, and forward to serve his master, his country and friends, cheerfull in his conversation, his discourse ever pleasant mixt with the sayings of wise men, and their histories, repeated as occasion offered; yet so reserved that he never shewed the thought of his heart in his greatest sence, but to myself only . . . . (102)

What might strike the modern reader as slightly affected or effete ("he never used exercise but walking, and that generally with some book in his hand") is a sign of Fanshawe's intellectual accomplishments and his calm, gentlemanly temperament.[8] The elder Fanshawe is exemplary not only in his personal relations ("the tendrest father imaginable, the carefullest and most generous master" (103) but also in religion – "a true Protestant of the Church of England" (102) – and in politics: "ever much esteemed by his two masters, Charles the First, and Charles the Second" (103). Given the active role Fanshawe played in public affairs, as counselor, ambassador to Spain and Portugal, and translator, it is remarkable that so much atten- tion is given here to his mildness, cheerfulness, gentleness (he seems to have lacked the hot temper of John Hutchinson), and personal attractive- ness. But these qualities are the outward manifestation of an inward temperament, harmonious in a classical sense, and embodying the virtues of a Christian gentleman. In accord with its didactic purpose, the initial portrait of Sir Richard concludes with an exhortation to his son that becomes a prayer: "so you may imitate him in his patience, his prudence, his chastity, his charity, his generosity, his perfect resignation to God's will . . . Amen" (103).[9]

As Ann Fanshawe proceeds to the rest of the family, the idealizing strain continues, although the accounts necessarily become briefer, and sometimes perfunctory: "Your uncle Henry . . . was killed in fighting gallantly in the Low Countrys with English colours in his hand. He was very handsom and a very brave young man, beloved and lamented of all that knew him" (106); or, of another kinsman, "He married the daugh- ter and heir of Sir Edward Heath, a pretty lady and good woman" (107). This remarkable family has, in Lady Fanshawe's account, nary a black sheep, with the possible, gracefully elided example of "Sir Simon Fan- shawe, a gallant gentle man, but more a libertin than any one of his family" (106). Occasionally her illustrations may strike the reader differently from what she intends: for example, her assertion that Sir Henry Fanshawe "had great honour and generosity in his nature" is demonstrated by an anecdote in which he is asked to sell a horse by someone who then quibbles at the price: each time the amount he names is refused, he raises his price and so obtains more for a fine horse than he had originally asked (105). Although there is a form of honor here, it is manifested in pride, determination, persistence, and stubbornness rather than generosity.

Turning to her own family, Ann Harrison Fanshawe portrays figures not merely exemplary but nearly saintly. She begins the account of her mother with a story told "before many hundreds of people" at her funeral:

That my mother being sick to death of a feavour 3 months after I was borne, which was the occasion she gave me suck no longer, her friends and servants thought to all outward appearance that she was dead, and so lay almost two days and a night, but Doctor Winston coming to comfort my father went in to my mother's chamber and, looking earnestly on her face, sayd, "She was so handsome, and now looks so lovely, I cannot think she is dead"; and suddenly took a lancet out of his pocket and with it cut the sole of her foot, which bled. Upon this he immediatly caused her to be lain upon her bed again, and to be rubb'd, and such means used as she came to life. (108–9)

Later her mother relates how, finding herself in a peaceful place, she was nevertheless troubled by "the sence of leaving my girle, which is dearer to me than all my children." Seeing two figures "cloathed in long white garments," she begs, ""O let me have the same grant given to [Hezekiah], that I may live 15 years to see my daughter a woman." To which they answered, "it is done"; and then at that instant I awaked out of my trance.' And Dr. Howlsworth did then affirme that that day she dyed made just 15 years from that time" (109).

Whereas we might place this vivid anecdote in the context of other near-death experiences, Ann Fanshawe clearly has other conceptual models – the beauty of the apparently dead woman as a sign of her virtue, the biblical precedent of fifteen years of life granted to King Hezekiah,[10] and the raising of Lazarus. Like the prophetic dream of a star by Lucy Hutchinson's mother,[11] the reawakening of Margaret Harrison to watch over her daughter marks not only providential beneficence toward the mother but a special care or concern for the daughter. It is therefore altogether appropriate that Ann Fanshawe, when her mother's death comes, suddenly grows into adulthood. She records that at first

I was wild to that degree that the houres of my beloved recreation took up too much of my time, for I loved riding in the first place, and running, and all acteive pastimes; and in fine I was that which we graver people call a hoyting girle [an awkward, silly girl, a hoyden]. . . . But upon my mother's death I then begun to refflect, and as an offering to her memory, I flung away those little childnesses that had formerly possest me, and by my father's command took upon me the charge of his house and family, which I so ordered by my excellent mother's example, as found acceptance in his sight. (110)

However much one might lament Ann Harrison's metamorphosis at fifteen from a tomboy into a woman, she herself represents the change as an actively willed choice, undertaken in response to her mother's example and as an act of duty to her father. By the time she writes the account, thirty-six years later, Ann Fanshawe has joined the ranks of those she terms "graver people" (110); she describes her new behavior as a tribute to a woman earlier characterized as "a loving wife and most tender mother, very pious, and charitable to that degree that she reliev'd . . . many with her hand dayly out of her purse" (109), the result of reflection and in obedience to "my father's command." Her acceptance of adult responsibility is finally sealed four years later when, at her marriage to Sir Richard Fanshawe, "my dear father . . . by my mother's desire gave me her wedding ring, with which I was married" (111). The rather general devotional opening of this narrative, then, acquires a more specific form as Ann Fanshawe discovers in her own life patterns that she sees as divinely ordained or assisted.

Mary Beth Rose has noticed, not altogether positively, the ease with which Ann Fanshawe merges her identity with her husband's, never deviating from the model of "idealized partnership to identical emotions and goals,"[12] and becoming a figure finally lacking in individuality and initiative. But the judgment that these memoirs are merely conventional, which can emerge easily from twenty-first-century assumptions, gives too little weight to the positive value of Fanshawe's conceptual models. In contrast to Anne Halkett, whose narrative models are more in sympathy with our own – so much so that they anticipate fiction published after her time – a number of Ann Fanshawe's models are iconographic, patterns less familiar and perhaps less agreeable to us. But for Fanshawe these admired forebears and established scenes are indispensable: she sketches an ideal marriage, an image of perfect amity, intimacy, and mutual satisfaction: "*Glory be to God* we never had but one mind through our lives, our soules were wrapped up in each other, our aims and designs one, our loves one, and our resentments one" (103). She describes Sir Richard as "so reserved that he never shewed the thought of his heart in his greatest sence, but to myself only, and this I thank God with all my soul for, that he never discovered his trouble to me but went from me with perfect cheerfulness and content, nor revealed he his joyes and hopes, but would say that they were doubled by putting them in my brest" (102).

But important as these patterns are in framing her narrative, Ann Fanshawe does not simply follow them blindly. Although the Fanshawe marriage seems to have been unusually happy, an attentive reading of the memoirs might yield a number of instances in which husband and wife were not altogether "one" – in their attitude to the Earl of Clarendon, for example, whom Lady Fanshawe consistently resented and with whom Sir Richard seems to have worked amicably,[13] or her dislike of their traveling separately, of which she says, "My husband thought it convenient to send me . . ." (122). Most dramatically, in flat contradiction of her husband's instructions, she appeared on the deck of a ship under attack (127–28). But the point about these discrepancies is not that the Fanshawes did not in the main get on well, nor even that Ann Fanshawe did not often subordinate her role to her husband's, but that in her family history she takes upon herself the role of guardian, preserver, and presenter of her husband's memory. She fashions him and their marriage as she wishes them to be remembered. Conventional her choices may be, but rather than being a woman whose "goal is not to act, as a subject, but to be loved, as an object of devotion,"[14] she presents their union as ideal and herself within that context as remarkably resilient, brave, and resourceful. It is against this background that we should understand Ann Fanshawe's representation, discussed below, of the crucial and formative instance in her life in which she becomes a wife worthy of her husband's confidence.

Beyond the devotional opening and the idealized family history, Ann Fanshawe uses a variety of other models in shaping her narrative. One is the tale of the mercantile adventure: of her early life with her husband she says, "both his fortunes and my promised portion . . . were both at that time in expectation, and we might truely be called marchant adventurers, for the stock we sett up our trading with did not amount to 20 pounds betwixt us" (112). She also conveys the excitement of their setting out on what is both figuratively and sometimes literally a military campaign: the sum of £20 "was to us as a little piece of armour is against a bullet, which if it be right placed, though no bigger than a shilling serves as well as a wole sute of arms; so our stock bought pens, ink, and paper, which was your father's trade, and by it I assure you we liv'd better than those that were born to 1200olb a year as long as he had his liberty" (112).

Throughout her narrative, Ann Fanshawe frequently represents the vicissitudes of her family in biblical terms. She reminds her son of the necessity of rendering an account of his actions to God; her own memoir might also be regarded in this light.[15] She describes the extremity of the family's change in fortune from good to bad: "we, that had till that hour lived in great plenty and great order, found ourselves like fishes out of the water and the sene so changed that we knew not at all how to act any part of obedience" (111); "no mony, for we were as poor as Job, nor clothes more than a man or two brought in their cloak bags. . . . alwaies want, yet I must needs say that most bore it with a martyrlike cheerfulness. For my owne part I begun to think we should all like Abraham live in tents all the days of our lives" (111). With the examples of Job's deprivation and the nomadic life of Abraham before them, Ann Fanshawe finds a conception that leads not to desperation but the acting of the "part of obedience." The series of adventures and mishaps that make a substantial portion of the memoir (pp. 116–39) seem episodic but are part of that conception of trials undergone: "Now we appeared upon the stage to act what part God desined us, and as faith is the evidence of things not seen, so we upon so righteous a cause cheerfully resolved to suffer what that would drive us to, which afflictions were neither few nor small, as you will find" (113).[16] The notion of life as a kind of play directed by God becomes the impetus to a resolved cheerfulness, guiding both actions and the interpretation of those actions.[17]

However drastic the representation of misfortune ("little though[t] I to leap into that sea that would tosse me until it had racked me"; 115), Ann Fanshawe's representation of good fortune is also dramatic. The blissful union of the two lovers after their first separation intriguingly recalls the joy of Solomon and the Queen of Sheba in the Song of Songs:

he with all expressions of joy received me in his arms and gave me an hundred pieces of gold, saying, 'I know that thou that keeps my heart so well will keep my fortune, which from this time I will ever put into thy hands as God shall bless me with increase.' And now I thought myself a qween, and my husband so glorious a crown that I more valued myself to be call'd by his name than borne a princess, for I knew him very wise and very good, and his soule doted on me. (115)

The images of gold, of passion, of excess, even the language of "his soul doted on me," all echo the representation of an earthly passion that, in the later allegorizing of the text, was read as the union of Christ with his bride the Church; and the tribute of gold offered by a husband to his wife here demonstrates confidence as well as love. Into this context Lady Fanshawe precisely and deliberately puts the story of temptation and near-betrayal: "upon which confidence I'll tell you what happened" (115).

This incident, in which Richard Fanshawe refuses to tell his wife affairs of state, has also been taken as an instance of his patronizing, limiting attitude to her.[18] But in Ann Fanshawe's account this episode, long considered and carefully retold, is crucial in her marriage; it too is about reaching maturity. The newly married Ann Fanshawe is urged by Lady Rivers, a kinswoman and older member of her circle, to solicit information from her husband with the intention of passing it on, perhaps merely as self-aggrandizing gossip. The story as Fanshawe tells it has enough of the classic elements of temptation to make us recall Milton's Eve: Lady Rivers flatters the younger woman, "tacitly commend[ing] the knowledge of state affairs" and suggesting that "none was at first more capable than I" (115). Fanshawe emphasizes both her own naiveté and her desire to rise in her husband's esteem: "I that was young, innocent, and to that day had never in my mouth, 'What news', begun to think there was more in inquiring into buseness of publick affaires than I thought off, and that it being a fashonable thing would make me more beloved of my husband (if that had been possible) than I was" (115).[19]

Ann Fanshawe represents vividly her persistent soliciting of information, eating nothing at supper, crying herself to sleep, and accusing her husband of not caring about her feelings. In this scene, she depicts her husband as the wise counselor, loyal to his King, clearly aware of the demarcations between personal and public life. To her complaint, "Thou dost not care to see me troubled," she recalls, "he, taking me in his armes, answered, 'My dearest soule, nothing upon earth can afflict me like that; and when you asked me of my busines, it was wholy out of my power to satisfy thee. For my life and fortune shall be thine, and every thought of my heart, in which the trust I am in may not be revealed; but my honour is my own, which I can not preserve if I communicate the Prince's affaires, and pray thee with this answer rest satisfyed'" (116).[20] It is possible to see in the ending of this story a patronizing husband, an infantilized wife, and a lack of conjugal confidence. But one must agree with the older Ann Fanshawe that it would be inappropriate for the King's counselor, particularly in the midst of a civil war, to share the latest news of state affairs with his twenty-year-old wife. Indeed much of the tone of this incident points to the considerable discrepancy in age – seventeen years – between the two partners. Moreover, as Lady Fanshawe tells the story some thirty-one years later, it is not so much a faithful picture of her marriage as an exemplary tale, a paradigm for her son, and a story of how she became a worthy partner. In her account, she finds reason and goodness on her husband's part, folly on her own; like Eve, she realizes "How beauty is excelled by manly grace / And wisdom which alone is truly fair."[21] Having aspired like Eve to greater knowledge so that she may rise beyond her present state, Ann Fanshawe with the benefit of hindsight likewise corrects that belief, affirming that no station can be higher than that of the loyal wife. She concludes that "So great was his reason and goodness, that upon consideration it made my folly appeare to me so vile that from that day until the day of his death I never thought fit to aske him any business, but that he communicated freely to me, in order to his estate or family" (116).

Although Ann Fanshawe here resolves never to pry into her husband's affairs and elsewhere articulates the notion of accepting the part that God "desined" for them to play, she is anything but passive in the experiences that befall her; rather, her expressed attitudes derive from belief and choice rather than innate weakness or timidity. She is the woman who climbs up to see marching soldiers and is nearly shot (115). She escapes the threat of plague and an attack of fleas (126), dons male clothing in order not to miss the attack of a Turkish man-of-war, "as free from sickness and fear as, I confess, from discretion" (128). Having survived shipwreck she revels in simple food and drink: "we had very good fires and Nance white wine, and butter and milk, and wall nuts and eggs, and some very bad cheese. And was not this enough with the escape of shiprack to be thought better than a feast? I am sure untill that houre I never knew such pleasure in eating" (131). Denied permission to leave England as Ann Fanshawe, she impersonates a merchant's wife to get a pass under her maiden name (Harrison), which she then boldly transforms to Fanshawe, thereby ensuring safe passage for her three children, herself, and two servants. When her husband is imprisoned in Whitehall, she visits him daily, coming alone at four in the morning, standing outside to talk to him even when drenched with rain; later she secures a certificate of his ill health and presents it to Cromwell to gain his release. And when Richard Fanshawe is replaced as Charles's ambassador to Spain and dies shortly thereafter, she manages the family financial affairs and the arduous journey back to England. The only challenge she is on record as refusing is the gift of a young lion from the Conde de Molina, "saying I was of so cowardly a make I durst not keep company with it" (161). Although she chooses not to emphasize her own accomplishments (she fears that "to commend my better half . . . methinks is to commend myself and so may bear a censure" [103]), Ann Fanshawe was clearly a person of courage, determination, and resourcefulness, and she recounts these incidents with a vividness of detail and degree of relish that makes them thoroughly memorable. She could, had she wished, confined her history to such incidents alone.

Rather than seeing her courage and resolve and her capacity for independent action as opposed to her wifely role, one might find them closely connected, since some of her boldest actions are undertaken in response to her husband or on his behalf. Although his position and the Civil War often made separation necessary, and although she always found these periods uncomfortable, she also bore additional responsibility during them.[22] She describes sailing to meet him "very cheerfully towards my North Starr, that only had the power to fix me" (122) and notes, "I had the discomfort of a very hasardous voyage, and the absence of your father, he then being upon business at Corke" (123). When the city she inhabits is taken by Parliamentary forces, she takes charge, immediately writing to her husband, "blessing God's providence that he was not there with me, perswading him to patience and hope that I should gett safely out of the town by God's assistance" (123). Urging *him* to be vigilant, she promises to secure his papers:

Immediatly I packed up my husband's cabeenet, with all his writings, and near a 1000lb in gold and silver, and all other things both of clothes, linnin, and household stuff that were portable and of value; and then, about 3 a clock in the morning, by the light of a tapour and in that pain I was in [her recently broken wrist had been improperly set], I went into the market place, with onely a man and maid, and, pasing through an unruly tumult with their swords in their hands, searched for their chief commander, Jeffreys. . . . He instantly writt me a pass, both for myself, family, and goods, and said he would never forgett the respects he owed your father. (123–24)

Her escape, "through thousands of naked swords," by means of a neighbor's cart at 5 a.m., caused Cromwell the utmost chagrin (124). Mary Beth Rose sees such incidents as an imitation of male quest narrative, but in presenting this material Ann Fanshawe joins rather than opposes her dual positions as loyal wife and bold initiator of action.

Fanshawe recounts a second, equally dramatic incident that involves a degree of disobedience and might have led to censure, yet it meets with praise. While she and her husband are at sea, they encounter a Turkish galley; the captain, fearing that they will be captured as slaves and hoping to be taken for a warlike vessel, orders all women below decks.

This beast captain had locked me up in the cabine. I knocked and called long to no purpose, untill at length a cabine boy came and opened the doore. I, all in teares, desired him to be so good as to give me his blew throm cap he wore and his tarred coat, which he did, and I gave him half a crown, and putting them on and flinging away my night's clothes, I crept up softly and stood upon the deck by my husband's side as free from sickness and fear as, I confess, from discretion; but it was the effect of that passion which I could never master. By this time the 2 vessels were ingaged in parley and so well satisfyd with speech and sight of each other's forces that the Turk's man-of-war tacked about and we continued our course. But when your father saw it convenient to retreat, looking upon me he blessed himself and snatched me up in his armes, saying, "Good God, that love can make this change!" And though he seemingly chid me, he would laugh at it as often as he remembred that voyage. (127–28)

Whatever Ann Fanshawe learned in the incident with Lady Rivers, it was not mindless acquiescence. She clearly relishes action and, like a cross-dressing Shakespearean heroine, enjoys appearing on deck, so perfectly disguised that her husband doesn't notice her gender or identity until the battle is over. Her freedom from sickness, fear, and discretion she attributes to "that passion which I could never master," that is, not to wifely obedience, but to love. In what must be a favorite family story, here retold for her eleven-year-old son,[23] it's clear that her husband is as pleased with her feat and with her adoption of this romantic role as she is. If one adds to these instances the powerful, if not equally dangerous, image of Ann Fanshawe, wet with rain, standing outside her husband's prison at dawn to speak with him, it is evident that even though she presents herself in the role of a devoted wife who respects her husband's judgment and is inspired by his example,[24] she is fully capable of independent action and remarkable courage.

Given this abundant evidence of Ann Fanshawe's vivacity and independence, perhaps the most puzzling part of the memoir is the quality of her extended account of Sir Richard's term as ambassador, which includes innumerable details of congratulatory, condoling, and welcoming visits, of gifts given and received, of ceremonial processions, complete with minutiae of dress, equipage, and attendance. Such details, which come in nearly mind-numbing profusion, all but crowd out personal feelings and leave no evidence of an inner life. For example she describes her husband's audience as ambassador with the King of Spain, including two pages in which she attempts to summon up the pageantry of his visit:

[My husband] about 11 of the clock sett forth out of his lodgings thus: first went all those gentlemen of the town and pallace that came to accompany my husband; then went 20 foot men all in new liveryes of the same colour we used to give, which is a dark green cloath with a frost upon green lace; then went all my husband's gentlemen, and next before himself his camaradoes, two and two: . . . then my husband in a very rich suite of cloathes of a dark fillemoate imbrocad laced with silver and gold lace, nine laces, every one as broad as my hand, and a little silver and gold lace layd between them, both of very curious workmanship. His sute was trimed with scarlet taffeta ribbon, his stockings of white silk upon long scarlett silk ones, his shoes black with scarlett shoes' strings and garters, his linnen very fine laced with very rich Flanders lace, a black beavour button on the left side, with a jewell of 1200lb, a rich curious wrought gold chaine made in the Indies, at which hung the King his master's picture richly sett with diamonds, cost 300lb, which His Majesty in great grace and favour had been pleased to give him at his coming home from Portugal. (163–64)

By contrast the events of family life in 1660, even the death of a child, receive only cursory notice: "This year I sent for my daughter Nan from my sister Buttler's in Kent, where I had left her. And my daughter Mary dyed in Hartfordshire in August and lyes buried in Hartford Church in my father's vault. In the latter end of this summer I miscarryed, when I was near half gone with child, of 3 sons, 2 houres one after the other. I think it was with the great hurry of business I then was in, and perpetuall company that resorted to us of all qualitys, some for kindness and some for their own advantage" (141). In the account of the events of 1664, the illness of her two daughters with smallpox receives one sentence, sharing a paragraph with her inability to receive the ladies of the Spanish court:

On the 29th we returned home to our house at Madrid, where on Saturday after my little child Betty fell sick of the small pox, as had done my daughter Anne in the month of September, but both of them (God's name be praysed) recovered perfectly well without blemish. But as I could not receive (for want of capacity of roome) the ladys of this court in my lodgings at the Conde de Irvia's, so I could not receive them here by reason of the small pox in the family, and they having twice a piece offered to visite me and I refused it, upon that account. (169)

In these passages, Ann Fanshawe, who earlier in the narrative could provide succinct and lively accounts of landscapes, menus, and incidents, of the beauty of the Alhambra or the color of Tyrian dye, seems totally caught up in the formalities of life and in its ceremonial details. And she appears as concerned over her inability to entertain Spanish noblewomen as over the grave illness of her daughters. This might strike the present-day reader as at least as much a betrayal of value and independent judgment as her decision not to try to gain information about state secrets. Although there are still accounts of the palaces and monasteries of Spain, the manners and customs of the country, and the excellence of its food, much of the life and energy – and nearly all personal emotion – are missing from this section of the memoir. Rose describes this section as "a shallow catalog of ceremonies and gifts" (69) and believes that the memoir shows that "she assigns a secondary value to those material aspects of her experience that are uniquely female" (70).[25]

Is such emphasis the result of Fanshawe's decision to cede the affairs of state to her husband, leaving only the externals for herself, or of her habitual subordination of herself and her maternal role to his public function? A number of the situations recounted are those in which she in fact participated in the ceremonial aspects of her husband's career: while he engaged in negotiations for peace between England and Spain, she continued to bear children, pay and observe state visits, and record the architectural and cultural beauties of the country. While in the presence of her husband, Ann Fanshawe played a secondary role, in contrast to the instances elsewhere recounted in which his absence forced her to bold independent action. A case in point is her report of a visit to the Queen of Spain, with its painful attention to the minutiae of ceremony and state, right down to the placement of cushions and the delivery of curtseys.

Through infinite number of people I passed to the Qween's presence where Her Majesty was seated at the upper end under a cloath of state, upon 3 cushins, and on her left hand the Emperesse, and 3 more. The ladyes were all standing. After making my last reverence to the Qween Her Majesty, and the Emperesse rising up and making me a little curtsy, sate downe – again. Then I, by my interpreter Sir Benjamin Right, said those complements that were due from me to Her Majesty; to which Her Majesty made a gracious and kind reply. Then I presented my children, which Her Majesty received with great grace and favour. Then Her Majesty speaking to me to sitt, I sate down upon a cushion lay'd for me above all the ladys who sate, but below the Camerera Mayor (no woman taking place of Her Excellency but princesses). The children sate on the other side, mingled with court ladys that are maides of honour. Thus after having passed half an houre in discourse, I tooke my leave of Her Majesty and the Emperesse, making reverences to all the ladyes in passing. I returned home in the same order as I came. The next day the Camerera sent to see how I did, in complement from Her Majesty. (165–66)

In contrast to earlier sections, this seems only the shell of an account, focused on the external and formal, with attention to the rituals of hierarchy and ceremonial. Can the person who wrote this have any sense of proportion, any real interest in human nature? Another factor that may contribute to the lack of personal engagement is that much of the latter section of the memoir (though probably not the passage just quoted) seems to be drawn from earlier notes, perhaps in the form of a diary: many sections or paragraphs begin with a date and visits paid or received, on the occasion of birthdays, deaths, or births. Reporting these encounters long after the fact, Ann Fanshawe is able to transmit the details that she had recorded without whatever spark of enthusiasm the event might originally have aroused in her. These may indeed be events that, fifteen years hence, have lost their lustre.

Several explanations might be advanced for the different tenor of the latter part of the narrative. First, since this text is, by Ann Fanshawe's account and intention, the memorial to her husband's life and accomplishments, these outward symbols of success may well seem to her important evidence of that achievement. She describes her husband's coach of state "with four black horses," as "the finest that ever came out of England (none going in this court with 6 but the King himself)" (164), and she reports of the mutual salutes of the English and Spanish that "His Majesty had commanded that his ships and forts should first salute the King Of England's Embassadour . . . as if His Majesty were there in person" (155). In other words, the honors given to Sir Richard and Lady Ann Fanshawe are tributes not only to them but also to their King and must be duly reported; moreover, the degree of welcome given to the Fanshawes is, as she emphasizes, appropriate to royalty itself: "The richnesse of the guilt and silver plates which we had in great aboundance, as we had like wise of all sorts of very fine household linnen, was fit onely for the entertainment of so great a prince as His Majesty, our master, in the representation of whose person my husband received this great entertainment" (156). With regard to the tendency to record details of dress, costume, and placement, Ann Fanshawe has from the beginning of her narrative shown a strong sense of the material, the tactile – the bed floating in water, the wine and Nantes cheese, the biting fleas.[26] She has been able to live vividly in the moment and even, as she advised her son, "to be content in that state of life which it hath pleased God to call you to." In citing these details, Ann Fanshawe may have miscalculated what might interest a reader; but if the events of her later life tended to courtly audiences rather than midnight escapes, she herself should not be blamed.

Yet there is also a sense in which material gifts and possessions have a strong symbolic value: for the woman who early in her marriage reports receiving gold from her husband as a token of his love, such subsequent gifts have a similar, if less emotionally charged function. She reports how the Queen of Spain "for my person and the delight that Her Majesty took in my conversation, . . . for a token there off . . . sent me a jewell of diamonds that cost the Qween 8550 ducats plate, which is about 2000lb sterling" (174). The gift is given with further adulatory comments by the Duchess of Medina de les Torres. Such gifts indeed seem to have had psychological and symbolic as well as material value for Fanshawe. Only occasionally are there signs of weariness, as in the apparent relief that Sir Richard need not pay a return visit to thank for a visit already thanked for (168), or the assertion that, despite the luxury of their accommodations in Spain, "your father and myself both wisht our selves in a retired country life in England, as more agreable to both our inclinations" (156).

If the diplomatic encounters in Spain are recorded with an attention to the surface and less personal involvement than before, in the final section of the text, Ann Fanshawe once again creates a more unified and forceful narrative; she herself conveys a new energy and independence, forced as she is by circumstances to assume responsibility for herself, her family (including a ten-month-old son), and her servants. Having described at length the outward pomp of their residence in Spain and the success of Sir Richard in negotiating a peace treaty between Spain and England, Ann Fanshawe recounts a succession of losses and deaths. The series begins with the death on September 17, 1665, of Philip IV of Spain; in the midst of mourning for the King comes news that Sir Richard is to be replaced as ambassador; his successor, the Earl of Sandwich, arrives; Sir Richard himself dies within a month; and Lady Fanshawe begins her arduous journey back to England. She herself sees a tragic pattern to events as she records them: "I may truly say, never any ambassadoure's family came into Spaine more glorious or went out so sad" (187).

Ann Fanshawe's immediate recorded response to her husband's death is twofold: she inserts part of an ode of Horace (in Sir Richard's English translation) on the imperturbable man of integrity, able to bear all conditions;[27] this is followed by her own impassioned prayer for divine aid: "Have pitty on me, O Lord . . . See me, O Lord, with five children, a distressed family, the temptation of the change of my religion, the want of all my friends, without counsell, out of my country, without any means to returne with my sad family to our own country, now in warr with most part of Christendom" (185). In the final pages of her narrative, Ann Fanshawe admirably performs the role of head of household, mother of their children, and guardian of his memory.

But before this final state of sufficiency is achieved, Ann Fanshawe records what she sees as a final temptation, one that stands in symmetrical relation with the earlier encouragement to meddle in state affairs. If the initial temptation, in which she figures as Eve, is that of pride, the hope to rise above her station, this might be seen as the danger of despair or sloth, giving in to the easier way. After her husband's death, before she returns to England, she is offered security in Spain, with her material needs supplied: "The 5th of Ju[ly], 1666, St.N., the Qween Mother sent the Master of the Ceremonyes of Spaine to invite me to stay with all my children in her court, promising me a pension of 30 thousand ducats a year, and to provide for my children, if I and they would turne our religion and become Roman Catholicks" (186).

Interestingly, whereas Fanshawe vividly represented her psychological state in the earlier contest with her husband, here she merely records her answer:

I answered, I humbly thanked Her Majesty for her great grace and favour, the which I would ever esteeme and pay with my service, as far as I was able, all the days of my life. For the latter I desired Her Majesty to believe that I could not quitt the faith in which I had been borne and bred in, and which God had pleased to try me for many years in the greatest troubles our nation hath ever seen. (186)

Although Ann Fanshawe earlier expresses a good deal of enthusiasm for Spain – its lavish courtesy, food, landscape, and monuments (her account of the monastery of the Escorial, for example, is altogether positive) – she depicts this decision simply as a matter of conscience and national loyalty.

One might conclude from the lack of psychological detail that the temptation was not a very strong one (though certainly faced by more than one English person abroad),[28] or perhaps that Ann Fanshawe as we see her late in the memoirs is so caught up in the surface that there is no need to depict the struggle of conscience (if there was one) that took place under her perfect politeness to the Queen of Spain. Fanshawe concludes with a compliment "for this so great favour which Her Majesty was pleased to offer me in my greatest afflictions" (186). But the placing of this event late in the memoir also demonstrates the challenges of her later life and her ability to deal with them. In spite of her description of herself as "the most distressed wretch upon earth" (185), Ann Fanshawe's response to her situation is hardly passive. She firmly positions herself, as she had earlier in the memoirs, in a drama overseen by Divine Providence, and this time she rejects what she plainly regards as a dangerous temptation, offered to a vulnerable subject. After a penitential petition which includes the altogether orthodox acknowledgment of her own lack of merit and dependence on divine grace, she reminds her Creator of his promise to widows and orphans: "O my God, look upon me through the merits of my Saviour, and for his sake save me. Doe with me and for me what thou pleasest, for I doe wholly rely upon thy mercy, beseeching thee to remember thy promises to the fatherlesse and widow, and enable me to fullfill thy will cheerfully in the world" (185).

Once this temptation is overcome, Ann Fanshawe vigorously and effectively discharges her duties as head of the family and preserver of her husband's memory. She sees to the embalming of his body; receives numerous visits of condolence; sells what she can to fund the return voyage; and arranges passage for herself, five children, and accompanying household of ten by land and sea from Madrid to London, a journey of four months. She even refuses the Earl of Sandwich's offer of escort for her husband's body, "desiring to goe out of that place as privately as I could possibly" (187); in other words, she stages her departure and her account of it even as she had shaped the representation of their arrival. Upon reaching England, she arranges for burial in the family vault and the inscribing of her husband's funeral monument, energetically seeks payment of what is owed him, and adjusts her household expenses in the light of her new situation. This section includes a strong element of resentment for what Ann Fanshawe regards as her family's mistreatment, particularly by the Earl of Clarendon and the Commissioners of the King's Treasury. But the detailed account of her attempts to secure the money owed, spiced with her antipathy to those she feels have cheated her ("I wish I had given [a bribe], though I had *poured* it down his throat, for the benefit of mankind" [189]), chiefly emphasizes the integrity of her husband's and her own behavior throughout, as loyal to their King and to their faith.

In this great distress I had no remedy but patience. How far this was from a reward, judge ye, for near 30 years suffering by land and sea, and the hasard of our lives over and over, with the many services of your father, and expence of all the monyes we could procure, and 7 years' imprisonment, with the death and beggery of many eminent persons of our family, that when they first entered the King's service had great and clear estates. (189)

In a cascade of details, Ann Fanshawe records not only her own difficulties ("[I] was forced to sell 1000lb worth of our own plate, and to spend the Qween's present of 2000 doublons in my journey into England; not oweing or leaving a shilling debt in Spaine, I thank God"; 189) but also the financial decline of her family, consistent with the circumstances of the English nobility:

About this time dyed my brother Lord Fanshaw's widow. . . . She was buryed in the vault of her husband's family in Ware Church. Within a year after that her son the Lord Fanshawe sold Ware Park for 26 thousand pounds to Sir Thomas Bide, a bruer of London. Thus in the fourth generation of the chief of our family since the[y] came in to the south, they, for their sufferings for the crown, sold the flower of their estate and of near 2000 a year more. (191)

Consonant with her final injunction to her son, "Manage your fortune prudently, and forget not that you must give God an account here after, and upon all occasions" (102), Ann Fanshawe's narrative constitutes a reckoning of her and her husband's activities. She recalls her straitened circumstances and her attempts to act accordingly, dismissing members of her household to economize (190). Her guiding principles are a characteristic balancing of pragmatism and religious faith. We see her struggling with her own impulses and preferences, her sense of her maternal role, and her conception of life taking place on a stage managed by divine direction: "I resolved to hold me fast by God, untill I could digest in some measure my afflictions. Sometimes I thought to quitt the world, as a sacrifice to your father's memory, and to shut my self up in a house for ever from all people; but upon the consideration of my children, who were all young and unprovided for, being wholy left to my care and dispose, I resolved to suffer as long as it pleased God the stormes and flowes of fortune" (190).

In keeping with Fanshawe's sense of rendering an account to God and to her son, the final section of the text deals with accounts in several senses of the word: Ann Fanshawe means to correct the record on her husband's tombstone "if God permit," thus reminding her reader that all human activity is subject to divine dispensation. She includes a characteristic detail – a note of what the festivities cost when her husband became Burgess for the University of Cambridge – and the text, from which something is missing at the end, trails off in a detail having to do with her straitened financial circumstances.[29] In the balancing of her concern with integrity and honor on the one hand and economics and detail on the other, these existing final lines reflect the structure and emphasis of the narrative as a whole. The last lines of the text record Sir Richard's honor, in this case freely given and unsolicited, and his widow's attempt to correct the record.

If Ann Fanshawe does not construct a single and unified autobiographical narrative, she nevertheless employs a number of powerful conceptions – the portrait of the ideal husband, diplomat, and public servant; the pilgrimage of a family, loyal to God and King, through a difficult period in history; a story of development from girlhood (a hoydenish phase), to a young wife learning the appropriate limits of her influence and knowledge, to a mature and successful (if subordinate) partner. The narrative begins in adventure, rises to glory and success, and concludes in honorable loss. Perhaps with a different audience or in another time, Ann Fanshawe might have shaped her text to conform more fully to a single one of these several patterns; she might have given herself greater prominence. But what her account may lack in consistency it does not lack in interest, for it gives a strong sense of the conceptual frameworks available to her – biblical, exemplary, providential, mercantile, romantic, devotional – and the ways in which each in its turn proves useful or appropriate. Rather than finding "an inhibited, repressed story,"[30] we find the story that she chooses to tell, of a life of success, honor, and hardship, the strong history of her family and her place within it.

CHAPTER 5

Romance and respectability: the autobiography of Anne Halkett

In the autobiography of Anne Murray Halkett we come to a text that is more fully fashioned, more self-conscious and focused in its presentation than those I have been discussing. Unlike Lucy Hutchinson, who gives herself a number of (albeit important) scenes within the life of her husband, or Ann Fanshawe, who tells her story in the context of a family history that centers on her husband's professional career and places her in a supporting role, Anne Halkett sets out to tell her own story, perhaps with the intention of justifying her actions to posterity. Although Halkett resembles her contemporaries in having no single biographical model available to her – indeed, the shifting generic patterns are an important feature of her work – her presentation has a strength and coherence of narrative line that takes it beyond the episodic and moves at times to a style surprisingly close to that of the eighteenth-century English novel. In what follows, I shall concentrate on the diverse models of self-presentation and narrative used by Halkett in her autobiography, strategies that partake of devotional treatise, family history, and romance.[1]

Anne Murray Halkett, daughter of Thomas Murray, provost of Eton College and tutor to Charles I, was born January 4, 1623, a few months before the death of her father. In her early twenties, she was courted by Thomas Howard, eldest son of Thomas, Lord Howard of Escrick: the match was forbidden by her mother on the grounds of inequity of fortune, the Howards having much more to offer and hence to expect than the Murrays. In 1647–48 Anne Murray, acting on her strong royalist sympathies, assisted in the daring escape of the Duke of York from St. James's Palace: in the process she became politically and romantically involved with Colonel Joseph Bampfield, agent for Charles I. In the early years of their acquaintance Bampfield presented himself as a widower: the relationship faltered when Anne Murray learned – after a sequence of conflicting reports – that his wife was still alive. Although Bampfield attempted to maintain the connection, Anne Murray at last married Sir James Halkett, a widower with four children, in 1656. She herself bore four children and survived her husband, who died in 1670, by twenty-nine years. Besides overseeing her children's education, one of the chief occupations of her later years seems to have been the writing of devotional literature, in particular meditations on biblical passages – the miracles of Christ, the Psalms, the good women of scripture – and on festival days of the Church of England. Lady Halkett's account of her life was compiled in 1677–78, after the death of her husband: it is preserved in a manuscript in the author's hand in the British Library.[2]

As Sidonie Smith has pointed out, the genre of autobiography as often defined – a story of a success, the achieving of a goal, a picture of a representative life, a life that reflects the times more generally – is not very helpful as a model for a woman writer. Women's autobiographical writings tend rather to be about personal encounters, about family life: insofar as they are about broader social experience, a number of them – like Fanshawe's and Hutchinson's – were undertaken to inform children of their fathers' character and accomplishments. Because the first page of the manuscript of Anne Halkett's text is missing and the second mutilated, we are lacking information – including her opening statements – that might allow a more confident generic identification. Two models, the conversion narrative and the family history, available to both men and women in the seventeenth century, seem relevant to Halkett, though neither is fully adequate for this text, which displays a yet broader range of methods of self-understanding and self-presentation.

While the opening of the narrative, even in its truncated form, clearly expresses a devotional intent, Anne Halkett's autobiography certainly does not conform to the single-minded focus of the conversion narrative, an account that assumes a particular direction, a plot in which a life of dissipation (as perceived by the author) or of spiritual lethargy and insensitivity precedes a spiritual awakening and transformation. The first surviving paragraph of the manuscript incorporates a statement of faith, biblical quotations, and invocation of divine aid. Halkett prepares to recount her life's story, perhaps in retrospective evaluation of her own actions, but also as if to place these actions before a divine tribunal. Although especially pronounced at the beginning, the dual notion that human actions are subject to divine judgment and that individual human beings may be blessed with divine guidance is an important principle throughout this text.

The opening paragraph is a tissue of biblical language, some of which had found its way into the Anglican *Book of Common Prayer*: "And since wee have an advocate with the Father of Christ the righteous, hee will plead for mee wherin I am inocentt and pardon wherin I have beene guiltty."[3] These passages, part quotation, part paraphrase, of several important texts by someone who would have heard and read them repeatedly, indicate the interactive and devotional nature of this enterprise. Anne Halkett takes stock of past actions, asserting not so much that she is justified in what she has done (as she does in later passages of the text) as that her errors and wrongdoing will be pardoned. And she anticipates future events with a prayer for divine protection: "And if the Lord sees fitt to continue mee still in the furnace of affliction, his blesed will bee done so that I may bee one of his chosen" (9). This introduction is at once a private statement of faith and a testimony with public implications (rather like the service of the Prayer Book, from which Halkett draws), suggesting that she intended her memoirs to be read, if only within her own family, as a representation of the values and events of her life.[4]

After this devotional opening, the narrative goes on to place Anne Halkett in the context of her family. This part of the text, though unfortunately preserved only in fragmentary form, seems to mingle pride in and justification of her forebears. (I have added in square brackets possible readings for the missing text.) Some objection has apparently been raised against them and is here emphatically countered.[5]

> For my parentts I need nott say much, since they were [known]
> [to many] And I need nott bee ashamed to owne them
> [It] was mentioned as my reproach that I was of [a low]
> stat]ion, whereas hee that now succeeds to that fa [vor]
> was once which was a good a gentleman as any
> [af] ter, I shall ever bee sattisfied with what can [be said]
> [to] the advantage of that familly, but some that [belong]
> to, both by father and mother would take itt ill nott
> [to be] thought gentlemen: for my father claimed [the distinction]
> of beeing derived from the Earle of Tillibardin's familly and my mother
> from the Earle of Perth's.

Despite the missing words and syllables, it is clear that Halkett defends her family's rank and reputation. She represents her parents as persons of worldly distinction and high moral character, the first being the consequence of the second: "Hee was thought a wise King who made choice of my f[ather] to bee tuter to the late King of blessed memory: and what the excellentt Prince learnt in his youth kept him stedfast in his relligion though under all the temptations of Spaine, temperate in all the exceses that attend a court" (10). Indeed, her parents are not only valued by their contemporaries but also taken as models, being strong enough to resist the social, political, and religious pressures of their times. Besides instructing her in the rather limited skills (French, drawing, music, and dancing) deemed appropriate for a lady, Halkett's mother instilled the habit of religious practice: "I was seldome or never absentt from devine service att five a clocke in the morning in the summer and sixe a clocke in the winter till the usurped power putt a restraintt to that puplicke worship so long owned and continued in the Church of England" (11). Anne Murray Halkett's virtues, as recounted here, are also those of her family: she presents herself as the scion of a virtuous and noble race.

That model gives way in the next section to another, even more powerful and more appropriate to the subsequent narrative: an upright young heroine, fulfilling the obligations in which she has been instructed, is nevertheless subject to misunderstanding and misprizing. Here the text departs markedly from the mold of spiritual autobiography, in which the scandal and vice of one's earlier life are reversed by one's turning to faith. Even the possibility of self-examination suggested by the devotional opening is dismissed as a possible affront to the writer's honor: "What my childish actions were I thinke I need nott give accountt of here, for I hope none will thinke they could bee either vicious or scandalous" (11).

As one reads this text, it becomes increasingly evident that Halkett has constructed not merely a memoir filled with factual detail but a narrative governed by certain conceptions of her character and her role.[6] Perhaps surprisingly in relation to the gesture of religious self-examination with which the text opens, most of what follows is not confession of fault but rather justification of the author's actions. Moreover, the narrative focuses on her in a quite romantic and dramatic way, setting her against a variety of backgrounds, in relation to her mother and her several suitors, and in the context of the confusion, danger, and adventure of the Civil War. Halkett recounts her life in chronological fashion, dealing first with her parentage, then with her early life, which included two quite dramatic love affairs, and concluding, or rather breaking off, not long after her marriage to Sir James Halkett.[7] Although the narrative might be marketed as "The Life and Loves of the Lady Anne Halkett," the dominant ideological motif or concern is the protagonist's integrity, her attempt to evaluate and ultimately justify her own actions.[8]

Anne Murray Halkett begins her account with an emphasis on her sense of honor, her integrity *vis à vis* her family, in accordance with the values in which she has been raised. She prides herself on exemplary obedience to her mother, her only surviving parent: "till the yeare 1644 I may truly say all my converse was so inocentt that my owne hart cannott challenge mee with any imodesty, either in thought or behavier, or an act of disobedience to my mother, to whom I was so observantt that as long as shee lived I doe nott remember that I made a visitt to the neerest neibour or went any where withoutt her liberty" (11). But it is precisely this sense of filial obedience, as well as a concern with her own reputation, that is tested in the first major incident of the narrative. Anne Murray forms a romantic attachment explicitly forbidden by her mother, to a young man three years younger than herself: in her mother's, and even in her own view, the interest of his family required him to marry a woman with a larger dowry than the Murrays could provide.

Anne Murray's relationship with Thomas Howard is more fully treated than the uneventful and dutiful years of her youth: it receives eleven pages in contrast to the two pages devoted to parents and family. This experience seems critical in the process of her self-definition – as a young woman who abides by her principles, even though she is urged otherwise by someone she loves, and is maligned and misunderstood by those nearest to her. The account, composed some thirty years after the event, is remarkably circumstantial, involving dates, vivid descriptions of actions, and direct quotation. It focuses on the pressures placed on Anne Murray and the nature of her inner debate.

After announcing that none of her childish transgressions could be worth mentioning, Halkett writes, "In the yeare 1644 I confese I was guilty of an act of disobedience" (11), signaling an important shift in the narrative. But much of what follows seems calculated to explain and justify these actions, to assert that what she has done is "neither vicious nor scandalous." The narrative features a passionate young man, urging an engagement or marriage on a young woman who attempts to moderate his behavior. Their initially unremarkable acquaintance leads to an outburst of uncontrollable emotion: "hee was halfe a yeare in my company before I discovered any thing of a particular inclination for mee more then another, and as I was civill to him both for his owne meritt and his sister's sake, so any particular civility I receaved from him I looked upon itt as flowing from the affection hee had to his sister and her kindness to mee" (11). But of course Halkett's linguistic patterns ("hee was . . . before," "and as I was . . . so. . .") anticipate, as they would in fiction, a shift in action and in understanding from the past to the present: "After that time itt seemes hee was nott so much master of himselfe as to conceale itt any longer" (12). In a crescendo of dramatic actions, Howard first employs an intermediary "to tell mee how much hee had indeavored all this time to smother his passion"; he then has recourse to desperate measures: "if I did nott give him some hopes of faver hee was resolved to goe back againe into France . . . and turne Capucin" (12).

If this threat by the eighteen-year-old Thomas Howard evokes a smile, it is because we feel we have encountered these situations and characters somewhere before: precisely where has been the subject of considerable critical discussion.[9] After an interval of ten days (during which Howard's friend begs Anne Murray to listen to his suit), a yet more dramatic encounter ensues. As in the best tradition of romantic fiction, the lady is reluctant, the gentleman importunate: she, like a Petrarchan mistress, says, "I did yield so farre to comply with his desire as to give him liberty one day when I was walking in the gallery to come there and speake to mee" (12). When he does speak, his behavior and appearance recall the courtly lover: "What hee said was handsome and short, butt much disordered, for hee looked pale as death, and his hand trembled when hee tooke mine to lead mee, and with a great sigh said, 'If I loved you lese I could say more'" (12). Thomas Howard's behavior as recounted by Halkett places him in a long line of distraught lovers, stretching from Dante and Petrarch through Hamlet to, somewhat surprisingly, Jane Austen's Mr. Knightley.[10]

It may well strike the reader as remarkable, even incredible, that conversations that occurred thirty years before can be retold verbatim (although a sufficiently significant conversation might be remembered).[11] Halkett might have recorded such incidents in a diary or journal that she then consulted in composing her memoirs. But whatever the source of such details, the series of incidents – one is inclined to say the scene – is so completely shaped that it acquires the dramatic impact of a play or novel and so supportive of one view of the matter that it has the persuasive force of a rhetorical treatise.

On several occasions, Anne Murray gives her word on a matter – once to her mother and once to her suitor – knowing that her statement means something different to her than to them, a technique that anticipates the cleverness and moral earnestness of Richardson's heroines. For example, in response to Thomas Howard's begging her to marry him, she agrees not to marry at all until she sees him married first. This he joyfully takes as a promise on her part rather than – as she sees it – a means to *avoid* a promise: "Upon this wee parted, both well pleased, for hee thought hee had gained much in what I promised, and I looked upon my promise as a

cure to him, butt noe inconvenience to myselfe, since I had noe inclination to marry any" (13).

Such a dual interpretation of a verbal agreement also leads to an
amusing stratagem, in which Anne Murray – in self-defense or self-
interest – abides by the letter though not the spirit of the law. Having
been forbidden by her mother ever to see Mr. Howard again, under threat
of being turned out of doors and disowned (15), and faced with a counter
oath by Thomas Howard, who will not leave for France until he has seen
her, Anne Halkett recalls dramatically:

> I laid my hand upon my eyes and with a sad sigh said, "Was ever creature so
> unfortunate and putt to such a sad dificulty, either to make Mr. H. forsworne if
> hee see mee nott, or if I doe see him, my mother will be forsworne if shee doth
> nott expose mee to the uttmost rigour her anger can inventt." In the midst of this
> dispute with my selfe what I should doe, my hand beeing still upon my eyes, itt
> presently came in my mind that if I blindfolded my eyes that would secure mee
> from seeing him, and so I did not transgrese against my mother. And hee might
> that way sattisfy himselfe by speaking with mee. I had as much joy in finding
> outt this meanes to yeeld to him withoutt disquiett to my selfe as if itt had beene
> of more considerable consequence. (18)

Whether one smiles at the sophistry here or applauds the heroine's ingenuity, one must be struck by the detail of the recollection and the dramatic –
even melodramatic – method of presentation. Anne Murray's reputation is
important to her, as is her sense of integrity: she feels an obligation, if not an
inclination, to obey her mother, whom she represents as harsh and vindic-
tive. She even has leisure in this account to ponder the difficulty that her
mother and her lover will be in if she does not provide an escape for them
from the oaths they have sworn. And she carefully details her movement
from physical gesture (covering her eyes) to imaginative breakthrough (a
way to resolve the difficulty). But the main thrust of this part of the
narrative is to recount her actions in such a way as to make them appear
justified, to depict herself as the virtuous and ingenious heroine coping
with unreasonable constraints. Though we may find both trivial and
obviously self-deceptive aspects to this exchange, it represents a cultural
moment in which struggles with one's own conscience and with external
authority are crucial elements. Moreover, the representation of that
moment significantly anticipates the complicated circumstances of life
and conscience that we see in the fiction of the next century.[12]

Anne Murray Halkett's account of her relationship with Thomas
Howard involves struggles of conscience, tension between parent and

child over the suitability of a particular match, the conflicting concerns of love and property, and a contest over who shall determine a young woman's destiny.[13] It represents, with the sharpened perspective of thirty years, events that the writer has fashioned into a narrative that both examines and justifies her life. Although certain dates and facts (the date of her birth and her father's death, for example) can be independently verified, most of what she relates is so personal that no second account exists, making the question of factuality or "creativity" in the writing of a memoir indeterminable.

Yet for my purposes the important point is clear: Anne Halkett shaped these events and incidents, not only, I believe, as she wrote about them but also as she thought about them, turning them over in her mind, perhaps for years. Her autobiography has not only detailed reminiscence and dramatic language but also fashioning of character that suggests a ruling conception if not an actual generic type. So virtuous is Anne Murray that "Lord H.," the father of her suitor, is willing to overlook the relative financial disadvantage to his son in marrying her, while Anne Murray's mother assumes the harsh authoritarianism of old Capulet, saying "shee [would] rather I were buried then bring so much ruine to the familly shee honored" (19).[14] Anne Murray herself, a young woman of passion and integrity, is torn between her own wishes and her sense of family obligation: she is clearly dependent on her mother not only for financial and social support but also for esteem. Her situation uncannily recalls, even as it anticipates, that of Clarissa Harlowe:

Many were imployed to speake to mee. Some used good words, some ill: butt one that was most seavere, after I had heard her with much patience raile a long time, when shee could say noe more, I gave a true accountt how inocentt I was from having any designe upon Mr. H. and related what I have allready mentioned of the progrese of his affection: which when shee heard, shee sadly wept and beged my pardon and promised to doe mee all the service shee could. (19)

And her suitor comes to resemble the too easily gallant young men of Jane Austen: the man who promises never to marry marries first. Upon his return from France he visits other women, paying them attentions in public while ignoring Anne Murray, to whom he sends a private message excusing his actions: finally, he finds the charms of an heiress irresistible and marries her.[15] Upon learning of Thomas Howard's infidelity, Anne Murray dramatically flings herself down on a bed, saying, "'Is this the man for whom I have sufred so much? Since hee hath made himselfe unworthy my love, hee is unworthy my anger or concerne.' And rising, imediately I wentt outt into the next roome to my super as unconcernedly as if I had never had an interest in him, nor had never lost itt" (22).

Although the extent to which Halkett shapes her narrative varies, much of the gesture here seems to be life – or life recollected – imitating art, as Halkett employs images of the implacable parent, the romantic heroine, the courtly lady, the virtuous but poor woman insufficiently prized by her fickle suitor. Much of the vividness of this section of the memoir derives from the use of patterns that, however accurately they may reflect Anne Murray's own actions, are familiar to us from fiction. Given the enormous popularity of romances for readers of this period, one might argue that, rather than Halkett providing the model for Richardson, as James Sutherland suggests, the heroines of popular fiction may have contributed to Halkett's sense and depiction of herself, and that her acts of self-understanding relied not only on the biblical and devotional models with which she begins but also on the secular literature associated with women readers, texts that feature both dramatic episodes and melodramatic speeches.[16]

If the first part of Halkett's narrative represents her as the heroine of romance, articulating her moral dilemma in ways that recall that genre, an equally important aspect is the process of self-evaluation and self-examination, which sometimes yields clear vindication and at other times a more ambiguous result, both morally and rhetorically. Much of the account of Halkett's relationship with Howard seems calculated to regain her mother's esteem (psychologically rather than actually, since her mother was dead by the time the autobiography was written). The object of reproachful speeches, Anne Murray replies in a way that evidently will not satisfy her mother but that maintains her own moral rectitude: "I said I could nott butt regrett what ever had occationed her displeasure or his punishmentt, butt I was guilty of noe unhandsome action to make mee ashamed; and therfore, what ever were my presentt misfortune, I was confident to evidence before I died that noe child shee had had greater love and respect to her, or more obedience" (17). Only a letter to a cousin, written in an attempt to escape to a Protestant convent in Holland, persuades her mother of her honest intentions: "from that time shee receaved mee againe to her faver, and ever affter used mee more like a friend then a child" (20). Although this incident would seem to confer adult status on Anne Murray, she recounts as a primary concern, than which "Nothing troubled mee more," her "mother's laughing att mee" (22) after learning of her former suitor's marriage. And even after Mrs. Murray's death in August 1647, she remains a kind of moral arbiter, a part of the larger community whose good opinion her daughter seeks to maintain. The need to justify herself, first to her mother and then to a broader audience, is one of the dominant motifs of this narrative.

As we have seen in the cases of Ann Fanshawe and Lucy Hutchinson, as well as Margaret Hoby and Anne Clifford, the manuscripts of women writers are subject to editing and censorship – whether in the taciturnity and self-control of Hoby and Clifford, or the crossing out of lines of Fanshawe's text, or the loss or deletion of whole pages or sections, as in Clifford and Hutchinson. In Halkett's case too, material is obviously missing: in the first instance, from the beginning of the manuscript and from the end, presumably through simple fraying or tearing, but also more significantly at two points in the body of the text. These medial gaps come at highly sensitive points in the narrative, strongly suggesting that a leaf was removed to excise details later thought too intimate or too embarrassing. The first of these excisions comes as Halkett turns to her relationship with Colonel Joseph Bampfield, an agent for the King, and later in the service of Parliament.[17]

Although we lack an account of their initial meeting, the first recorded encounters already suggest Anne Murray's interest in Bampfield. The narrator recounts these interactions with somewhat less assurance than those with Howard, in which she manipulates her material for rhetorical effect. Halkett records qualities in Bampfield as she first perceived them, not as she later understood them. She reports his conversation as full of morality, perhaps a little too full, given subsequent events: "his discourse was serious, handsome, and tending to imprese the advantages of piety, loyalty, and vertue" (23). While Halkett's account of her own conversation may be intended to convey the impression of upright and correct behavior, the challenge she issues to Bampfield sounds in retrospect rather arch, even potentially flirtatious:

Affter I had beene used to freedome of discourse with him, I told him I aproved of his advise to others, butt I thought his owne practise contradicted much of his proffession, for one of his aquaintance had told mee hee had nott seene his wife in a twelvemonth; and itt was imposible, in my opinion, for a good man to bee an ill husband, and therefore hee must defend himselfe from one before I could beleeve the other of him. (23)

In contrast to her earlier attempts to justify her actions to her mother, there is here a less clearly defined opponent, the forces of society vaguely expressed in the passive voice and the conditional: "I know I may be condemned as one that was too easily prevailed with, butt this I must desire to bee considered: . . . " (28). Halkett also acknowledges her motives and their negative effects:

> The earnest desire I had to serve the King made mee omitt noe opertunity wherin I could bee usefull, and the zeale I had for His Majesty made mee not see what inconveniencys I exposed my selfe to: for my intentions beeing just and inocentt made mee nott reflect what conclusions might bee made for the private visitts which I could nott butt nesesarily make to C. B. in order to the King's service. (27)

The dramatic story that follows, in which Anne Murray helps the Duke of York escape in women's clothes from St. James's Palace, shows her courage and inventiveness. But this dangerous undertaking also brought her into prolonged and sometimes intimate contact with Bampfield, into situations that clearly require some explanation: "One evening when I wentt to see him I found him lying upon his bed, and asking if hee were nott well, hee told mee hee was well enough . . ." (27). Interestingly, Halkett does not comment directly on this rather surprising scene, but presents it as part of the larger whole – her unguarded intimacy with Bampfield.

Anne Halkett's attitude toward her narrative is complicated not only by hindsight, which provides a more sober perspective on her earlier actions, but also by a tendency to agree with her censurers, or at least to agree that appearances could easily have led to their conclusions. But the tone and direction of the narrative are also curiously mixed, as Halkett combines her early impressions of Bampfield with her later realizations, presenting an alternating rather than a consistent point of view. In contrast to her account of Thomas Howard, in which she had a dominant position for much of the time and, even when abandoned, found an acceptable role to play, her account of this relationship is mired in circumstance and uncertainty, reflecting her inability to pass a final, definitive judgment on Bampfield:[18]

> hee was one who I had beene conversantt with for severall yeares before; one that proffesed a great friendship to my beloved brother Will; hee was unquestionably loyall, handsom, a good skollar, which gave him the advantages of writting and speaking well, and the cheefest ornamentt hee had was a devoutt life and conversation. Att least hee made itt appeare such to mee, and what ever

misfortune hee brought upon mee I will doe him that right as to acknowledge I learnt from him many excellentt lessons of piety and vertue and to abhorre and detest all kind of vice. This beeing his constantt dialect made mee thinke my selfe as secure from ill in his company as in a sanctuary. (28)

Even after nearly thirty years, Halkett's sense of Bampfield's attractions remains strong enough that she at first states the positive impression, before modifying it – "Att least hee made itt apeare such to mee" – and following up with another tribute to what she has learned from him – "many excellentt lessons of piety and vertue and to abhorre and detest all kind of vice." Even at this remove, and after what she now understands as his duplicity, Bampfield remains, ironically, a kind of moral marker for Halkett.

While Halkett's account of her relationship to Bampfield involves moral self-examination, and while it, like her relationship with Howard, leads to a self-proclaimed verdict of innocent, the handling of this relationship is less economical and less assured, reflecting a degree of doubt about her own actions and leading to a weaker organization of her text. For example, the suspense about Bampfield's marital state is not soon resolved, and involves a sequence of episodes that a writer of fiction would have pruned to make the narrative line more focused and less ambiguous. At first, having supposedly learned of his wife's death, Bampfield puts on mourning, but "desired the gentleman who had first aquainted him with itt nott to make itt puplicke" (27). A few lines later Bampfield proposes marriage, and Anne Murray soon accepts (28). But twenty-five lines later, in a highly dramatic gesture, Bampfield places her on one side of the room and himself on the other, "for I have had news since I saw you that, if itt bee true, my distance from you must bee greater and I must conclude my selfe the most unfortunate of men" (28–29). Fourteen lines later, considerably less dramatically, it is reported that Bampfield's servant has "brought word that his wife died att the same time that hee first gott knowledge of itt, and that hee was att her grave where shee was buried" (29).

Subject like Anne Clifford to the vicissitudes of fortune, Anne Halkett here records events episodically, rather than shaping them firmly into a plot. She recounts in chronological order the death of her brother Will and the illness of the child of a friend;[19] but soon there are allegations against Bampfield from her brother and sister, "both representing C. B. under the caracter of the most unworthy person living, that hee had abused mee in pretending his wife was dead" (32). This news sends her into a severe, prostrating illness. Yet despite what seems a clear connection between her physical and psychological state, Halkett protests that "I gave nott the least creditt to [this report] because I thought there information might come from such as might report itt outt of malice or designe" (33). In short, in contrast to the highly romanticized account of her wooing and ultimate desertion by Thomas Howard, Halkett's narrative here shows her at the mercy of circumstances and Bampfield's duplicity,[20] and the lack of assurance in her narrative handling of it reflects her own ambivalence and perhaps self-deception. The question of Bampfield's marital status is not finally resolved until late in the narrative when Sir James Halkett himself brings her word that "C. B.'s wife was living and was now att London, where shee came cheefely to undeceave those who beleeved her dead" (72). Part of Halkett's inability to deal with these events, either emotionally or rhetorically, stems from her ongoing involvement and her sense that she is – understandably – the subject of unfavorable comment: "I aprehended every one that saw mee censured mee, and that was noe litle trouble to mee when I reflected on my misfortune that gave them butt too just grounds" (72).

But if Halkett does not fully control this part of her story, there are other subtler indications of narrative pattern and conception, of her attempts to shape the unruly materials of life. The suspenseful but ragged tale of her relation with Bampfield is interrupted and complemented by another instance of deceit, one that allows her to demonstrate her integrity. Halkett recalls in detail how a hypocritical clergyman and tempter, Mr. Nicolls, spreads rumors about her and Sir Charles Howard, her host and the husband of her friend and sister of her former suitor.[21] In this episode, which acts as a counterpoint to Anne Murray's involvement with Colonel Bampfield, the narrator is totally blameless: the inclusion of this incident thereby underscores her innocence in the previous case as well. The account also gives a somewhat more favorable cast to the character of Bampfield, whose motives are not so clearly malign as those of Mr. Nicolls, though their modes of self-defense are similar: Bampfield wants to take the sacrament as evidence of his faithfulness; Nicolls swears on the Bible even though Anne Murray knows him to be lying.

What has been taken as a mere digression – to Delany an instance "of neurotic oversensitivity," "a tempest in a tea cup, to which no male autobiographer would give so much importance"[22] – and which is rather apologetically represented by Halkett as tangential – "I am sory I cannott relate my owne misfortunes withoutt reflecting upon those who was the occation of them" (35) – serves an important purpose in the narrative.

Rather than simply delaying the conclusion, this incident reinforces the claims of Halkett's integrity made elsewhere in the narrative: it represents the virtuous protagonist belied, and only at length vindicated and believed. In the midst of this extended tale of deceit, Anne Halkett offers small but significant tokens of her reliability: she is awakened by an earthquake; she tells her hosts of her experience, only to have her story at first rejected and then independently verified. Characteristically but misleadingly, she introduces the incident as a mere curiosity: "By the way I cannott omitt to mention what was remarkeable the time I was in that familly" (41). Despite the lack of clear rhetorical signals, the incident is an important marker of her truthfulness and reliability as a witness, and is even confirmed in the next paragraph by a second earthquake, which both she and Lady H. experience.

Anne Halkett's narrative, which certainly involves patterns of behavior and consistent attitudes, is neither so clearly shaped as fiction, in which one character might serve as a foil to another, nor is it altogether lacking in meaningful structure. Sometimes strongly fashioned, sometimes episodic, this narrative does not manifest a single consistent pattern but rather a suggestive structure of events, framed by Anne Halkett as she attempts to understand her own life, and perhaps reinforced by the reader's searching for structure in a given text. In the cases of Mr. Nicolls and Colonel Bampfield, there is a direct confrontation of the hypocritical or double-dealing offender and written evidence to support the narrator's position: Mr. Nicolls, confronted by Anne Murray in the presence of Lord and Lady Howard, is finally confounded by a letter in his hand which she produces; there is a weak analogue in the mention that her brother-in-law has fought a duel with C. B. (as she habitually calls him), and in the response: "C. B. knew very well I could nott butt heare of itt and that itt would very much afflict mee, and therfore hee writt a long letter in his owne vindication" (48).[23]

The latter section of the autobiography, which centers on Anne Murray's travels among her royalist friends and acquaintances and her encounter with the King, is generally less consistent, less focused, and less highly patterned than the earlier part of the narrative.[24] But Halkett's keen awareness of her own behavior and of the view that others take of it persists, contributing to the thematic unity of the text.[25] This section of the narrative also vividly reflects her energy, courage, and resourcefulness, as she dresses the wounds of soldiers (55–56); serves as a physician for the community; debates the nature of Divine Providence with the Parliamentary Colonel Overton (60–61); boldly faces down English soldiers in the house of Lady Dunfermline and again in Edinburgh (58–59, 63–64); and secures the house and aids in the escape of the Earl of Dunfermline (May 1653) as he is pursued by Parliamentary cavalry (73).

The chronological account of Halkett's activities in the period 1650–53 moves somewhat haphazardly between the uncertainty over Bampfield's marital status and her own travels in Scotland, suspended as she is between an anticipated marriage and her involvement in daily activities. But although the latter part of the narrative is less strongly focused than the initial section, a second center of interest develops when she meets Sir James Halkett, an honorable widower much attracted to her. She initially discourages Halkett's attentions because she considers herself committed to Bampfield (67); later she inquires about Halkett's character and politics, while encouraging him to marry someone else (71). The narrative vividly sketches character: in contrast to Bampfield, whose chief interest (aside from his activities as spy and courier) is maintaining his influence over Anne Murray, Sir James Halkett is disinterestedly eager to serve both herself and Bampfield. The latter's superficially polite response to Halkett's courtesy is worthy of Richardson's Lovelace himself: "C. B. understood very well upon what accountt itt was that hee receaved these testimonys of kindnese and did regrett the misfortune of nott having itt in his power to obleige him, for hee knew noe thing could doe itt more then his resigning his interest in mee; and that was nott posible for him to doe, though hee would often tell mee if any thing should arive to deprive him of mee, hee thought in gratitude I was obleiged to marry Sir J. H." (68–69). For the reader who knows the ending, this ironic comment is also prophetic.

Besides narrative patterns or generic motifs of fiction – the artful deceiver, the belied heroine, the virtuous lady facing down the unruly mob – Halkett uses instances of prophecy and faith in her attempt to discover meaning and coherence in her own life, an attempt that in turn helps shape her text. She recounts, for example, the prophecy of one Jane Hambelton "who they say had the second sight" (69), first of sorrow to come (which is speedily fulfilled) and then of the impossibility of her marrying Bampfield: "And remembring how truly butt sadly fell outt what shee had foretold before, made mee the more aprehencive of this separation, though I was one that never allowed my selfe to inquire or beleeve those that pretended to know future eventts" (70). Halkett also finds, rather like Defoe's characters, that things happen providentially.[26]

Importuned by a man "who had not beene used to seeke butt was now . . . forced to aske my charity to keepe . . . from starving" (70), even though "all I had was butt one poore shilling nor knew I where to borrow two pence," she gives him the shilling "and refferred my selfe to His hands for no whom I did itt. . . . And I doupted nott butt God would provide for mee" (70). The next morning, as if miraculously, she receives a letter from her sister containing twenty pounds. Later, having assisted in the escape of Lord and Lady Dunfermline, she falls so ill that "I concluded that the Lord had determined now to putt an end to all my troubles. . . . Butt itt seemes itt was only sentt for a triall and to lett mee find the experience of the renued testimony of God's favor in rasing mee from the gates of death" (74).[27]

These serious illnesses – a pattern in Halkett's life as well as in her narrative – are frequently associated with the stress of romantic relations, in particular with crises in her relationship with Bampfield: the first follows the report of his imprisonment (32) and the news from her brother and sister that Bampfield's wife is alive; the second (57) is the result of the "conflict betwixt love and honor," her strong feelings for Bampfield and her determination not to see him until he has proved beyond all doubt that he is a widower. Later, as she is recovering from another illness, she is visited by Sir James Halkett. Perhaps it is a hopeful sign of emotional investment in this new relationship that she falls "into a feaverish distemper" after Halkett leaves, though she records with annoyance that her illness "gave occation to some people to say that I fell sicke with hartbreake because Sir James H. was gone to London to marry my Lady Morton" (78).

The latter part of Anne Halkett's narrative, which recounts her wooing by and acceptance of Sir James Halkett, is analogous to the initial relationship with Thomas Howard, although Anne Murray is now a reluctant and considerably older woman and James Halkett a less impetuous but no less earnest suitor than Howard. While Halkett presses his suit, she persists in her resolution never to marry: "I told him I was sencible that the civillity I had receaved from him were nott of an ordinary way of freindship and that there was nothing in my power that I would nott doe to exprese my gratitude. Butt if hee knew what disturbance any discourse like that gave mee, hee would never mention itt again" (75). Interestingly from the point of view of narrative, although Anne Murray Halkett represents the debate between Halkett and herself in vigorous terms ("I told him, since hee had left caring for himselfe, I was obleiged to have the more care of him, which I could evidence in nothing more then in hindring him from ruining himselfe"; 77), she no longer quotes directly, as she had her earlier dramatic debates with the impassioned Thomas Howard, but instead provides a vivid summary.

The external circumstances are also somewhat muted. In contrast to the earlier relationship, this one has no disapproving mother and no censuring society, but rather a kindly group of well-wishers: "Itt is so usuall where single persons are often together to have people conclude a designe for mariage, that it was noe wonder if many made the same upon Sir James and mee" (75).[28] Yet Anne Murray continues in uncertainty toward Bampfield, so much so that she consults a clergyman about the appropriateness of marriage to Halkett (Mr. Dickson, of whom she "had a great esteeme of his judgementt"; 76), apparently believing that he will discourage her from it. On this point, the manuscript as we have it is tantalizing, and once again, at a critical moment, a leaf is missing. The manuscript breaks off just as she learns from James Halkett that "undouptedly C. B.'s wife was living . . . att London" and resumes with her lament that "none living could condemne mee more then I did my selfe" (72). Anne Murray describes no action on her part that would make a marriage to James Halkett inappropriate, but she clearly feels that there is a major obstacle – that "I had beene so farre ingaged to another that I could nott thinke itt lawfull for mee to marry another; and so told him all the story of my beeing unhapily deceaved and what lengh I had gone, and rather more then lese" (76).

Some things here are ambiguous: was Anne Murray so deeply involved with Bampfield that she could not legally marry anyone else, or was this a matter of emotional entanglement? To "what lengh . . . had [she] gone"? Clearly she had agreed to an engagement, perhaps undertaken a civil marriage, yet she refers to "the concealing of my *intended* marriage" (72; emphasis mine). Does the "rather more then lese" refer to the extent of her actions toward Bampfield or, as the text seems to imply, the extent of her revelations to Mr. Dickson? This, she says, is a "relation, which I could nott make withoutt teares" (76). Yet in responding, the clergyman refers not to a transgression but "an unusuall tryall," and seems to go further than necessary in absolving Anne Murray of wrongdoing: "since what I did was suposing C. B. a free person, hee nott proving so, though I had beene puplickely maried to him and avowedly lived with him as his wife, yett the ground of itt failing, I was as free as if I had never seene him" (76). In the absence of evidence, Mr. Dickson's "though" suggests that Anne Murray has not done these things, but her discourse and her distress leave the extent of her involvement uncertain.[29] In a narrative in large part devoted to self-examination and self-justification, this critical incident in her relation with Bampfield brings the text literally to the breaking point.

Although less dramatically than in her relationship with Thomas Howard, in this final section of the narrative Anne Murray is the reluctant mistress who at last agrees. She takes Sir James's daughters into her home, on the grounds that she was "obleiged to doe all I could to sattisfy him, since I could nott doe what hee cheefely desired" (75). She professes to herself and to the reader that this action does not make their marriage any more likely, that "I had noe thoughts of what others concluded as done" (75). The degree to which Anne Murray here partly deceives herself is fascinating: like the first-person narrator of a novel, she accurately records her actions yet, so far as one can judge, fails to understand her own motives, leaving the reader to observe her moving ineluctably toward a marriage with Halkett while denying that she has any intention of doing so.

Although this text is the record of Halkett's life rather than a work of fiction, it manifests so many tendencies toward narrative shaping that I have been prompted to ask questions about it appropriate to fictional genres. Particularly interesting is the extent to which Halkett achieves perspective on or distance from her earlier life, a question that applies also to first-person narratives in early novels (as for example, *Moll Flanders*). In writing her life with herself as heroine, Anne Halkett is reticent about important elements of the situation and deeply conflicted: clearly she has been very strongly attracted to Bampfield; clearly marrying Halkett is the prudent thing to do, but she emphasizes other aspects of her decision to marry. As before in the narrative, she constructs herself as a person of integrity who refuses to cause injury to anyone, particularly to someone well disposed to her, an honorable suitor "whose eyes were so perceptable as to see and love injured vertue under so darke a cloud as incompassed mee aboutt" (77). Hence she finds a suitable final obstacle in her indebtedness rather than in her feelings: as in her relationship with Howard, Halkett represents herself as the scrupulous and disinterested party:

When I found hee made use of all the argumentts I used to lessen his affection as motives to raise itt higher, I told him, since hee had left caring for himselfe, I was obleiged to have the more care of him, which I could evidence in nothing more then in hindring him from ruining himselfe; and therfore told him I would bee ingenious [frank] with him and tell him my resolution was never to marry any person till I could first putt my affaires in such a posture as that if I brought no advantage where I maried, att least I would bring noe trouble. And when ever I could doe that, if ever I did change my condittion, I thought hee was the only person that deserved an interest in mee. (77)

Curiously, Halkett's phrase "interest in me" has both financial and personal meanings, signifying the convolutedness and complexity of her feelings at this point.

Finally, as the narrator represents herself moving – in conscience and practical affairs – toward marriage with James Halkett, Bampfield surfaces again, coming to her lodging uninvited to inquire "whether or not I was maried to Sir J. H." Anne Murray, who "hated lying," but who sees "there might bee some inconvenience to tell the truth," again manifests the ingenuity of an eighteenth-century heroine – or of an early modern Jesuit – saying "'I am' (outt aloud, and secrettly . . 'not')" (82).[30] And there ends her association with Bampfield. This encounter, the final dramatic scene in this relationship, might have been treated more fully than it is, or it might be seen as analogous to her observing the letter if not the spirit of her mother's prohibition of her seeing Thomas Howard, as a legally defensible act of deception. But as the narrative proceeds inevitably, if not always with rhetorical certitude, toward her marriage, this moment is handled as a brief interruption rather than a climactic event.

Anne Murray's final "mental reservation" with Col. Bampfield is an instance of the practice of equivocation, "a mode of discourse legitimate under certain (dire) social circumstances: it consists of one proposition made for two different audiences but uttered in full only to one of those audiences."[31] According to its defenders, since "the statement is true in its entirety [it] . . . is a legitimate mode of discourse for God's servants to employ when they find themselves in certain difficult situations of interrogation." Keith Thomas argues that in the course of the seventeenth century, debates over questions of conscience moved toward a simpler approach, one based on "general moral character" and individual integrity rather than "a series of discrete problems, each to be solved separately in accordance with the rule-book."[32] If Halkett's equivocation with Bampfield is an instance of a practice associated with the Jesuits, and employed earlier in the century, one might see her autobiography as a whole, with its emphasis on the integrity of the writer, as an instance of the transition described by Thomas. Halkett manifests grave concern over her marriage to Sir James Halkett, concern over whether she is violating divine law, as well as offending the mores of the community she values. But she also seeks to explain particular acts and the motives behind them in the light of general assertions about character, assertions supported by an array of encounters and incidents, prophecies and fulfillments.

In the final sections of the narrative, some of the same motifs that have marked Anne Murray Halkett's earlier life are applied to her and her new husband. Leaving London shortly after their marriage, they are miraculously – or providentially – delivered from a coaching accident. The account includes lively circumstantial detail: the coach is overbalanced by the weight of "a big fatt gentleman whose name I forgott, butt hee was one that had imploymentt under the Bishop of Durham" (85); a mysterious "good angell . . . who, seeing the danger we were in, held the coach . . . till itt was off the bridge"; their deliverance "was so extreordinary . . . that wee knew nott how to bee thankefull enough to God Allmighty who had given itt" (86). And in the very last incident recorded, Sir James, like Anne Murray, is the victim of attempts to embarrass him or to force him into a position against his conscience, to make him serve as a Justice of the Peace under the commonwealth despite his strong royalist sympathies or be forced to a public refusal.

But these last sections, though marked by attitudes and narrative techniques similar to those found earlier, are also clogged with details that blur their general outlines. Halkett's narrative of her life, it will be clear, is autobiography, not fiction, and particularly in these latter sections it seems to be shaped in the moment of telling rather than as part of a large design. In these sections even the willing reader, hoping to find a coherent structure, may be disappointed. But as I have argued, Halkett's text also includes many elements of dramatic presentation, commentary, direct dialogue, conception of character and event, repetition and pattern that, while they do not render this an aesthetically consistent whole, certainly move it beyond a mere chronicle of events. Moreover, these techniques are not merely patterns of narrative structure but of understanding, reflecting the view the writer came to have of her own life and the process by which she achieved it. Recording perhaps for herself, perhaps for members of her family, perhaps for a wider audience, she constructs a history of her actions that is ultimately an apologia, supported by elements representing divine providence as her guide.

While the features I have described suggest an editorial hand or an authorial awareness of considerable sophistication, as a literary manuscript

Anne Halkett's autobiography manifests another kind of editing that complicates consideration of it. As I have noted above, the first leaf of the manuscript is missing and the second mutilated, and the last page of the manuscript breaks off in mid-sentence, in an account of events twenty years before the date of composition; we have no way of knowing how much is lost. Thus, the narrative begins in the midst of Lady Halkett's devotional introduction and it breaks off in the midst of an account of Sir James Halkett's attempts to avoid service as Justice of the Peace. Even more important, a leaf has been torn from the manuscript at two crucial points – after the marriage of Thomas Howard, which is also the beginning of her relationship with Joseph Bampfield (23), and when she ultimately learns, from the man who would become her husband, of Bampfield's false claims regarding the death of his wife.

The beginning and the end of a manuscript can easily be lost over time, but given the nature of the other omissions, it seems clear that someone – perhaps one of Halkett's heirs – thought that she had been a little too frank on the subject of her relations with Bampfield and hence removed what are arguably the most interesting pages in the manuscript. Anne Halkett herself is unlikely to have done so, since she could have exercised whatever control she thought appropriate in writing the original. Still, she might have had second thoughts on rereading what she had written. Our utter lack of knowledge leaves us with perplexing questions about censorship and self-censorship.

Beyond the issue of censorship remains the question of how to view a text that is obviously incomplete, partly through the ravages of time, partly through deliberate action. Do we as readers simply regard it as fragmentary, frustrating, perplexing? Do we try to make a whole of what is left, filling in the gaps with our imagination? Or do we see the omissions here as reflective of the very nature of such a text, one in which the material can never be as fully fashioned as in fiction, and in which our attempts to see the kinds of shapes, repetitions, or patterns familiar to us from fiction are necessarily to be disappointed? In short, to counterbalance what I have been arguing about the shaping of Anne Halkett's autobiography, let me, perhaps perversely, suggest that what has happened to it is appropriate to the kind of text it is, one that attempts to make sense of life, to see it as an affair with purpose and direction, but that must also reckon with uncertainty, indeterminacy, and chance, that may be pruned or amplified not just by its author but by life itself.

CHAPTER 6

Margaret Cavendish: shy person to Blazing Empress

The women writers I've been discussing represent a developing sequence of strategies of self-representation: from Margaret Hoby, whose character and daily activities are glimpsed through the record of her devotional life; to Anne Clifford, whose strength emerges in the struggle to maintain property, custody of her daughter, and a sense of herself, expressed first in brief diary entries and later in more connected and controlling narrative accounts; to Lucy Hutchinson and Ann Fanshawe, who, though casting themselves within a larger narrative in which their husbands figure prominently, nevertheless manage to occupy important and central roles. Anne Halkett comes closest of all to a coherently shaped narrative of her own life, one that uses motifs associated with more fully developed narrative forms – the novel and the romance – and sometimes achieves a striking degree of psychological realism or dramatic flair. The earlier texts, those of Hoby and Clifford, depend more clearly on devices of time, being written in the form of a daily record, or establishing connections through momentous anniversaries or in significant places. The subsequent texts – of Hutchinson, Halkett, and Fanshawe – rely more heavily on motifs associated with character, judgment, or action. Using forms that are deeply connected to the writers' process of understanding, these accounts present the influence of providence or bear the marks of romance, develop the argument for integrity or family pride. If the fit between the details of the writer's life and the interpretive strategies she adopts is sometimes inexact, that is an indication that the writer's understanding of her experience is more complex than the simpler outlines of fiction, or that the process is incomplete, and that life is not yet art.

In the spectrum of these writers Margaret Cavendish – a legend in her own time and once again in ours – represents a new order of self-depiction, one that takes both autobiographical and fictional forms and uses them with unprecedented flamboyance. I shall consider two texts, first Margaret Cavendish's brief version of her own life, *A True Relation of my Birth, Breeding, and Life*, attached to her collection of tales, *Nature's Pictures*, printed in 1656,[1] and second, the images of her that emerge in the utopian science-fiction fantasy, *The Blazing World*, published in 1666 along with her *Observations upon Experimental Philosophy*.

Margaret Lucas Cavendish, born in 1623, was the youngest daughter of Thomas Lucas of Colchester and his wife Elizabeth. After the outbreak of the Civil War in 1642, the family took refuge in Oxford, where Margaret became a maid of honor to Queen Henrietta Maria. In 1644 she followed the Queen into exile in Paris, where she met and soon married the lately widowed William Cavendish, Marquis of Newcastle, thirty years her senior. The Lucases and Cavendishes suffered great losses during the Civil War: St. John's Abbey, the Lucas family home, was ransacked by Parliamentary forces in 1642; Margaret's youngest brother Sir Charles Lucas was executed in 1648; and Newcastle, who had been commander of Charles I's army in the North (defeated at the battle of Marston Moor), had his estates confiscated. Margaret and William Cavendish remained in Europe until the Restoration, living as extravagantly as they could and entertaining such important contemporary thinkers as Hobbes, Gassendi, and Descartes. Although Margaret Cavendish received little formal education, these contacts provided her with intellectual stimulation and a sense of the significant questions of the day, if not a systematic framework for considering them. In 1651–52, having gone to England to petition for the income from her husband's estates, Margaret Cavendish began her writing career with *Poems and Fancies*; she continued in a variety of genres – letters, plays, works engaging ideas of science and philosophy, and fantasy – until her death in 1673.[2]

In contrast to Hoby, Clifford, Halkett, and Fanshawe, who wrote essentially private documents, or who intended them simply as contributions to a family history, Margaret Cavendish not only wrote *A True Relation of my Birth, Breeding, and Life* for publication but also joined it with other texts of her own production, tales that connect in striking ways with her own life and interests, manifesting elements of autobiography and wish fulfillment. According to Kate Lilly, in these fictional tales "Margaret Cavendish was rewriting the narrative of her own history as romance. . . . In particular she charts the difficult progress of the exceptional, and exceptionally chaste, woman to her just reward: a brilliant marriage and her own title."[3] In a variety of texts, then, Cavendish demonstrates not only an interest in publishing that sets her apart from most women of her time but also an interest in presenting her own biography. In *A True Relation* that interest is manifested as anxiety, as an existential need to appear in print.

Cavendish herself raises the question with which I began: "why hath this Ladie writ her own Life?" In its context at the end of *A True Relation*, the question is rhetorical, suggesting in fact a lack of general interest in the answer: "Readers will scornfully say, why hath this Ladie writ her own Life? since none cares to know whose daughter she was, or whose wife she is, or how she was bred, or what fortunes she had, or how she lived, or what humour or disposition she was of?"[4] Cavendish then acknowledges her own deep interest in self-presentation, an admission that leads to a flood of facts intended to preserve her place in history:

> I answer that it is true, that 'tis to no purpose, to the Readers, but it is to the Authoress, because I write it for my own sake, not theirs; neither did I intend this piece for to delight, but to divulge, not to please the fancy, but to tell the truth, lest after-Ages should mistake, in not knowing I was daughter to one Master *Lucas* of *St. Johns* neer *Colchester* in *Essex,* second Wife to the Lord Marquis of *Newcastle,* for my Lord having had two Wives, I might easily have been mistaken, especially if I should dye, and my Lord Marry again. (63)

Not only does Cavendish acknowledge that she writes for herself rather than for a public eager for details; her concluding remarks also suggest a fear that if she does not present herself, no one will; that if she does not present herself, no one will care; that if she does not present herself, she will cease to exist. The balanced syntax of her imagined retort to the uninterested reader gives way to a less ordered flow of details, a desperate attempt to stem the tide of oblivion. Indeed, the oddly inconclusive ending of this text suggests a desire to continue to hold the floor, not to yield to the next speaker or to let the curtain fall – lest some contingency should arise that might require further speech from the Duchess of Newcastle. With the possible exception of Anne Clifford, in no other writer I've considered do we get such a sense of the text as a means of self-representation and self-construction, of the power of print as a way to preserve one's "place in the story."[5]

In fact, one of the most dramatic and conclusive statements on Cavendish's writing comes in the midst of her praise of her own qualities, which rises to a climactic declaration of her considerable ambition. Balancing between what she has been taught (not to envy others) and what she feels (the desire to excel), she begins: "I repine not at the gifts that Nature, or Fortune bestows upon others, yet I am a great Emulator;

for though I wish none worse than they are, nor fear any should be better than they are, yet it is lawfull for me to wish my self the best, and to do my honest endeavour thereunto" (61). As in the passage that concludes *A True Relation*, we see Cavendish beginning with a syntactic weighing of qualities (signaled by clauses joined by *yet*) that then cascades into a list of absolutes:

for I think it no crime to wish my self the exactest of Natures works, my thred of life the longest, my Chain of Destinie the strongest, my mind the peaceablest; my life the pleasantest, my death the easiest, and the greatest Saint in Heaven; also to do my endeavour, so far as honour and honesty doth allow of, to be the highest on Fortunes Wheele, and to hold the wheele from turning, if I can, and if it be commendable to wish anothers good, it were a sin not to wish my own; . . . (61)

In this breathless account, marked by a sequence of end-linked clauses and parallel phrases, we see that writing for Cavendish is no accident, no trivial pursuit, but rather the expression of a powerful and deep-seated desire, not only to be known in her own time, but also to rise to "Fames Tower, which is to live by remembrance in after-ages" (62). The point is surely climactic, but it is characteristic of Cavendish's style that she does not stop here but merely pauses for breath before plunging on.

If Cavendish is unusually eager to present herself, her life, and her family in print, it remains to be asked what kind of picture emerges, and what conceptual or organizational method she uses. In contrast to the devotional beginning of Anne Halkett's autobiography or the grand cosmic setting of Lucy Hutchinson's brief account of herself, Margaret Cavendish's opening, like the rest of *A True Relation*, is much more personal and idiosyncratic. Cavendish presents the topics of her discourse in a rather *ad hoc* manner, beginning with her father, proceeding to her brothers, her sisters, her familial relations, and on to a narrative of her own life; she recounts her coming to court where she meets Newcastle, and proceeds to a eulogy for her brother-in-law Charles Cavendish; she offers an account of his helpfulness, a description of her husband, and finally of herself, her characteristics, her method of writing, and her considerable ambitions as a writer. The early sections of the narrative are organized under a series of headings not necessarily of equal importance; Cavendish moves rather abruptly from one to the other, opening paragraphs with indicative phrases: "As for my breeding"; "As for our garments"; "As for tutors"; "As for my Brothers, of which I had three"; "But to rehearse their Recreations" (42–45). Her sentences are long, even by seventeenth-century standards, and a third of the way through *A True Relation* she gives up paragraph breaks altogether, moving by free association from one topic to the next. Readers of this text can attest that its methods of organization (if that's not too strong a term) and presentation are neither ordinary nor obvious; yet *A True Relation*, though often bewildering, is remarkably vivid and forceful.[6] I want to consider the reasons for this mixture of impressions.

Perhaps the first thing to notice about Cavendish's self-presentation is its volubility and enthusiasm: the difficulty of deciphering the person who emerges from or through the language is that her account of herself, her family, and her upbringing is profuse, full of assertions and specifics, yet nonetheless confusing. In fact, the more closely one attends to Cavendish's text, the more perplexed one is likely to be, for the sheer mass of data and statements blurs the image. Although it has been argued that Margaret Cavendish is deeply divided and unable to decide who she is, I'm more interested in the complex self she constructs in her texts.[7]

One might begin with the opening of the document itself, in which Cavendish's initial statement, "My Father was a Gentleman," yields to a rush of details, a frontal assault:

My Father was a Gentleman, which Title is grounded and given by Merit, not by Princes; and 'tis the act of Time, not Favour: and though my Father was not a Peer of the Realm, yet there were few Peers who had much greater Estates, or lived more noble therewith: yet at that time great Titles were to be sold, and not at so high rates, but that his Estate might have easily purchased, and was prest for to take; but my Father did not esteem Titles, unless they were gained by Heroick Actions; and the Kingdome being in a happy Peace with all other Nations, and in it self being governed by a wise King, King *James*, there was no imployments for Heroick Spirits . . . (41)

Although Cavendish's syntax appears to set one clause or phrase against another in antithetical style, the effect is not one of balance and order but of a self-generating sequence tending in one direction. In part her father is defined by what he is not, although in Cavendish's assertion he is as good as those who are (whatever he is not): "not a Peer of the realm, yet there were few Peers who had much greater Estates, or lived more noble therewith." Some explanation is in order, for Thomas Lucas "unfortunately fortunately kill'd one Mr. *Brooks* in a single Duel," an act that led to his exile; "for my Father by the Laws of Honour could do no less than call him to the Field to question him for an injury he did him" (41). Cavendish's phrase "unfortunately fortunately" presumably refers to her father's good fortune in not having been killed himself, and his misfortune in killing another, an action that led to six years in exile. Cavendish omits the further unfortunate fact that as a consequence the eldest son failed to inherit his father's estate.[8] Each apparent conclusion leads to a new development, as in the following example; the initial parallel sequence sounds definitive, but is steadily qualified by the subsequent clauses beginning *yet*, *for*, and *but*: "though my Father by Honour challeng'd him, with Valour fought him, and in Justice kill'd him, *yet* he suffered more than any Person of Quality usually doth in cases of Honour; *for* though the Laws be rigorous, *yet* the present Princes most commonly are gratious in those misfortunes, especially to the injured: *but* my Father found it not, . . ." (41, emphases mine). Cavendish's presentation as a whole is breathless, hurried, and strongly defensive, as she musters an array of qualities to parry any criticisms that might be brought against her father. Margaret Lucas herself does not appear until the very end of this extended paragraph: exiled by Queen Elizabeth in 1597 for the killing of Brooks, Thomas Lucas was finally allowed by King James "to return home to his Native Country, wherein he lived happily, and died peaceably, leaving a Wife and eight Children, three Sons, and five Daughters, I being the youngest Child he had, and an Infant when he died" (42).

This method of presentation – the rush of details, the syntactical balance that cascades into an endless series of statements, the assertion of absolutes that on occasion turn out to be mutually exclusive – is characteristic not merely of the opening of *A True Relation* but of the text as a whole. A particularly striking example is Cavendish's account of her "breeding," i.e., her education and upbringing:

As for my breeding, it was according to my Birth, and the Nature of my Sex, for my Birth was not lost in my breeding, for as my Sisters was or had been bred, so was I in Plenty, or rather with superfluity; Likewise we were bred Vertuously, Modestly, Civilly, Honorably, and on honest principles: as for plenty, we had not only, for Necessity, Conveniency, and Decency, but for delight and pleasure to a superfluity; 'tis true, we did not riot, but we lived orderly; for riot, even in Kings Courts and Princes Palaces, brings ruin without content or pleasure, when order in less fortunes shall live more plentifully and deliciously than Princes, that lives in a Hurlie-Burlie, as I may terme it, in which they are seldom well served, for disorder obstructs; besides, it doth disgust life, distract the appetites, and yield no true relish to the sences; for Pleasure, Delight, Peace, and Felicitie live in method, and Temperance. (42)

From this long sentence consisting of end-linked phrases and clauses, a series of thoughts and after-thoughts, one thing is clear: Margaret Cavendish means to assert that her breeding was exemplary. But just how was it exemplary? It was appropriate to her birth (she's just told us that her "Father was a gentleman"; 41) and to her sex. Precisely what difference that might make is not specified; presumably she refers to the gap between the academic expectations for female and male children, but she offers an affirmation based on assumptions rather than a description.[9] Cavendish repeatedly locates herself within the range of examples of her family: she is educated in the same manner as her sisters and differently from her brothers. She emphasizes moral and social virtues: "we were bred Vertuously, Modestly, Civilly, Honorably, and on honest principles"; in other words, she conforms to an accepted – but still undefined – norm. The question of wealth and privilege is perhaps most vexed: "for as my Sisters was or had been bred, so was I in Plenty, or rather with superfluity"; "as for plenty, we had not only, for Necessity, Conveniency, and Decency, but for delight and pleasure to a superfluity." On the one hand Cavendish wants to assert sufficiency to the point of abundance (which then becomes superfluity); on the other, she wants to stress a kind of balance and temperance.

But this passage leaves one wondering just how the Lucas family lived. What degree of luxury did they enjoy? Cavendish seems to move through a series of designations that change as she considers them: her family had enough, in fact they had abundance, in fact they had more than enough; but they did not misuse that abundance: "superfluity" did not lead to "riot" or excess. Finally, they lived "in method, and Temperance." But what is the relationship between the superfluity that is asserted toward the beginning of the paragraph and the temperance that is asserted at the end? Is there a contradiction here? While it is possible to have more than enough and yet live temperately, the impression created by the two terms is certainly different. It is as if Cavendish, looking hard at the implications of one, shifts to the other, wanting to assert the virtues of both without realizing – or acknowledging – the contradictions implied. The point for Cavendish is less to fix the moving target than to assert excellence, to affirm altogether positive, normative behavior, even as the content of these assertions shifts.

The syntactic pattern of Cavendish's prose also contributes to this blurring of images. It is on the one hand additive and sequential, as Cavendish relies on co-ordinating conjunctions such as *and* and *for* to construct an extended sequence without subordination. But she also employs balance and antithesis: "as my sisters was or had been bred, so was I"; "'tis true we did not riot, but lived orderly." So while the balanced syntax leads us to expect a weighing of one quality against another, a coming to rest somewhere in between, the additive mode in fact constantly adjusts the picture we see, and the lack of subordination makes it nearly impossible to gain a comprehensive picture.

This method – a series of often-absolute assertions that are not altogether consistent – is characteristic of Cavendish's self-presentation. She uses it again in describing her brothers – about whom she asserts initially that she knows little, but ultimately that they were essentially perfect (one can discern a shift after the colon): "As for my Brothers, of which I had three, I know not how they were bred, first, they were bred when I was not capable to observe, or before I was born; likewise the breeding of men were after different manner of wayes from those of women: but this I know, that they loved Virtue, endeavour'd Merit, practic'd Justice, and spoke Truth; they were constantly Loyal, and truly Valiant" (43–44). Perhaps most paradoxical is the account of her youngest brother, Sir Charles Lucas, described as an ideal soldier (though "cut off before he could arrive to the perfection thereof"; 44). Thus the ultimate proof of his innate soldiership must be found in his "Treatise of the Arts in War," but this unfortunately remains a closed text "by reason it was in Characters, and the Key thereof lost, we cannot as yet understand any thing therein, at least not so as to divulge it" (44). The supposedly definitive proof of excellence remains unavailable, sealed in cipher. Sir Charles Lucas was indeed a distinguished soldier, and Cavendish might have cited particular evidence to support the point, but her method is to assert rather than to demonstrate, to construct a rhetorical effect rather than a documented case.

Since Cavendish admits to little first-hand knowledge of her brothers' early life, she must rely to some extent on reports, though she also questions their value, especially if they should be negative. The result is an account, full of praise, that undermines itself at every step: "neither had they skill, or did use to play, *for ought I could hear,* at Cards or Dice, or the like Games, nor given to any Vice, *as I did know,* unless to love a Mistris were a crime, *not that I knew any they had, but what report did say, and usually reports are false, at least exceed the truth"* (44; emphases mine). On the one hand, there are no reports of gaming or card playing (therefore her brothers can't have been gamblers), yet there are reports of their relationships with women, which she rejects since "usually reports are false, at least exceed the truth." The result is strong assertion, coupled with a body of evidence that vanishes before our eyes.

Clearly, Margaret Cavendish did not subject her own writing to the kind of critique I've just been making, and it may seem pointless or superfluous to demonstrate that she is not a logical thinker and writer. Cavendish herself anticipates our critique: the epistle to the reader that precedes this memoir asserts that such forgetfulness as we may see here is inherent in creativity. After citing her husband as the example of a forgetful creator, she goes on: "Indeed it's against nature, for natural wits to remember; for it is impossible that the brain should retain and create; and we see in nature, death makes way for life; for if there were no death, there would be no new life or lives."[10]

But Cavendish is not merely forgetful or inconsistent in her presentation of herself and her family: her prose is so full of positive assertions as to leave this reader, at least, thinking that there must be a comprehensible position here, even as I struggle to define it. Perhaps most intriguing is Cavendish's assertion, repeatedly offered, that she is "naturally bashful."[11] As a young woman Margaret Lucas begged her mother for permission to serve as a lady-in-waiting to Queen Henrietta Maria, even over the objections of her brothers and sisters. She reports the fact with characteristic complexity and assertiveness, and in the antithetical style seen earlier: "for though they knew I would not behave my self to their, or my own dishonour, yet they thought I might to my disadvantage, being unexperienced in the World, which indeed I did, for I was so bashfull when I was out of my Mothers, Brothers and Sisters sight . . ."; she depicts herself as simultaneously withdrawn and ambitious that "they should approve of my actions and behaviour" (46).

While the word *bashful* may seem to us in flat contradiction to Cavendish's behavior, the *OED* provides a clearer sense of what the word may have meant to her:

1. Wanting in self-possession, daunted, dismayed (uses recorded from 1552–1674);
2. Of persons: shrinking from publicity, shamefaced, shy. Sometimes used in a good or neutral sense, to mean "Sensitively modest in demeanour"; but sometimes depreciatively, meaning "Excessively self-conscious, embarrassed and ill at ease in society, 'sheepish'" (1548–1810);
3. Of things, actions, etc.: characterizing or characterized by extreme sensitiveness or modesty (1595–1816).

In fact, this lack of social aptitude is precisely what Cavendish ascribes to herself. Ambition leads her to seek a place at court, while modesty (or bashfulness) keeps her from expressing herself, or even learning what she might in this situation: "I durst neither look up with my eyes, nor speak, nor be any way sociable, insomuch as I was thought a Natural Fool, indeed I had not much Wit" (46). The very attempt to avoid dishonor leads to the perpetuation of this hesitant and doubtful behavior: "indeed, I was so afraid to dishonour my Friends and Family by my indiscreet actions, that I rather chose to be accounted a Fool, than to be thought rude or wanton" (46). Remarkably, or perhaps not so remarkably, this strategy captivated William Cavendish, the 51-year-old widowed Marquis of Newcastle, who "did approve of those bashfull fears which many condemn'd, and would choose such a Wife as he might bring to his own humours, and not such an one as was wedded to self conceit, or one that had been temper'd to the humours of another, for which he wooed me for his Wife; and though I did dread Marriage, and shunn'd Mens companies, as much as I could, yet I could not, nor had not the power to refuse him, by reason my Affections were fix'd on him, and he was the onely Person I ever was in love with" (47).

The self-confessed reticent maiden is wooed by Newcastle; she both dreads marriage and "glories" in her love for him; she "shunn'd Mens companies" yet cannot resist him. One is tempted to find here at least a degree of self-deception, or to suspect that the growth of this relationship might be described differently by others (as indeed it was). Sara Mendelson argues strongly that Margaret Lucas played a clever and active role in the courtship, and Sidonie Smith, in an illuminating essay, sees a deep psychic division in Cavendish's self-presentation.[12] But consistent throughout this welter of inconsistencies is the method of self-definition – a series of strongly worded assertions that modify, complicate, or even confuse the picture as we go along, a sequence of general and definitive statements that create a kaleidoscopic series of images. And in the case of this picture, as in the account of Cavendish as writer, the sequence is climactic: not only was Newcastle "the onely Person I ever was in love with," but her definition of the nature of that love is also progressive and triumphal:

Neither was I ashamed to own it, but gloried therein, for it was not Amorous Love, I never was infected therewith, it is a Disease, or a Passion, or both, I onely know by relation, not by experience; neither could Title, Wealth, Power or Person entice me to love; but my Love was honest and honourable, being placed upon Merit, which Affection joy'd at the fame of his Worth, pleas'd with delight in his Wit, proud of the respects he used to me, and triumphing in the affections he profest for me, which affections he hath confirmed to me by a deed of time, seal'd by constancy, and assigned by an unalterable decree of his promise, which makes me happy in despight of Fortunes frowns; . . . (47)

In this sequence Cavendish uses a series of parallel phrases to assert the power and nobility of her feelings for William Newcastle, and his for her.

She moves from a refutation of anything that might be construed negatively ("Amorous Love," which "is a Disease, or a Passion, or both") to her positive declaration ("my Love was honest and honourable"). And her self-presentation again involves a considerable degree of defensiveness, a pre-emptive barrage against the possible critique of the world at large. Yet in contrast to other sections in which new thoughts blur the image created by prior thoughts, the effect here is strongly and consistently affirmative.

Cavendish's use of preemption – the notion that the best defense is a strong offense – is a marked characteristic of her prose, amusingly evident in an account of her siblings in which she imagines (and rejects) all the things that could possibly be wrong with them. Of her mother's eight children,

> three sons and five daughters, there was not any one crooked, or any ways deformed, neither were they dwarfish, or of a Giant-like stature, but every ways proportionable, likewise well featured, cleer complexions, brown haires, but some lighter than others, sound teeth, sweet breaths, plain speeches, tunable voices, I mean not so much to sing as in speaking, as not stuttering, nor wharling in the throat, or speaking through the Nose, or hoarsly, unless they had a cold, or squeakingly, which impediments many have: neither were their voices of too low a strain or too high, but their notes & words were tuneable and timely; . . . (48–49)

Not content with a positive description ("tunable voices"), Cavendish proceeds to delineate the qualities her siblings have not ("not stuttering, nor wharling in the throat, or speaking through the Nose, or hoarsly, unless they had a cold, or squeakingly, . . ."), following the point wherever it leads her, through quirks and variations, until she rounds up her thoughts at the end: "but their notes & words were tuneable and timely."[13] This catalogue, worthy of Burton's *Anatomy of Melancholy*, both in its accumulation of details and in its digressing from its original direction, seems designed to ward off all possible criticism.[14] But of course the list of negative traits is so extensive as to become an object of attention itself and hence profoundly, if delightfully, counter-productive.

If the author of this text can accurately be called a shy person, it is in the sense of being proactively defensive, warding off social intercourse even while attracting attention. This is a quality that she may have shared with her family, for she describes them as a group of remarkably agreeable people ("I do not know that ever they did fall out, or had any angry or unkind disputes"; 45) whose sociability is oddly self-contained. Although Cavendish describes how her siblings used to go "to Plays, or to ride in their Coaches about the Streets to see the concourse and recourse of

People; and in the Spring time to visit the Spring-garden, Hide-park, and the like places; and sometimes they would have Musick, and sup in Barges upon the Water" – in other words they engaged in a considerable degree of display – nevertheless "they did seldome make Visits, nor never went abroad with Strangers in their Company, but onely themselves in a Flock together agreeing so well, that there seemed but one Minde amongst them." This degree of exclusiveness extends even to in-laws: "my Sisters . . . had no familiar conversation or intimate acquaintance with the Families to which each other were linkt to by Marriage" (45–46).

This picture of an attractive, apparently agreeable, and privileged family, whose members are sociable only among themselves, set apart from the rest of society like a little cameo picture, is curious and paradoxical. But that image is quite consistent with the reports we have of Margaret Cavendish herself – a woman who liked display, but who was not very good at conversation; who made the journey to England to seek an improvement in her husband's fortunes, but who was so offended by an accusatory description of him that she aborted the mission, never to try again: "I whisperingly spoke to my brother to conduct me out of that ungentlemanly place, so without speaking to them one word good or bad, I returned to my Lodgings, & as that Committee was the first, so was it the last, I ever was at as a Petitioner" (51).

Cavendish constructs a persona in *A True Relation* that manifests bashfulness, modesty, and reticence. Rather than being treated as negative, these qualities are associated with her assertion that she is contemplative by nature: "I being addicted from my childhood, to contemplation rather than conversation, to solitariness rather than society, to melancholy rather than mirth, to write with the pen than to work with a needle, passing my time with harmless fancies, their company being pleasing, their conversation innocent, in which I take such pleasure, as I neglect my health, for it is as great a grief to leave their society, as a joy to be in their company" (57). Yet for all these assertions, the course of her prose, like the course of her life, seems to have drawn her repeatedly into the public eye, in a movement that she describes as nearly obligatory: "although for my part I had rather sit at home and write, or walk, as I said, in my chamber and contemplate; *but I hold necessary sometimes to appear abroad*" (59; emphasis mine). Like her brothers and sisters, Cavendish goes "to see and to be seen," and it is notable how her phrases and clauses enact a gradual, almost irresistible movement: "but because I would not bury my self quite from the sight of the world, I go sometimes abroad, seldome to visit, but only in my Coach about the Town, or about some of the streets, . . .

where all the chief of the town goe to see and to be seen, likewise all strangers of what quallity soever, as all great Princes or Queens that make any short stay" (57).

Some biographers have seen Margaret Cavendish's public persona as compensation for her shyness;[15] the inference, though intriguing, is not inevitable. But my chief interest is in the connections, whether casual or explanatory, that Cavendish herself establishes in her prose. She tells, for example, how her contemplative inclinations extend to solipsism: "when I was in the company of my Naturall friends, I was very attentive of what they said, or did; but for strangers I regarded not much what they said . . ." (59).[16] And her confessed disregard of others leads, as if naturally, to her love of display: "also I never took delight in closets, or cabinets of toys, but in the variety of fine clothes, and such toys as onely were to adorn my person" (59). Just as bashfulness is linked with ambition earlier in the account, here love of contemplation yields in an unbroken syntactic series to extravagantly extroverted behavior:

I was never very active, by reason I was given so much to contemplation; . . . but my serious study could not be much, by reason I took great delight in attiring, fine dressing and fashions, especially such fashions as I did invent my self, not taking that pleasure in such fashions as was invented by others: also I did dislike any should follow my Fashions, for I always took delight in a singularity, even in acoutrements of habits, but whatsoever I was addicted to, either in fashion of Cloths, contemplation of Thoughts, actions of Life, they were Lawfull, Honest, Honorable, and Modest, of which I can avouch to the world with a great confidence, because it is a pure Truth.[17] (60)

As in the earlier passages that we have considered, this one constitutes a remarkable journey, if not of self-understanding, surely of self-depiction and self-fashioning. Cavendish records an impression, followed by another, and another, until the picture as a whole is quite different from that with which she began. She first asserts her contemplative nature, suggesting a kind of inwardness that resembles a scholarly vocation. But in fact, she reads little, partly because she understands little (and must ask her brother Lord Lucas for advice), but chiefly because she would rather be adorning herself. What Cavendish calls contemplation, others might call day-dreaming. She continues to consider herself one who shuns the world, yet she takes "great delight in attiring, fine dressing and fashions," and indeed is rather put out if "any should follow my Fashions, for I always took delight in a singularity." This remarkable display – which on the face of it seems the very reverse of modest or bashful behavior – culminates in an absolute affirmation of those qualities, a definition of her character as she understands it: "whatsoever I was addicted to, either in fashion of Cloths, contemplation of Thoughts, actions of Life, they were Lawfull, Honest, Honorable, and Modest, of which I can avouch to the world with a great confidence, because it is a pure Truth" (60).

Margaret Cavendish cites her self-fashioned image as "pure Truth" with apparent confidence and conviction even as she presents bits of evidence that would support a contrary interpretation of situation and character. This voluble woman who delights in fine dressing, and who hopes "my Readers, will not think me vain for writing my life" (and then goes on to find her models in Caesar, Ovid, Aristotle, and Vergil), concludes with yet another image of herself, complete with costume: "though I desire to appear at the best advantage, whilest I live in the view of the publick World, yet I could most willingly exclude my self, so as Never to see the face of any creature, but my Lord, as long as I live, inclosing myself like an Anchoret, wearing a Frize-gown, tied with a cord about my waste" (62–63). This final declaration calls to mind several other dazzling acts of literary self-transformation: that of Richard II, who if he couldn't be King, would be a pilgrim, giving "my jewels for a set of beads, . . . / My gay apparel for an almsman's gown" (*Richard II* 3.3.147, 149); or Lady Wishfort in *The Way of the World*, urging her supposed friend Marwood, "let us leave the world, and retire by ourselves and be shepherdesses" (Act 5). In other words, the voice of *A True Relation* invites comparison less with other human beings than with literary characters. And that is perhaps how we can best understand this text – not as a window on Margaret Cavendish's soul, nor as a failed attempt at self-knowledge and accurate recording, but rather as a remarkable feat of textual self-construction.

As we've seen in the examples cited, Cavendish's earnest efforts at self-depiction are subject to revision, and her attempts at a balanced style are forever tipping into imbalance and enthusiasm for a new position. In addressing a whole host of subjects – the family's relation with servants, her mother's tendency to anger or lack thereof, whether the education of the Lucas children was encouraged or neglected, whether Margaret Cavendish is prodigal or covetous or neither, whether she cares about dress greatly or not at all – Cavendish creates an endless series of statements, modifications, and qualifications. This is remarkable prose, not for its control, but for its imitation of a mind in action, a mind asserting an ideal or a perfect mean, and then moving quickly and irresistibly into one of the poles of the argument (or both): as, for example, in her admission late in the text: very well – I am prodigal, but being prodigal is good, at least in the way I am prodigal – besides I am not too prodigal, not harmfully so. Cavendish's combination of fervent assertion and sequentially organized syntax repeatedly implies that she's given us the last word, even while perpetually changing it.

Cavendish clearly contradicts herself – and with enthusiasm – but she does so in a number of fairly predictable ways. She persistently asserts, without an overview, but with a degree of energy and conviction that make her a force to be reckoned with. Rather than a stable image of Cavendish, the text presents a familiar series of oppositions – the relationship between reserve and ambition, shyness and display – expressed in syntax that refuses to stop, thereby creating not only confusion but also vivid and kaleidoscopic impressions. An authority on herself who hardly pauses for breath (perhaps because she fears interruption or dissent), she is far more than an autobiographer; she is a vibrant literary character. In that sense Cavendish's strategy in *A True Relation* is but the prelude to her even more dramatic self-imaging in *The Blazing World*, a text in which she breaks the bonds of fact and autobiography to create herself not once but twice.

Margaret Cavendish confesses, late in *A True Relation*, that her desire to write "her own life" is driven not just by anxiety that she will disappear but by full-fledged ambition to be remembered in history. That ambition is articulated far more strongly in *The Description of a New World, Called the Blazing World*, in which she appears in a world, indeed worlds, of her own making. Even in our own time, when women are no longer taught to be "chaste, silent, and obedient," Cavendish's sheer effrontery and ebullience remain remarkable. In the preface to *The Blazing World* she takes female ambition not as extraordinary but as to be expected, and resolves to be in the front rank of such striving beings:

I am . . . as Ambitious as ever any of my Sex was, is, or can be; which makes, that though I cannot be *Henry* the Fifth, or *Charles* the Second, yet I endeavour to be *Margaret* the *First;* and although I have neither power, time nor occasion to conquer the world as *Alexander* and *Caesar* did; yet rather then not to be Mistress of one, since Fortune and the Fates would give me none, I have made a World of my own: for which no body, I hope, will blame me, since it is in every ones power to do the like. (153–54)

If in Anne Halkett's autobiography we see a tendency to self-dramatizing and romanticizing that helps shape her self-presentation, in *The Blazing*

World we find a fiction whose acknowledged purpose is to give greater
scope to its author. And whereas in other texts we might cautiously reflect
on apparent connections between the author's life and the story she tells,
in Cavendish the resemblances are so great as to constitute a whole new
order of things.[18] Cavendish offers no pretense, no reticence about the
degree of her self-interest or self-representation; rather she creates a world
and a set of characters that reflect her attitudes, her activities, and her
preoccupations.

  The Blazing World is described by Cavendish as having three parts –
"romancical, philosophical, and fantastical" – and indeed it opens with a
romance narrative, moves into a playful section of questions about science
and the natural world, and concludes with a tale that provides perspective
on Cavendish's life and her views of society. Yet neither the three-part
division announced in the preface nor the formal two-part division of the
text itself accurately captures the variety of one's experience of reading.
There are elements of wish fulfillment in the central female figure who is
powerful, respected, and loved; of utopian fantasy in the creation of a
well-ordered and prosperous monarchy with a capital city called Paradise;
a probing of scientific, philosophical, and theological questions in discussions with a group of fanciful characters – Bear-men, Worm-men, Fly-
and Fish-men, and others; there is perspective on Cavendish's own time
and place in the voyages to the Blazing World and back; and there are
amusing self-revelations (and revelings) in the representation of "the
Duchess of Newcastle" and her more spectacular alter ego, the Empress.
The narrative sections are often distinctly improvisatory: one feels that
Cavendish, more intent on imaginative self-indulgence and inquiry than
on the shaping of a consistent narrative, is making it up as she goes along.
As the text moves rather abruptly from one mode to the next – narrative
or romance to fantasy or philosophical speculation – a reader whose
expectations are formed by a particular section may be surprised to find
herself deep in another kind of text twenty pages on.[19]

  Although readers today may see ways in which Cavendish's tale anticipates other fantastic voyages in English literature – the voyage to an unknown land of extreme cold, the death of characters subordinate to the
author's interest in the protagonist, as in *The Rime of the Ancient Mariner*,
the emphasis on the possibilities and follies of science in *Gulliver's Travels* –
it also grows out of contemporary interest in other worlds, manifested in
such works as John Wilkins's *Discovery of a World in the Moone* (1638)
and Henry More's *Essay upon the Infinity of Worlds out of Platonick
Principles* (1647).[20] Besides the interest in scientific questions that occupy

approximately a third of the narrative, the wildly improbable story that Cavendish creates seems driven chiefly by a desire to present characters like herself – or herself as she would wish to be. There is little development of character; rather, dialogue and episode take second place to a pursuit of the author's own interests – in the natural world, theology, and political systems – and in her wish to redress her husband's grievances, restore his fortunes, and praise his accomplishments.

To this end Cavendish creates a world both strange and convenient: a beautiful young lady, a figure that one can hardly avoid regarding as Cavendish's self-image, is admired by a merchant who abducts her and sails into a mysterious northern land. Subject to extreme cold, the lady's captors freeze to death, while she is sustained "by the light of her Beauty, the heat of her Youth, and Protection of the Gods" (154). Taken off the ship by creatures that appear dangerous but are in fact well-mannered and admiring ("in shape like Bears, onely they went upright as men"; 156), she is instantly accepted, even adored, by the Emperor and his subjects, "who could hardly be perswaded to believe her mortal" (162). Married to the Emperor within the space of a sentence (he needs only to be assured that she is not a goddess), she is given "absolute power to rule and govern all that World as she pleased" (162). Margaret Lucas was of course not abducted by a merchant, but her marriage to William Cavendish brought her into a realm of wealth and potential influence far greater than that of her own family. (The subsequent disappointment of Newcastle's hopes is in fact an important motif in *The Blazing World.*) In contrast to Cavendish herself, who had little facility with languages, the young lady very quickly picks up enough of the language of the Blazing World to be able to converse easily with its strange creatures.[21] Whereas Margaret Cavendish was invited to attend a single meeting of the Royal Society in 1667 (a year after the publication of *The Blazing World*), making an appearance that met with decidedly mixed reviews,[22] the Empress of the Blazing World converses at length with the Bird-men (on matters of astronomy and climate), the Bear-men (on matters of telescopes and microscopes), the Fish-men, and sundry others about questions of the natural world that intrigue her. Even though the answers do not always satisfy her, her inquiries fully engage the authorities she consults. Clearly Cavendish has constructed a world more favorable to female scientific inquiry than the one in which she lives.[23]

Since the Empress's conversations in effect allow Margaret Cavendish to pose any question that comes into her mind, they give a fair sample of her interests in natural phenomena and her attitudes toward experimentation and technology.[24] These sections indicate that Cavendish, like many of her contemporaries, was intrigued by the powers of the microscope, the possible existence of other worlds, and the nature of cycles – whether of generation, movement of the tides, or circulation of water. She rejects some inquiries as fruitless, declaring abstruse mathematics both incomprehensible and useless (188). And some questions are simply unanswerable – as whether the earth moves about the sun or the sun about the earth, and whether the heavens change or remain the same. She appears to show a bias toward nature over technology when she notes admiringly that the captains of the Blazing World navigate perilous waters without lodestones or compasses; yet she also describes with approval their use of a sort of jet engine (158). Again, the Empress's rebuke, that telescopes "are false Informers, and instead of discovering the Truth, delude your senses," seems to privilege nature, as does her command that the "Bear-men" "break them, and let the Bird-men trust only to their natural eyes, and examine Celestial objects by the motions of their own sense and reason" (170). But this position is modified by the sequel, for in response to the Bear-men's humble petition, the Empress allows them to keep their glasses, and they show her objects, microscopically enlarged, that clearly fascinate her. Despite Cavendish's concern about "artificial delusions," her evident engagement with the details she records suggest something other than a strict preference for unaided scientific observation.

The Blazing World allows Cavendish to represent her thoughts not only on science and theology but also on society: she emerges as a convinced monarchist and social conservative. When the residents of the Blazing World articulate the view that women, without holding direct power, have a large enough role in their influence on men (164–65), nothing in the text contradicts this statement. And when one recalls Margaret Cavendish's self-reported inability to plead for her husband before a Parliamentary Committee in *A True Relation*, suggesting a disinclination for overt political action or engagement, the position is not surprising. The Empress does erect separate religious facilities for women, who otherwise were not allowed access to public worship: "she resolved to build Churches, and make also up a Congregation of Women, whereof she intended to be the head her self, and to instruct them in the several points of her Religion" (191). But this move seems in equal measure a compliment to women, "which generally had quick wits, subtile conceptions, clear understandings, and solid judgments" (191) and an enlargement of her own power: "for the Emperess had an excellent gift of Preaching, and instructing them in the Articles of Faith; and by that means, she converted them not onely soon, but gained an extraordinary love of all her subjects throughout that World" (191). In her description of the Empress's policy decisions, Cavendish adheres to gender stereotyping: the Empress initiates a period of experimentation in the Blazing World, because it is the "nature of Women [to be] . . . much delighted with change and variety" (229), after which she decides to return to the original, single form of government, and eliminate factions.[25]

But these pages are far from a mere sober representation of Cavendish's positions on science, theology, philosophy, and society; they also display her sense of humor and wit.[26] The debate over whether offspring resemble their progenitors turns into a joke: in considering whether maggots bred out of cheese conform to the principle of likeness, the Empress first asserts that "Cheese has no blood, and so neither have Maggots; besides, they have almost the same taste which Cheese has" (177). When the experimental scientists, on the subject of motion, protest that "Maggots have a visible, local, progressive motion, which Cheese hath not," the Empress retorts "That when all the Cheese was turned into Maggots, it might be said to have local, progressive motion." The very designations of these characters are comic: Cavendish represents an orator (one of a group of "Magpie-, Parrot-, and Jackdaw-men") so caught up with "formalities and distinctions" that he is unable to speak at all (188). When the Empress's persistent questions exhaust the knowledge even of immortal spirits, she acknowledges that "It is the nature of Mankind to be inquisitive," and records their Miltonic reply: "Natural desire of knowledg . . . is not blameable, so you do not go beyond what your natural reason can comprehend" (206). While Cavendish depicts the Empress as fully capable of scientific discussion, giving "the Ape-men . . . better Instructions then perhaps they expected, not knowing that her Majesty had such great and able judgment in Natural Philosophy," she also, perhaps with a wry smile, spares her reader the full details of these conversations, engaging in an act of economy rare in her writing (183–84).

Although *The Blazing* World is a fully developed utopian science fiction, from my perspective the most intriguing and delightful part of it is the section in which the Empress, already clearly a manifestation of Margaret Cavendish's own fondest wishes, decides that she needs a scribe and sends for none other than the Duchess of Newcastle. In thinking about Cavendish's feat of self-representation, with its quite astonishing and unashamed need for prominence, I am reminded of an impromptu nativity pageant I once saw: the elder of two young children, unable to decide whether she wanted to be the infant Jesus or the adoring angel, chose the former role, but continued to direct her younger sister, the angel, from a prone position in the cardboard box that served as the manger.[27] Margaret Cavendish, having invented an improved version of herself – or at least an enviable female protagonist – can no longer remain on the sidelines but enters the main action as the assistant and adviser to, and ultimately the "Platonic friend" of, the Empress. Cavendish amusingly depicts the Empress's seeking a scribe for her "Cabbala": while she would very much prefer "the Soul of some ancient famous Writer, . . . *Aristotle, Pythagoras, Plato, Epicurus,* or the like," or, failing that, "the Soul of one of the most famous modern Writers, as either of *Galileo, Gassendus, Des Cartes,* . . . ," she is warned by a spirit of the arrogance and recalcitrance of all of these great thinkers, and chooses instead "the *Duchess of Newcastle,* which although she is not one of the most learned, eloquent, witty and ingenious, yet she is a plain and rational Writer, for the principle of her Writings, is Sense and Reason" (208). Just as in Lucy Hutchinson's biography of her husband the text moves inexorably toward his choice of her as the ideal mate, so Cavendish's account homes in on the Duchess of Newcastle as the ideal scribe for the Empress. But the reasons given for the choice – Cavendish's reputation for sense and reason – are so at odds with what we know of that reputation as to bring a smile.[28]

It's hard to know just how to read this passage: Cavendish may (for once) be attempting modesty, disavowing great learning, eloquence, wit, and ingenuity, while claiming the more basic qualities of sense and reason that would make her an agreeable assistant to the Empress, or – this seems more likely – she may be smiling with us. The Duchess is distinguished from the great thinkers who "were so wedded to their own opinions, that they would never have the patience to be Scribes" or so "self-conceited, that they would scorn to be Scribes to a Woman" (208), in phrases that raise issues that Cavendish herself, mocked as a writer, must have been sensitive to. And indeed, though there is a further joke about what seems to be the Duchess's chief liability – the appalling quality of her handwriting – she does offer the Empress sensible advice: to avoid such excessively ambitious projects as the construction of a "Jewish Cabbala," or even a philosophical, political, or moral Cabbala, and rather to choose a project more akin to Cavendish's own talents and interests: "to make a Poetical or Romancical Cabbala, wherein you can use Metaphors, Allegories, Similitudes, *etc.* and interpret them as you please" (210).

In advising the Empress, the Duchess generally recommends simplification rather than the elaboration of tradition: for example, "The only thing . . . in morality, is but to fear God, and to love his Neighbour, and this needs no further interpretation" (210). But once we get beyond this basic counsel, the exchange becomes the stage for Cavendish's overpowering ambition – to "be a great Princess." There's a nice touch of humor as the Empress attempts to persuade the Duchess that she is really very grand already (211) before yielding to her wish to be an Empress as well. This desire for power and domination seems on the one hand particularly strongly felt by Cavendish (her soul tells the Empress that "neither she her self, nor no Creature in the World was able to know either the height, depth or breadth of her ambition"; 211), and yet it is a power, she asserts, open to all human beings: "we wonder, proceeded the Spirits, that you desire to be Emperess of a Terrestrial World, when as you can create your self a Celestial World if you please . . . for every humane Creature can create an Immaterial World fully inhabited by immaterial Creatures, and populous of immaterial subjects, such as we are, and all this within the compass of the head or scull" (212). Besides avoiding the bloodshed of military conquest, the creation of a world allows more complete enjoyment of that world "in whole and in parts, without controle or opposition" (213).

There is in this section of *The Blazing World* a curious, slightly disorienting multiplication of these worlds: Cavendish shows us two characters – or rather their two souls – creating worlds of their own in a tale in which Cavendish herself has already created a world of her own. And although we might presume that the Empress who so strongly resembles Cavendish and the Duchess who bears her name both come from the same world, they do not – allowing Cavendish to show several aspects of Restoration England. There are little games of rivalry and one-upmanship throughout: the Duchess, summoned by the Empress, brings her imagined world with her, which so impresses the Empress that she wants to live in it – but she is in effect warded off by the Duchess and urged to "make such another World in her own mind" (216). Although the Empress of the Blazing World is native to the world we know, she uses the world she creates in her imagination as a laboratory for possible improvements in the Blazing World ("which yet she could hardly do, by reason it was so well ordered that it could not be mended"; 216).

Cavendish uses the world she imagines to seek redress for the ills of her own world, particularly the injustices done to her husband in the course of the Civil War and the slurs on her own reputation. She depicts a courtroom scene in which the Duchess pleads the cause of the Duke of

Newcastle against Fortune, perhaps repairing her failure to speak on his behalf before the Parliamentary Commission in 1651.[29] The stables of the Duke, a renowned horseman, become the model for the far more splendid stables constructed by the Emperor, in a passage that allows Newcastle to be both exemplary and unjustly deprived.[30] Likewise, Margaret Cavendish's plays are the model for the theater that the Emperor wishes to erect, giving her an opportunity to defend her dramatic practice as more suited to the Blazing World than to "the Blinking World of Wit," where her plays are out of favor (247). The world from which the Duchess comes is both a place of trouble, "very much disturbed with factions, divisions, and wars" (216), that she tries to dissuade the Empress from visiting, and also a place to be emulated for a monarch such as Charles II, who "governs so justly and wisely, that his subjects are the happiest people of all the Nations or parts of that world" (218). Cavendish builds into her fantasy grand images of herself, as when the Empress returns to her homeland to restore peace and order, guiding a magical armada to defeat her country's enemies, and being received as "an Angel, or some Deity," by all who kneel before her (237).

Given these multiple themes, vagaries, and inconsistencies, one might regard *The Blazing World* as simply a vehicle for imagination, social commentary, self-defense, or courtly compliment, as the writer is at any moment inclined. Even though Cavendish, unlike Halkett or Hutchinson, is ostensibly writing fiction, she does not develop characters of believable depth, but rather generates multiple images of herself. The text lacks an obvious formal organization or strong narrative line (one might find a partial resemblance in Swift's *Tale of a Tub*), yet it creates an absorbing and engaging experience – as if we inhabit a hall of mirrors, with the imaginary worlds created reflecting and intensifying each other. Since the souls of the Duchess and the Empress are (not surprisingly) so much alike, such kindred spirits, it is often difficult to remember just whose soul or whose world we are inhabiting at a given moment, and since both Empress and Duchess are in fact aspects of Cavendish, it is sometimes hard to remember which is the Duchess of Newcastle. But the constant tendency throughout is the magnification of Margaret. Cavendish builds into her fantasy grand images of herself, discussions with herself of herself, and ideal scenarios in which she repairs the mistakes she has made in life. These images include a powerful warrior princess, the savior of her country and the adviser to her King, and a natural philosopher who spends "most of her time in the study of Natural Causes and Effects" (249); they conclude with the Emperor and Empress in a kind of paradisiacal cavalier society, passing time to the accompaniment of music, as if at the Cavendish estates at Welbeck or Bolsover.

In the Epilogue to the Reader, Cavendish comes full circle: having created a world to give herself full scope, she finds it so filled with images of herself that she may need to repeat the process and begin again: since the Empress of the Blazing World is "my dear Platonick Friend; I shall never prove so unjust, treacherous and unworthy to her, as to disturb her Government, much less to depose her from her Imperial Throne, for the sake of any other; but rather chuse to create another World for another Friend" (251). Unlike Alexander the Great, who is reputed to have wept that there were no more worlds for him to conquer, Margaret Cavendish seems prepared to go on infinitely, imagining new worlds for her own delight and prominence. Having admitted her great ambition, she constructs a dialogue to answer the Empress's question: "why she did take such delight . . . in being singular both in Accoustrements, Behaviour and Discourse? The Duchess's Soul answered, she confessed that it was extravagant, and beyond what was usual and ordinary; but yet her ambition being such, that she would not be like others in any thing if it were possible; I endeavour, said she, to be as singular as I can; for it argues but a mean Nature to imitate others" (245).

Until recently readers and critics were slow to acknowledge the scope of Margaret Cavendish's achievement as an imaginative artist, accepting too easily the contemporary account of her as simply eccentric or worse, and regarding her as merely undisciplined and self-indulgent. In 1962, Douglas Bush referred to "the Duchess of Newcastle, voyaging through strange seas of Thought, alone," a comment reinforced by Paul Salzman in 1985: "the work has been derided by the few scholars who have read it."[31] That of course is no longer the case. But if Cavendish's wit (as Jonson said of Shakespeare) was not always under her own control, she was nevertheless a remarkable performer, in her life and in her writing.[32] Having begun in *A True Relation* with self-confessed (if not always evident) bashfulness and reticence, in *A Blazing World* she takes center stage as actor, director, and writer of the script. If *A True Relation* ends with an anxiety that if the author ceases speaking all memory of her will be lost, *The Blazing World* provides a structure in which the self – that is a Margaret Cavendish embellished and improved by art – can constantly be reinvented in new forms and locations.

Conclusion: "The Life of Me"

At the end it seems appropriate to return to some of the questions posed at the beginning, and to measure the distance we have traveled from the diary of Margaret Hoby to the *Blazing World* of Margaret Cavendish. I have focused on a sequence of representations of the self, from daily entries to more extended narratives, beginning in the life of the writer, in claims of factual representation, and moving toward more fully elaborated and persuasive accounts. Taken as a whole, these texts offer a view of the development of seventeenth-century women's writing and raise questions about our strategies for reading such texts.

In considering a variety of texts and their ways of recording and interpreting life experiences, I have tried to notice generic clues without imposing rigid expectations, but also to avoid taking generic differences for temperamental differences, aspects of function for matters of choice or expression (or failure of expression). Margaret Hoby's diary, for example, is plainly intended as an aid to her spiritual life rather than as mode of personal expression: a lack of emotion or personal detail in the text does not mean the absence of these things in life. Yet once we have made these adjustments, there is a good deal to be learned from such a sparse and limited text. There is, of course, information: through myriad details in the text the patient reader gets a fair idea of the scope and nature of Hoby's responsibilities and even of her recreations. But this text is more than a transparent conduit of fact. On repeated readings I was struck by syntax and rhythm that create an all-inclusive account of the writer's time, even though the activities it describes seem severely limited. And through this syntax – the patient repetition of "and," "when," "then," "then" – comes the sense that all time is to be accounted for, a sense of the completeness of the record. The form in this case may be generated by religious function – the Puritan diary of devotional observance – but form also generates meaning, as we feel Hoby's careful attention to the details of life, her stewardship of time. Moreover, constrained as Hoby may be by her choices – most notably the choice to lead a life shaped by prayer and devotion – her text also conveys a considerable sense of agency, not only in what she does, and in the significant responsibilities she bears on the estate she inherited, but also in the simple repetition of the pronoun "I." This is of course the consequence of her personal recording – but it also reminds us of the extent to which these are willed activities, carried on independently or with the assistance of others.

In looking at the diverse life records of Anne Clifford, more questions and answers emerge. Less formulaic than Hoby's, Clifford's early diaries are more likely to record events, conversations, even emotional reactions of the writer. But similar challenges in reading remain, since Clifford is as likely to withhold information or personal feeling as to express it. In some ways the 1616–19 diaries resemble the text of a drama rather than a narrative: the effect of reported events, sometimes owing to their cumulative weight, sometimes to their contrasting nature, is as powerful as particular statements about events. Once again we are confronted with a document not much like present-day forms of record-keeping, and once again we need to find appropriate ways of reading and responding, seeing all that is there, without distorting or over-reading the text.

In my discussion of Clifford I argued both for the restraint of her text and for its informative qualities. If we are attuned to its nuances, we will appreciate more fully the psychological state of the writer, buffeted or encouraged as she is by events. And just as we read Clifford's text, she herself is reading the events of her life, looking for meaning, pattern, and direction in them. As she reads, she rewrites, not at first in the sense of recopying the text but rather by adding marginal notes, sometimes about contemporary events, but often information she could not have had at the time, entries that establish connections that grow in significance. In these less personal summaries, Anne Clifford, like Margaret Hoby, tends to bring all her experience under the control of her narrative, creating a kind of completeness that, though lacking in one kind of individual expression, is nevertheless a potent image of the interests and concerns of the writer, making finally a just and complete circle of her life and that of her family.

The extended narratives of Halkett, Fanshawe, and Hutchinson present new challenges of interpretation. These texts represent the self in a more detailed, more coherent form, but like the diaries and records of Hoby and Clifford, they too raise questions about the degree to which a writer reveals herself, her reasons for doing so, and the extent to which this self-presentation is an instrument in some larger purpose. For Halkett, I have argued, justification of her own actions seems primary, as she offers an account of events, an explanation of motives, a clarification partly to herself but also to an inquiring world. This strategy seems clear from the outset, where Halkett begins – "I need not be ashamed to owne them" – setting herself in the context of her family and their distinguished achievements and going on to explain actions of her own that might be open to question. The motifs of Ann Fanshawe's narrative focus on her growing to maturity – beginning with a "hoydenish" phase until, after the death of her saintly mother, she begins to assume adult responsibility. The theme is repeated in her marriage, when she comes to understand her function as the ambassador's wife – a role that implies limitations on what she is privy to but also demands considerable resourcefulness and courage. Lucy Hutchinson, whose relatively brief autobiography, when set against the longer life of her husband, might suggest subordination (as statements in the text do), nevertheless creates a narrative in which she plays a central role, first as the object of her husband's love, the helpmate to whom Providence leads him, and then as the defender of his integrity and faithfulness.

Although there is some independent information against which we might judge these narratives, I have considered not their "accuracy" but rather their strategies of self-presentation. It has seemed to me that both the writer and the reader look for shape, coherence, and meaning in the narrative: these are texts in which women try to make sense of their lives. And while these autobiographical texts, true to the vicissitudes of life, have not been pruned and shaped as a fictional narrative might be, they certainly show signs of theme, motif, and explanation. They are often tendentious, and it might be useful to consider them both as argument and as autobiography. They also make use of fictional forms in their vivid representation of action, particularly the forms of romance, but also those of prophecy, fulfillment, and the sense of providential guidance.

In short, what makes these texts challenging and interesting is the mixture of tendencies they display: an accumulation of detail, a degree of untidiness and lack of clarity about the direction or significance of events, coupled with strong attempts by the writer to understand and to shape her experience. J. Paul Hunter has suggested that the habits of mind and expectations of autobiographers paved the way for early novels: "For someone like Defoe," he argues, "the awareness of recorded experience, habits of self-examination, and repeated readings of life experiences in quest of meaningful patterns clearly affected the way he organized things when he came to write lives, factual and fictional."[1] Further, "The two main stages of self-examination – the immediate recording of the self and the retrospective task of discovering patterns of meaning – are in fact both instructive to the novelistic process of making meaning from the interstices of events and attempts to understand them" (Hunter, 323). While not arguing that diaries and autobiographies give rise to novels, Hunter does assert that the habits of mind developed in the one prepare the way for the other. But it is also true that these early narratives, though based in fact, betray the motifs of fiction, so that it is not only a matter of greater interest in the private life, as Hunter argues, that is at issue in these texts, but also writerly attempts to understand that life, attempts that include fictional as well as religious models. These texts are marked by qualities of argument and persuasion: the writer's attempt to understand herself is joined with her attempt to present herself or her family as she wishes them to be understood.

To return to an issue I cited earlier: although the writers I've considered presented their lives and actions, and subjected them to interpretation, except for Cavendish's *True Relation* and *The Blazing World*, these texts were neither published nor intended for publication. Yet the autobiographies of Halkett and Fanshawe and the biography of John Hutchinson are clearly intended for other readers: Fanshawe addresses her narrative to her son, so that he will know – and perhaps emulate – the father who died when he was an infant; Lucy Hutchinson addresses her children, as she celebrates the life of her husband and defends his reputation against misinterpretation; Halkett's opening is devotional, rather than specifically addressed to an individual, yet she presents her case as if to a judging audience. Hence, even though these autobiographical texts were not published until many years later, they are all written *as if* for publication; they have all the forms of justification, of argument, of presentation that are appropriate for a somewhat wider circle of readers. The strands of writing from life, writing from memory, and writing for posterity are variously and intriguingly mingled in them.

Margaret Cavendish, who in contrast to the other writers considered, rushed into print with poems, plays, sociable letters, and *The Blazing World*, may then be seen as the natural development of the sequence I've outlined. Although in *A True Relation* she claims to write not for her readers but for herself, yet that self-regarding or self-pleasing act depends on a connection with the reading public, for it is precisely their awareness of her existence that she seeks. Publish or perish seems to be Cavendish's watchword: if she does not appear in print, we may forget her existence; she may even cease to exist.

Cavendish represents an extension of the pattern in another sense as well. Like texts that use the devices of art to comprehend chaotic fact and represent the truth of the self, Cavendish's *Blazing World* mingles fact and fiction, but with a reversal of emphasis, as she creates a "new world" with links to the old, and new characters – such as the Empress – with strong links to her creator the Duchess of Newcastle. In short, whereas Hutchinson, Halkett, and Fanshawe may depict scenes from life that seem to owe something to their familiarity with romance or drama, Cavendish creates a fiction with strong links to her life; she seems bound to reproduce her own interests, attitudes, ideas, and preoccupations in her fictions. In contrast to Margaret Hoby, who gives less of herself than the curious reader would like, Margaret Cavendish seems to give nothing but herself in all that she writes.

The very sequence in which I've considered these texts implies an argument about them, for it constructs a pattern from intensely private and personal spheres to more public and published ones – from Hoby who writes as a form of spiritual discipline; to Clifford, who writes to establish her claims to inheritance, individuality, and property; to Halkett, Hutchinson, and Fanshawe, who write of individuals in relation to their families, establishing a record fit for further dissemination; to Cavendish, who begins deep within the confines of her own family and moves to the stage of history and fantasy, romance and empire.[2] So we proceed from a group of texts that are secondary, an instrument in some other project, to texts that more fully and explicitly express the writer's concerns and personality. I might have gone on – but this is perhaps the subject of another study – to consider the intriguing case of Mary Carleton, who not only portrayed herself within a fiction but also appears to have invented herself out of whole cloth.

To look at these women and their texts in this sequence is to construct a narrative, a movement from severely factual, restrained self-examination to flamboyant self-presentation. Is this the way it was? Certainly. Is this the only pattern to be found? Probably not. One might note, for example, that the romantic Anne Halkett devoted her old age to the writing of religious tracts, and that Anne Clifford founded almshouses in later years (in addition to restoring castles and placing her name prominently on the façade). And despite what has been suggested about a growing interest in representations of the self, sympathy for women's writing was by no means universal: Margaret Cavendish, pathfinder that she was, was famously belittled by Dorothy Osborne, who remarked that "there are many soberer people in Bedlam."[3]

But although one might complicate the picture I've sketched, the texts I've studied show women writers demonstrating an increasing confidence in self-presentation, an increasing willingness to look within themselves and to construct a view of the self that is not simply literal but often tendentious, persuasive, and imaginative. These texts demonstrate the possibility, even the probability, that a woman would write of herself in ways that are increasingly bold, narrative in structure, even fanciful, and that some women would choose to publish this material. These texts begin as attempts to record and to understand; they become increasingly attempts to dramatize and to persuade. The title of this section, "The Life of Me," comes from Anne Clifford, who set out to write her family's history and ended writing the life of herself. But it also relates to Lucy Hutchinson, who represents her husband as Pygmalion, but who also places herself in the center, and to Margaret Cavendish, who set out to write "A True Relation" and ended in a new and blazing world, writing herself large, and repeatedly, into her work.

Notes

INTRODUCTION: MAPPING THE TERRITORY

1 Most especially of course the selection edited by Elspeth Graham, Hilary Hinds, Elaine Hobby, and Helen Wilcox, entitled *Her Own Life: Autobiographical Writings by Seventeenth-Century Englishwomen* (London: Routledge, 1989; rpt. 1992). Margaret Cavendish herself has also elicited unusual interest, being taken by some as the type of seventeenth-century women autobiographers. See, for example, the discussion by Leigh Gilmore in *Autobiographics: A Feminist Theory of Women's Self-Representation* (Ithaca: Cornell University Press, 1994), 44–49.

2 Virginia Woolf, *A Room of One's Own* (1929; New York: Harcourt, Brace and World, 1957), 51. For a recent statement contrary to Woolf, see Ursula Appelt's Introduction to *Write or Be Written: Early Modern Women Poets and Cultural Constraints*, ed. Barbara Smith and Ursula Appelt (Aldershot: Ashgate, 2001), which affirms that "there were many women who could read and even write" (xii).

3 James Olney, "Autobiography and the Cultural Moment: a Thematic, Historical, and Bibliographical Introduction," *Autobiography: Essays Theoretical and Critical*, ed. James Olney (Princeton University Press, 1980), 19.

4 See for example David Cressy, *Literacy and the Social Order: Reading and Writing in Tudor and Stuart England* (Cambridge University Press, 1981); Margaret W. Ferguson, *Dido's Daughters: Literacy, Gender, and Empire in Early Modern England and France* (University of Chicago Press, 2003).

5 J. Paul Hunter, *Before Novels: The Cultural Contexts of Eighteenth-Century English Fiction* (New York: W. W. Norton, 1990), 303.

6 See Margo Culley, "What a Piece of Work is 'Woman'? An Introduction," in *American Women's Autobiography: Fea(s)ts of Memory*, ed. Margo Culley (Madison: University of Wisconsin Press, 1992), 3.

7 Cf. Domna C. Stanton, "Autogynography: Is the Subject Different?" in *The Female Autograph*, ed. Domna C. Stanton (University of Chicago Press, 1987; originally New York Literary Forum, 1984), 10.

8 Georges Gusdorf, "Conditions and Limits of Autobiography," in Olney, ed., *Autobiography*, 30.

9 See Cynthia Pomerleau, "The Emergence of Women's Autobiography in England," in *Women's Autobiography: Essays in Criticism*, ed. Estelle Jelinek (Bloomington: Indiana University Press, 1980), 21; and Wayne Shumaker, *English Autobiography: Its Emergence, Materials, and Form* (Berkeley: University of California Press, 1954), 5: "Before 1600, autobiographies of the modern type are nearly impossible to find; after 1600, they follow one another at decreasing intervals, until at last, about 1800, their authors seem to be writing in a tradition instead of feeling their way into a new literary genre."

10 Paul Delany, *British Autobiography in the Seventeenth Century* (London: Routledge & Kegan Paul, 1969), 108.

11 Olney, "Autobiography and the Cultural Moment: a Thematic, Historical, and Bibliographical Introduction," in Olney, ed., *Autobiography*, 3–27.

12 Sidonie Smith, "Autobiography Criticism and the Problematics of Gender," in *A Poetics of Women's Autobiography: Marginality and the Fictions of Self-Representation* (Bloomington: Indiana University Press, 1987), 3–19; for Stanton, Jelinek, and Pomerleau, see notes 7 and 9. On the question of definitions, as well as the categorization by gender, see also Gabriele Rippl, *Lebenstexte: Literarische Selbststilisierung englischer Frauen in der frühen Neuzeit* (Munich: Wilhelm Fink Verlag, 1998), 13 ff.

13 Olney, ed., *Autobiography*. The single, illuminating essay is that by Mary G. Mason, "The Other Voice: Autobiographies of Women Writers," 207–35. Olney's earlier study, *Metaphors of Self: The Meaning of Autobiography* (Princeton University Press, 1972), includes no treatment of women authors. In this it resembles most earlier studies of autobiography, as noted by Estelle Jelinek, "Women's Autobiography and the Male Tradition," in Jelinek, ed., *Women's Autobiography*, 1–6. Similarly, John Sturrock, *The Language of Autobiography: Studies in the First Person Singular* (Cambridge University Press, 1993), defines that language without reference to women with the exception of St. Teresa of Avila. These accounts have been supplemented by others that redress the balance, including Mary Beth Rose, ed., *Women in the Middle Ages and the Renaissance: Literary and Historical Perspectives* (Syracuse University Press, 1986), now updated as Rose, *Gender and Heroism in Early Modern English Literature* (University of Chicago Press, 2002); Smith, *A Poetics of Women's Autobiography*; Sara Heller Mendelson, *The Mental World of Stuart Women* (Amherst: University of Massachusetts Press, 1987).

14 Susanna Egan, *Patterns of Experience in Autobiography* (Chapel Hill: University of North Carolina Press, 1984), x.

15 Stanton, "Autogynography: Is the Subject Different?", 4–5. Stanton also lists, p. 4, the many studies of autobiography that fail to consider texts written by women. A pleasant exception is Donald A. Stauffer's early study, *English Biography Before 1700* (Cambridge, MA: Harvard University Press, 1930), which includes a brief account of Halkett, Fanshawe, and Cavendish in a chapter on autobiography. Remarkably, Stauffer concludes that "as a class [autobiographies by women] . . . are far more interesting and important than

the autobiographies by men – more personal, informal, and lifelike," though his reasons for preferring them are the very reasons why other critics denigrate them: "Where the men tend to digress on questions of history, or grow prolix in controversial accounts, the women remain self-centered and confidential, engrossed in the more enthralling problems of their own lives" (209).

16 Smith, *A Poetics of Women's Autobiography*, 8–9, takes issue with another noted critic of autobiography, Georg Misch, who in his influential *History of Autobiography in Antiquity* (1907) emphasizes "the 'representative' nature of autobiography." Cf. Jelinek, *Women's Autobiography*, 7: "The consensus among critics is that a good autobiography . . . reveals [its author's] connectedness to the rest of society; it is representative of his times, a mirror of his era. . . . On the other hand, women's autobiographies rarely mirror the establishment history of their times."

17 Mason, "The Other Voice," in *Autobiography*, ed. Olney, 210.

18 Jelinek, "Women's Autobiography and the Male Tradition," in *Women's Autobiography*, ed. Jelinek, 17. This view is disputed by Rippl, *Lebenstexte*, 32–33, who finds women using a variety of literary patterns or modes, depending on the particular emphasis of the autobiography.

19 The point is well made by Leigh Gilmore, *Autobiographics*, 11: "The male autobiographies that many feminist critics have claimed as models of unity and coherence, such as Augustine's and Rousseau's, evidence the discursive and ideological tensions of the models of personhood they invoke. My own research has not borne out the claim that all men or all women do any one thing in autobiography all the time."

20 As Margaret P. Hannay notes ("'O Daughter Heare': Reconstructing the Lives of Aristocratic Englishwomen," in *Attending to Women in Early Modern England*, ed. Betty S. Travitsky and Adele F. Seeff [Newark: University of Delaware Press, 1994], 37), although the "stricture of chastity allowed no exceptions for rank, . . . silence and obedience were relative."

21 Sara Heller Mendelson, "Stuart Women's Diaries and Occasional Memoirs," in *Women in English Society, 1500–1800*, ed. Mary Prior (London: Methuen, 1985), 181–82. Mendelson appends a very useful list of these texts with a description of their contents.

22 Elspeth Graham, "Women's Writing and the Self," in *Women and Literature in Britain, 1500–1700*, ed. Helen Wilcox (Cambridge University Press, 1996), 212. Graham points to the difficulty of finding an appropriate term: "Even to use the term 'autobiography,' if this is seen to presume a specific set of generic features, becomes misleading. 'Self-writing' perhaps more clearly represents the variety of strategies and forms that are used by writers seeking to articulate and assert themselves through that very writing of the self" (213).

23 See the discussion by Ann E. Imbrie, "Defining Nonfiction Genres," in *Renaissance Genres: Essays on Theory, History, and Interpretation*, ed. Barbara Kiefer Lewalski (Cambridge, MA: Harvard University Press, 1986), 45–69.

24 Delany, *British Autobiography*, 18.

25 Hutchinson does preface the biography of her husband with a message to their children, but the claims made for his probity and competence imply a wider audience.

26 My experience of reading is like that of Laurel Thatcher Ulrich, *A Midwife's Tale: The Life of Martha Ballard, Based on her Diary, 1785–1812* (New York: Alfred A. Knopf, 1990), who began to discover in Ballard's diary significant connections not explicitly articulated in the text.

27 Germaine Greer, "The Tulsa Center for the Study of Women's Literature: What We Are Doing and Why We Are Doing It," *Tulsa Studies in Women's Literature* 1 (1982): 14. See also Nicky Hallett, "Anne Clifford as Orlando: Virginia Woolf's Feminist Historiology and Women's Biography," in *Women's History Review* 4 (1995): 505–24, who finds in Anne Clifford a feminist model for Virginia Woolf.

28 Margaret Ezell, *Writing Women's Literary History* (Baltimore: Johns Hopkins University Press, 1993), 20.

29 Suzanne Hull, *Chaste, Silent, and Obedient* (San Marino, CA: Huntington Library, 1982), takes as her subject books written for (and sometimes by) women; and the volume edited by Margaret Hannay, *Silent but for the Word*, has as its subtitle *Tudor Women as Patrons, Translators, and Writers of Religious Works* (Kent, OH: Kent State University Press, 1985). While there are obvious differences among the writers surveyed in Hannay's edition – from the limitations imposed by Vives to the boldness of Anne Askew – the volume as a whole helps correct the misconception noted at the beginning: "The problem of the woman writer has traditionally been not the anxiety of influence but the anxiety of absence" (1). It notes how women writers engaged in the subversion of existing texts and of existing attitudes (4). There are of course other more optimistic titles, such as Charlotte F. Otten, ed., *English Women's Voices 1540–1700* (Miami: Florida International University Press, 1992); Elaine Hobby, *Virtue of Necessity: English Women's Writing 1649–1688* (London: Virago Press, 1988); Anita Pacheco, ed., *Early Women Writers 1600–1720* (London: Longman, 1998); *The Renaissance Englishwoman in Print: Counterbalancing the Canon*, ed. Anne M. Haselkorn and Betty S. Travitsky (Amherst: University of Massachusetts Press, 1990); Constance Jordan, *Renaissance Feminism: Literary Texts and Political Models* (Ithaca, NY: Cornell University Press, 1990); Ezell, *Writing Women's Literary History*; and Hilda L. Smith, *Reason's Disciples: Seventeenth-Century English Feminists* (Urbana: University of Illinois Press, 1982).

30 Margaret J. M. Ezell. *The Patriarch's Wife: Literary Evidence and the History of the Family* (Chapel Hill: University of North Carolina Press, 1987), 63. See also Ezell, *Writing Women's Literary History*.

31 Ezell, *The Patriarch's Wife*, 65.

32 Cf. also Megan Matchinske, *Writing, Gender and State in Early Modern England* (Cambridge University Press, 1998), 2, on the necessity of reading particular actions in their complicating and enriching historical context.

33 Stuart Sherman, *Telling Time: Clocks, Diaries, and English Diurnal Form, 1660–1785* (University of Chicago Press, 1996), 31, inserts a caveat about Pepys's diary that might be widely applied: "Scholars who value the diary one way tend to ignore it another: they work from it, not on it. . . . Many raid the diary as a data base; fewer read it as a document with its own timings and textures, which inevitably get lost during the raids."

34 Stanton, "Autogynography: Is the Subject Different?", 10.

35 Cf. Janet Varner Gunn, *Autobiography: Toward a Poetics of Experience* (Philadelphia: University of Pennsylvania Press, 1982), 8: "Reading takes place at two moments of . . . the autobiographical situation: by the autobiographer who, in effect, is 'reading' his or her life; and by the reader of the autobiographical text." Gunn goes on to speak of "the autobiographical response of the reader" (18), at which point I would part company with her. While granting the importance of the reader's response, this formulation carries with it the danger of reading oneself into the text.

36 Cf. Mendelson, "Stuart Women's Diaries," 201, who sees in the travel diary of Celia Fiennes, c. 1685–1703, an indication that "Women's journals were ready to shift their attention from the inward contemplation of the soul to a lively appreciation of the world at large."

37 Howarth, "Some Principles of Autobiography," in Olney, ed., *Autobiography*, 86. For further discussion of the measure of creativity or fictionality to be found in autobiographies and memoirs, see also the essays by Gusdorf, "Conditions and Limits of Autobiography," 28–48; and Barrett J. Mandel, "Full of Life Now," 49–72, in Olney, ed., *Autobiography*. According to Mandel, "An honest autobiography puts its illusion of the past forward in good faith, not suspecting that it is but one angle of perception" (66).

1 MARGARET HOBY: THE STEWARDSHIP OF TIME

1 Whereas we tend to think of diaries as confessional, Hoby's diary obviously serves a quite different purpose. On the development of the genres of diary and autobiography, Sara Heller Mendelson, "Stuart Women's Diaries and Occasional Memoirs," in *Women in English Society 1500–1800*, ed. Mary Prior (London: Methuen, 1985), 181–210, is particularly helpful. See also Kim Walker, "'Busie in my Clositt': Letters, Diaries, and Autobiographical Writing," in *Women Writers of the English Renaissance* (New York: Twayne, 1996), 26–46, and note 9 below.

2 I have relied on two excellent editions of Hoby's diary, both with copious notes that gloss elliptical or obscure references and that place events and people in context: the *Diary of Lady Margaret Hoby, 1599–1605*, ed. Dorothy M. Meads (London: George Routledge & Sons, 1930), cited hereafter as Meads; and *The Private Life of an Elizabethan Lady: The Diary of Lady Margaret Hoby 1599–1605*, ed. Joanna Moody (Stroud: Sutton, 1998), cited hereafter as Moody. On the difficulty of teasing out information from these taciturn accounts, see Margo Culley, ed., *American Women's Autobiography:*

Fea(s)ts of Memory (Madison: University of Wisconsin Press, 1992), and Laurel Thatcher Ulrich, *A Midwife's Tale: The Life of Martha Ballard Based on Her Diary, 1785–1812* (New York: Alfred A. Knopf, 1990). Ulrich writes, 34, "In each case, the 'important' material, the passage or event highlighted in the accompanying discussion, is submerged in the dense dailiness of the complete excerpt," so that only by a careful study of the text can one become aware of the connections felt by the writer.

3 Meads, 4–9; Moody, xvii–xix. According to Diane Willen, "Godly Women in Early Modern England: Puritanism and Gender," *Journal of Ecclesiastical History* 43 (1992): 562, the distinctive qualities of Puritans in early Stuart England were "to be found in their religious fervour and their 'doctrine of daily practice'; in their personal encounters with God through Scriptures or through preaching as 'an instrument of reform.'" Willen argues that the practices of Puritanism – experiential religion, seeking assurance of salvation, and the practice of godly behavior – were especially appealing to women (563).

4 Thomas Sidney died July 26, 1595; Margaret married Sir Thomas Hoby, posthumous son of the translator of Castiglione's *The Courtier*, on August 9, 1596.

5 Meads, 9–12, 231; Moody, xix–xx.

6 British Library Egerton 2614, purchased in November 1883 from the Rev. C. St. B. Sydenham (Meads, ix). But Walker, "'Busie in my clositt,'" 39, finds in some of the oblique references of the diary a suggestion that a wider audience may have been imagined.

7 Mary Ellen Lamb, "Margaret Hoby's Diary: Women's Reading Practices and the Gendering of the Reformation Subject" in *Pilgrimage for Love: Essays in Early Modern Literature in Honor of Josephine A. Roberts*, ed. Sigrid King (Tempe, AZ: Arizona Center for Medieval and Renaissance Studies, 1999), 65, notes this lack of specificity and compares the diary to "a sort of household account book, with spiritual credits and debits for time well or badly spent."

8 The story of Herbert's deathbed dispatching of his poetry is told by Izaak Walton, "The Life of Mr. George Herbert," in *The Lives of John Donne, Sir Henry Wotton, Richard Hooker, George Herbert & Robert Sanderson*, ed. G. Saintsbury (London: Oxford University Press, 1927), 314.

9 On the function of such spiritual diaries, see Owen Watkins, *The Puritan Experience: Studies in Spiritual Autobiography* (New York: Schocken Books, 1972), 9–24; Willen, "Godly Women," 561–80; Mendelson, "Stuart Women's Diaries"; Lamb, "Margaret Hoby's Diary," 63–94; Effie Botonaki, "Seventeenth-century Englishwomen's Spiritual Diaries: Self-Examination, Covenanting, and Account Keeping," *The Sixteenth-Century Journal* 30 (1999): 3–21; Elspeth Graham, "Women's Writing and the Self," in *Women and Literature in Britain, 1500–1700*, ed. Helen Wilcox (Cambridge University Press, 1996), 209–33. Lamb describes Hoby's diary as "Addressing the question, 'Am I saved?'" and "primarily an exercise in the Puritan

discipline of self-examination, a pre-condition for 'assurance' or certain knowledge of election" (63–64). I see the diary rather as concerned with the more complicated question of stewardship, "How did I spend my time?" The "certain knowledge of election" was notoriously difficult to achieve.

10 Mendelson, "Stuart Women's Diaries," 186. Although Mendelson's source, John Featley's *A Fountain of Tears* (1646), was published nearly fifty years after Hoby's diary was written, there are other contemporary examples to indicate the widespread use of self-examination and self-monitoring. See also J. Paul Hunter, *Before Novels: The Cultural Contexts of Eighteenth-Century English Fiction* (New York, 1990), who cites John Norris's *Spiritual Counsel: or The Father's Advice to His Children* (1694), a recommendation for a "*Nightly Review*" (305).

11 *The Diary of Lady Margaret Hoby 1599–1605*, ed. Moody, 4. Unless otherwise indicated, all further quotations from Margaret Hoby's diary are from this edition. As Moody notes, p. 4, n. 7, "wrought" means "sewed or embroidered." Master Richard Rhodes is her chaplain.

12 Moody, p. 3, n. 3, glosses the word *lecture* or *lector*: "the formal reading aloud of a given passage, probably from the Scriptures or a sermon. Any literate member of the household may have given the lecture at public prayers."

13 In this respect it differs from the diaries discussed by Watkins, *The Puritan Experience*, 18–24, which are confessional as well as self-examining. As noted by Botonaki, "Seventeenth-century Englishwomen's Spiritual Diaries," 3–5, in the absence of a confessor, "self-surveillance" became particularly important for Protestants.

14 Willen, "Godly Women," 562, notes that "Most of the Puritan laity of early Stuart England, including . . . [Hoby], conformed to the Prayer Book."

15 Here I take a very different view from Lamb, who finds in the inclusion of events outside Hoby's life of prayer a sign that "She seems to have lost interest in her spiritual condition"; "Margaret Hoby's Diary," 71. Although it is indisputable that the diary entries become less frequent and that secular events are mentioned more frequently, there is no actual evidence that Hoby "increasingly neglects her pious exercises" and certainly none that she had ceased to care for her spiritual welfare, which would be nearly inconceivable for a woman of Hoby's time and religious convictions.

16 Moody, xxxi. Walker, "'Busie in my Clositt,'" 38–39, connects the change in the diary with Hoby's journeys to London: "The diary of one of God's chosen has been supplanted by the diary of a busy gentlewoman whose role is to support the public activities of her husband with her own domestic industry."

17 Graham, "Women's Writing and the Self," 226.

18 See, for example, Ralph Houlbrooke, ed., *English Family Life, 1576–1716: An Anthology from Diaries* (Oxford: Basil Blackwell, 1988); Anthony Fletcher, *Gender, Sex and Subordination in England 1500–1800* (New Haven: Yale University Press, 1995); *With Faith and Physic: The Life of a Tudor Gentlewoman: Lady Grace Mildmay 1552–1620*, ed. Linda Pollock (New York: St. Martin's Press, 1995). Willen, "Godly Women," 580, argues that the

practices of meditation and prayer that we see in Hoby "tempered patriarchy," allowing "godly women to transcend significant restrictions traditionally imposed on gender."

19 Here I concur with Marcia Pointon, *Strategies for Showing: Women, Possession, and Representation in English Visual Culture: 1665–1800* (Oxford University Press, 1997), 3, who says about the diary of Hester Lynch (later Thrale Piozzi): "What interests me about these entries is . . . their very ordinariness." She asserts that "the instrumental nature of representation as systematic and ideological, as well as affective, must be examined if we are to make sense of that social system" (2).

20 Mendelson, "Stuart Women's Diaries," has one answer: "early rising was reckoned as one of the spiritual graces," a fact that "helps explain how Stuart women managed to get through such a heavy load of secular responsibilities" (189). Walker, "'Busie in my Clositt,'" 40, also suggests that writing itself was "a proper activity for avoiding idleness."

21 Mendelson, "Stuart Women's Diaries," 182–91, very sensibly comments on the effect of the genre itself on what was recorded and what preserved, and cautions against taking surviving texts as altogether representative of what was written at the time or experienced by the author. See also Walker, "'Busie in my Clositt,'" 26–46, on the determinative effects of culture.

22 On the connection between an awareness of time and the development of the diary form in Hoby and others, see Stuart Sherman, *Telling Time: Clocks, Diaries, and English Diurnal Form, 1660–1785* (University of Chicago Press, 1996), 1–108. Sherman argues, 21–22, that "time-discipline" may be empowering.

23 Margaret P. Hannay emphasizes the sense of accomplishment and control for Hoby herself: "Hoby records her daily tasks in an effort to give shape to a life that was essentially fluid and repetitive; writing a list of tasks completed gives a sense of accomplishment, even if those same tasks must be repeated on the morrow"; "'O Daughter Heare': Reconstructing the Lives of Aristocratic Englishwomen," in *Attending to Women in Early Modern England*, ed. Betty S. Travitsky and Adele F. Seeff (Newark: University of Delaware Press, 1994), 46.

24 This attitude toward the prudent and disciplined use of time may also be seen in Lady Grace Mildmay's account of her own upbringing by her governess, Mistress Hamblyn: "when she did see me *idly disposed* [emphasis mine], she would set me to cipher with my pen and to cast up and prove great sums and accounts, and sometimes set me to write a supposed letter to this or that body concerning such and such things, and other times set me to read in Dr Turner's herbal and in Bartholomew Vigoe [a work of surgery], and other times set me to sing psalms and sometimes set me to some curious work" (Pollock, ed., *With Faith and Physic*, 26 (f. 11)).

25 As for example August 19, 1599, cited in the text below.

26 As Elspeth Graham argues in "Women's Writing and the Self," 226, "Juxtaposition of references to [Hoby's] religious duties with the details

of secular aspects of her life implies an integration of the spiritual into a daily routine. . . . Such a life should be directed by the spiritual, but there is no absolute division between spiritual and social aspects of virtuous femininity."

27 Margaret Hoby's attitude toward the work of this world, which constitutes a religious duty, may be compared with what Frances Dolan observes in the lives of Catholic women who were not martyrs but who endured; Dolan, "Reading, Work, and Catholic Women's Biographies," *English Literary Renaissance* 31 (2003): 343–72; Willen, "Godly Women," 568, notes a similarity between "the piety of godly women" and the "styles of devotion practiced by nuns."

28 See Sherman's perceptive account of the nature of the moment – or the minute – in Pepys, Donne, and Hoby; *Telling Time*, 29–54.

29 A trust was created with £3,000 from Margaret's father, £3,000 from the Earl of Essex for his brother Thomas, and £500 from the Earl of Huntingdon; Moody, xxi.

30 Linda Pollock, *With Faith and Physic*, describes in her account of Lady Grace Mildmay the essential role played by gentlewomen as medical practitioners, the extent of their knowledge in comparison with other would-be healers of the sick, and the high cost of medical care (92–100; 107–9). Anne Halkett also had considerable medical expertise.

31 Both Willen and Lamb point out ways in which the practice of piety counteracts patriarchy; as Willen puts it, "godliness tempered patriarchy: the need to follow Puritan strategies in their daily life allowed godly women to transcend significant restrictions traditionally imposed on gender. Far from isolating women within the confines of household religion, godliness integrated public and private spheres, allowed reciprocal relationships between laity and clergy and between men and women, and provided moral authority and increased status to elect ladies"; "Godly Women," 580.

32 Moody, 83, n. 159, suggests the reading of "a popeshe booke" on May 19, 1600 as a reflection of "the Hobys' need to keep themselves well-informed and even with 'the enemy.'"

33 In 1605 Richard Rhodes became parish priest (Moody, xxxvii); he had by then married a second time. The latter entries of the diary note that in his absence Mr. Ward presided at services (May 5, 1605). Lamb, "Margaret Hoby's Diary," 85, emphasizes the centrality of Rhodes to Hoby's devotional life, asserting that after his departure from her household, "Hoby's diary began its drift in purpose, recording social engagements and even gossip, rather than religious exercises."

34 Patrick Collinson, *The Birthpangs of Protestant England: Religious and Cultural Changes in the Sixteenth and Seventeenth Centuries* (New York: St. Martin's Press, 1988), 75.

35 Lamb, "Margaret Hoby's Diary," 85. See also Collinson, *Birthpangs*, 75: ". . . the frustrations arising from the subordination of women, exacerbated by the psychological as well as physical consequences of frequent and traumatic

child-bearing, led to sublimated outlets in the enthusiastic adoption and support of religious causes."

36 Megan Matchinske asserts that in the Tudor and Stuart periods, "Women begin to replace priests as regulators of conscience and bearers of secular and spiritual authority" (*Writing, Gender and State in Early Modern England* [Cambridge University Press, 1998], 4); and Diane Willen argues that "religious observance and religious education increasingly took place within the confines of the family, which was responsible for its own spiritual care," with important consequences for the influence of women ("Women and Religion in Early Modern England," in *Women in Reformation and Counter-Reformation Europe*, ed. Sherrin Marshall [Bloomington: Indiana University Press, 1989], 148). See also Lamb, "The Sociality of Margaret Hoby's Reading Practices and the Representation of Reformation Interiority," *Critical Survey* 12 (2000): 18–22, on the importance of Margaret Hoby in the religious life of her household. Moody, 8, n. 16, notes: "Children and servants were catechized about the preacher's utterances and note-taking was usual." According to the Bishop of Carlisle, Anne Clifford similarly cared for the spiritual welfare of her household, making sure that the Eucharist was provided to the household more than the three times a year required by the Church and offering books of devotion to her servants (*A Sermon Preached at the funeral of the Right Honorable Anne, Countess of Pembroke, Dorset, and Montgomery . . . by the Right Reverend . . . Edward Lord Bishop of Carlisle* [London: R. Royston, 1677], 33).

37 According to Moody, 119, n. 207, this was the Puritan divine Stephen Egerton, minister of St. Anne's Blackfriars (1598–1621). Hoby attended church at Blackfriars October 19 and 26, 1600, and November 16 and 17. On November 23, she went to Westminster, and then "kept in all that day, it being so stormy I Could not goe by water to the friers"; she returned on November 30, and not only heard the sermon but on arriving home "sett downe in my testement the cheffe notes deliuered by Mr Egerton"; she was again at Blackfriars to hear Egerton on December 7, 14, and 21; thereafter she was ill, but returned to hear Mr. Egerton on January 4; after another illness, she attended service on January 18; on January 25 and again on February 22, she had to make do with a summary: "Mr fuller Came in, and he repeated to vs the substance of Mr Egerton Sarmon."

38 Willen, "Godly Women," 577, notes a similar freedom of judgment in Lady Brilliana Harley, who strongly expressed her negative views on particular sermons and theological positions.

39 The precise nature of Hoby's concern is unclear. As a staunch Protestant she may have objected to infant baptism (as for example the Anabaptists did), or she may have thought the practice associated with Roman Catholicism. Early reformers, finding no basis for the practice in scripture, questioned the biblical validity of infant baptism; see "Anabaptists," *Encyclopaedia Britannica* (2005). As one reformer wrote in 1524, "infant baptism is a senseless, blasphemous abomination, contrary to all Scripture"; "Letters to

Thomas Müntzer by Conrad Grebel and Friends, Zurich, September 5, 1524," in *Spiritual and Anabaptist Writers*, ed. George H. Williams and Angel M. Mergal (Philadelphia: Westminster Press, 1957), 81.

40 See the account in Moody, xxii–xxviii, and the discussion by Lamb, "Margaret Hoby's Diary," 83–88.

41 Moody, xxvii–xxviii.

42 Ibid., xxix.

43 March 24–25, 1600.

44 It's not at all clear whether this designation has any significance, and if so, whether it indicates greater closeness, or a degree of subjection. It comes directly after an incident to be discussed below, the visit of young Mr. Eure.

45 As Moody notes, 11, n. 27, "Sir Thomas is regularly away, on matters of litigation, fulfilling his duties as Justice of the Peace in both the North and East Ridings of Yorkshire, and on various commissions . . . His absences increase over the period of the diary as he takes on a more significant role in the region."

46 Interestingly enough, Willen, "Godly Women," 571, concludes that the Hoby marriage was "less than satisfactory," whereas Mendelson, in a rough schematization of the twenty-three diaries she surveys, lists the Hoby marriage as among the "loving and companionable marriages" (193); and Fletcher, *Gender, Sex and Subordination*, 157, sees the Hobys "living contentedly together and enjoying each other's company." Pollock, *With Faith and Physic*, 6, provides historical perspective as she notes a similar lack of emotional warmth in the life writings of Grace, Lady Mildmay: "She does not record much contact between herself, her parents and her sisters after her marriage nor does she document much intimate rapport between herself and her husband. Her only child receives practically no mention in any of her papers. Yet to characterize this family life-style as indifferent to the welfare of individuals or as lacking in emotional support would not represent the whole truth, as an examination of her memoirs will reveal."

47 See the account in Moody's introduction, xlvi–l and in Meads, 269–72.

48 Margaret Hoby writes to Lady Eure on September 5, 1599, and July 14, 1600, and visits her on May 30, 1600.

49 See Meads, 194, n. 346; and 6, n. 12.

50 I am grateful to Yun Jin Lee for this suggestion.

51 The reference is August 18, 1599, but could come from multiple entries of the diary.

2   THE CONSTRUCTION OF A LIFE: THE DIARIES OF ANNE CLIFFORD

1 Pembroke was the younger son of Mary Sidney Herbert, sister of Sir Philip Sidney, but seems to have inherited little of his mother's love of literature. Clarendon reports that "he pretended to no other qualifications than to understand dogs and horses very well"; cited in George C. Williamson, *Lady*

Anne Clifford, Countess of Dorset, Pembroke & Montgomery 1590–1676 (Kendal: Titus Wilson & Son, 1922), 167. For an account of Clifford's life, see also Richard T. Spence, *Lady Anne Clifford, Countess of Pembroke, Dorset and Montgomery (1590–1676)* (Stroud: Sutton, 1997).

2 Anne recalls of her marriages, "The marble pillars of Knolle in Kentt and Wilton in Wiltshire, were to me oftentimes but the gay Harbours of Anguish"; cited by Williamson, *Lady Anne Clifford*, 173. On possible reasons for her separation from Pembroke, see Spence, *Lady Anne Clifford*, 99–103.

3 On the account book, see Williamson, *Lady Anne Clifford*, 58–60; on the later years, see Katherine Acheson, ed., *The Diary of Anne Clifford 1616–1619: A Critical Edition* (New York: Garland, 1995), 14. The title, "The Life of Me," used by Barbara Kiefer Lewalski in her *Writing Women in Jacobean England* (Cambridge, MA: Harvard University Press, 1993), 126 and passim, is perhaps misleading in conveying the impression of a separate volume or document. "The Life of Me" is part of the heading in the extensive, three-volume family record compiled by Anne Clifford. Placed at the top of the page of the section devoted to herself, it reads in full: "A summary of the Records, and a true memorial of the life of mee, the Ladie Anne Clifford, who by Birth being sole Daughter and heire to my illustrious Father George Clifford, the third Earle of Cumberland. By his Vertuous wife Margaret Russell my mother in right descent from him, and his long continewed noble Ancestors the Veteriponts, Cliffords, and Vescies, was Baroness Clifford, Westmorland, and Vescie, High-Sheriffess of Westmorland & Ladie of the honor of Skipton in Craven, and was by my first marriage Co. Dowager of Dorsett, and by my second marriage Co. Dowager of Pembrooke and Montgomery" (The Great Books of Record, vol. III; Cumbria Record Office, WD/Hoth 10). The emphasis here is less on Anne Clifford as an individual than on her place in a distinguished family. There are three copies of these family histories, two in Cumbria and another, an eighteenth-century copy, in the British Library (Harley 6177).

4 They are, for example, linked in the convenient edition of *The Diaries of Lady Anne Clifford*, ed. D. J. H. Clifford (Stroud: Sutton, 1990, 1992). The diary of 1616–19, transcribed by Vita Sackville-West in 1923, is usually referred to as the Knole Diary. A subsequent critical edition of the 1616–19 diaries, prepared by Katherine Acheson, is based on a manuscript in the Portland Papers (XXIII f 80–119) that she believes was the copy text for the Knole MS (15). Acheson, *The Diary of Anne Clifford*, 16, also notes that "the Portland copy clearly demarcates the two documents," namely the narrative account of 1603 and the diary version of 1616–19, and argues that they should be considered separately.

5 Edward Rainbow, Bishop of Carlisle, in his funeral sermon for Anne Clifford: "I have been informed that after some reviews, these were laid aside; and some parts of these *Diaries* were summed into *Annals*"; *A Sermon Preached at the funeral of the Right Honorable Anne, Countess of Pembroke,*

Dorset, and Montgomery . . . by the Right Reverend . . . Edward Lord Bishop of Carlisle (London: R. Royston, 1677), 51.

6 Anne Russell Dudley, Countess of Warwick, was the widow of Ambrose Dudley, 21st Earl of Warwick. As Clifford notes in her last diary, she died Feb. 9, 1604.

7 *The Knole Diary, 1603,* ed. D. J. H. Clifford, p. 21. All references to the 1603 diary are to this edition, cited as D. J. H. Clifford. All references to the diary for 1616–19 are to *The Diary of Anne Clifford 1616–1619: A Critical Edition,* ed. Katherine Acheson, cited as Acheson.

8 Martin Holmes, *Proud Northern Lady: Lady Anne Clifford, 1590–1676* (London and Chichester: Phillimore, 1975), 27, assumes that Margaret Clifford's anger resulted from fear of the plague ("he probably showed signs of illness – indeed, he collapsed and died next day – so that there would be an instant fear of infection"), but it's not clear from the text that the "Mr. Mene" with whom Anne Clifford rode ahead is the same as the "Mr. Minerill" whose death is reported two sentences later. This is one example of the dangers of interpretation of a text so elliptical and yet so evocative.

9 Acheson's reading of the two portraits in the Great Picture (see p. 50 and n. 33 below) suggests connections with both parents: "The younger Lady Anne resembles her mother in the attitude of her head, her hairstyle, and the dress which she wears. The older Lady Anne resembles her father: her black hood looks like his hair, her sombre clothes echo his dark outfit, and her stance is almost identical. In the right hand portrait she wears her mother's pearls, but in a fashion resembling her father's sword belt, rather than draped at the neck as Margaret Clifford wears them" (33).

10 Such references as this raise interesting questions about the process of composition. Often Anne Clifford includes notes, in her later years almost obsessively so, that refer to events later than the time being recorded. Many of these are marginal notes; the present sentence, which tells where she received word of the Queen's death, might have been added at the end of a paragraph. The text for 1603 sounds very youthful; it may have been copied later and the points of connection added.

11 Spence, *Lady Anne Clifford,* 63.

12 Spence also states, *Lady Anne Clifford,* 63–64, that Anne Clifford's version "is at variance with the standard interpretation," arguing that Clifford suppressed positive episodes in this period so as not to ruin "the impression of a beleaguered lady." But Spence also admits, 65, that "Dorset's treatment of Anne see-sawed, from apparent fondness to hostility according to whether or not his ambitions coincided with hers."

13 Lewalski, "Rewriting Patriarchy and Patronage: Margaret Clifford, Anne Clifford, and Aemilia Lanyer," *Yearbook of English Studies* 21 (1991): 96.

14 Spence in general sees Anne Clifford as shaping the diary in a way that puts her in the best possible light and her husband in a much more negative one. Cf. Kim Walker, "'Busie in my Clositt': Letters, Diaries, and Autobiographical writing," *Women Writers of the English Renaissance* (New York: Twayne,

1996), 42: "Clifford's diary is not only the record of a material struggle: it is also the record of a struggle for meaning."

15 The diary, as Mary O'Connor suggests in "Representations of Intimacy in the Life-writing of Anne Clifford and Anne Dormer," in *Representations of Self from the Renaissance to Romanticism*, ed. Patrick Coleman, Jayne Lewis, and Jill Kowalik (Cambridge University Press, 2000), 79–96, is an intriguing combination of the public and the private constructed at a moment when the lines between them were difficult to track. O'Connor makes this point about particular domestic tableaux in the diary, but it is true in a far broader sense.

16 "The Love Song of J. Alfred Prufrock," line 27, in T. S. Eliot, *The Complete Poems and Plays, 1909–1950* (New York: Harcourt Brace, 1958). Anne Clifford, of course, is far from being a Prufrock.

17 According to D. J .H. Clifford, xii, "family legend would have it that these entries were deliberately suppressed by a later member of the family."

18 Mary Ellen Lamb, "The Agency of the Split Subject: Lady Anne Clifford and the Uses of Reading," *English Literary Renaissance* 22 (1992): 352, describes a "split in subjectivity " and "shift of voice" in Clifford: "In a single sentence Clifford registers both protest and acquiescence, representing herself as simultaneously angry and 'content.'"

19 Lamb, "The Agency of the Split Subject," 352, speaks of Clifford having "internalized her position as a divided subject"; I see a greater degree of self-consciousness and control in Clifford's self-representation.

20 The note on the death of her mother, cited above, is in the margin; the reference to her death chamber, cited here, is part of the body of the text. The entry in the text is juxtaposed to a marginal note on Dorset's showing Anne Clifford his will, which is more positive than she had expected.

21 Lamb, "The Agency of the Split Subject," 357, cites the influence of Margaret Clifford on her daughter's diary: "The significance of this chronicle of her life was determined in part by its participation in a larger chronicle begun by her mother in her ambitious compilation of family documents in defense of her daughter's rights." This suggests that not only the keeping of a family chronicle but also its use as an interpretive device stems from Margaret Clifford.

22 On this point Acheson writes, "In his anger at her refusal to sign the agreement, Sackville is trying to effect the threatened separation by ordering his servants back to his side. The 'paper' was drawn in an attempt to show to the public that Clifford was not sending his men back to him of her own accord, by which it might appear that she had left him and taken refuge with her mother and open her to charges of desertion. . . . On reflection she deems this insufficient, sends after her retinue, and follows them" (145).

23 On the complicated matter of the inheritance, see the accounts in Acheson, 2–6; in Lamb, "The Agency of the Split Subject," 350–53; and the extended account in Spence, *Lady Anne Clifford*, 19, 23–73.

24 "This business" is a phrase frequently used to refer to the struggle over Clifford's inheritance – the attempt to get her to agree to a monetary

settlement and to renounce any claims to the northern castles willed by her father to her uncle. Margaret, daughter of George Clifford's sister Frances and her husband William, 3rd Baron Wharton, was the second wife of Sir Edward Wotton (Acheson, 140, n. 411).

25 These are servants in her own or her mother's household.

26 Mr. Edward Legge, Steward, is listed in the "Catalogue of the Household and Family of the . . . Earl of Dorset"; D. J. H. Clifford, 274.

27 Two such notes relate her mother's death to her husband's knowledge and whereabouts: "my Lord was at London when my Mother died, but he went to Lewes before he heard the news of her death" (next to May 17); and next to May 29 "on the 30ᵗʰ at night or the 31ˢᵗ my Lord was told the news of my mothers death he being then at Lewes with all this Company."

28 Her entry for May 12, 1616, articulates the extreme contrast between her husband's freedom of movement and social pleasures and her own: "All this time my Lord was at London where he had infinite & great resorte coming to him. he went much abroad to Cocking, to bowling Alleys, to Plays & Horseraces, & [was] Commended by all the World. I stay'd in the Country having many times a sorrowfull & heavy heart, and being condemn'd by most folks because I would not consent to the agreements, so as I may truly say I am like an owl in the Desert." The reference is to Ps. 102.6, AV: "I am like a pelican of the wilderness: I am like an owl of the desert." Interestingly, Arbella Stuart also uses this image of desolation and solitude in a letter to Sir Henry Brounker written March 9, 1603 (Ash Wednesday); *Letters of Lady Arbella Stuart*, ed. Sara Jayne Steen (New York: Oxford University Press, 1994), 162.

29 Clifford also sends a series of letters, asking her husband to visit her: "Upon the 14ᵗʰ [Feb. 1617] I sent Mr Edwards man to London with a letter to my Lord, to desire him to come down hither"; he comes two days later and stays from dinner until early the next morning. On March 3, 1617, she sends with two servants "a letter to my Lord to beseech him that he wou'd take Knoll in his way as he goes to London" from his estate at Buckhurst, where he is hunting.

30 *Work, wrought*: as noted with regard to Margaret Hoby, the general terms refer to that distinctively female occupation of sewing and stitching.

31 Similarly, in May 1617: "Upon the 8ᵗʰ I spent the day in working the time being very tedious unto me as having neither Comfort nor Company only the Child."

32 Acheson, 58; O'Connor, "Representations of Intimacy," 82–85, suggests that this tableau may be "a moment of intimacy" or "a public tableau of aristocratic union" and further that the references to needlework become "a trope, a synecdoche, for her sadness and her troubles."

33 For helpful and detailed readings of the triptych, which hangs at Appleby Castle and at the Abbot Hall Art Gallery in Kendal, see Lamb, "The Agency of the Split Subject," 347–68; and Nigel Wheale, *Writing and Society: Literacy, Print and Politics in Britain 1590–1660* (London: Routledge, 1999),

116–31. Both emphasize the role of the books in the portrait as defining Clifford's intellectual and religious interests and her social and cultural position.

34 There is a similar limitation on Clifford's observance of Lent as a period of fasting. In February, 1619, she makes pancakes (to use up butter and eggs) in the days before Lent; but while she notes that she had begun keeping Lent very strictly, after about ten days, she abandons her fast, apparently in response to her husband's and her physician's concerns about her health (101). On April 19, 1617, she notes: "all this lent I eat flesh & observed no day but good friday."

35 Rainbow, *A Sermon*, 62, notes that Anne Clifford "usually heard a large portion of Scripture read every day." Cf. Wheale, *Writing and Society*, 127, who asserts that "The theological works in the Great Picture reveal a piety characteristic of Clifford's family allegiance, generation – and gender. . . . Anne Clifford was . . . neither Puritan nor Laudian but a devout adherent of the established Church with Calvinist sympathies."

36 Rainbow, *A Sermon*, 53. On matters of clothing in this period, see Ann Rosalind Jones and Peter Stallybrass, *Renaissance Clothing and the Materials of Memory* (Cambridge University Press, 2000).

37 Quoted by D. J. H Clifford, 60.

38 Holmes, *Proud Northern Lady*, 120–21 ff.

39 Acheson 179; Spence, *Lady Anne Clifford*, 60, 66–71.

40 Although I sense strong emotion, I certainly do not share the view of Spence, *Lady Anne Clifford*, 70, on this entry – that here "Anne writes with glee and perhaps a little malice."

41 Spence, *Lady Anne Clifford*, 73–74, though aware of Lady Anne's pregnancy, emphasizes her "stubbornness" and "the independent streak . . . which at times could almost be termed eccentric."

42 Born February 2, 1620, the child lived only a few months. Marking the anniversary toward the end of her life, Anne Clifford wrote: "I remembered how this day was 56 years [since] about 12 of the clock in the day time, I was delivered of my little Son Thomas, Lord Buckhurst, in my owne chamber in Knowl house in Kent, where I & my eldest daughter the Lady Margaret then lay. And the same day John Conniston rid on horsback from thence to my first Lord to Great Dorset House in London towne to carry him the newes of the birth of that Son of his, who dyed in that house the 26th of July following" (D. J. H. Clifford, 246).

43 In a marginal note in early March 1619, Clifford writes: "about this time I caused the Book of the Cliffords to be newly copy'd out" (101). Clearly her family's history is a source of great interest and pride to her.

44 As for example in February 1616: "All the tyme I stay'd in the Country I was sometimes merry & sometimes sad, as I heard news from London" (40).

45 Holmes, *Proud Northern Lady*, 120–21 and passim, suggests that this last section of the diary is less well organized ("spasmodic") and implies that the reasons are psychological: "Her diary-keeping is no longer systematic, the

entries are few, listless and irrelevant, and it seems that even her indomitable spirit had come near to breaking under the strain and the frustration." As indicated, I do not find this slackening of interest in the 1619 record.

46 D. J. H. Clifford, 105–6. References to the diary from 1650–76 are to this edition.

47 D. J. H. Clifford, 106. Although D. J. H. Clifford's edition reads "I enjoyed myself," which one might take as an explicit indication of Clifford's pleasure in her inheritance, the Roxburghe edition and the original manuscripts in the British Library and in Kendal read quite clearly, "I employed myself." While I have no doubt that Anne Clifford fully enjoyed, in the modern sense, the activities of possession and rebuilding, she in fact used the more usual locution for a woman of her time: "I employed myself." I am grateful to grants from Smith College and the National Endowment for the Humanities that enabled me to examine the manuscripts and determine this point. Elizabeth V. Chew, "Si(gh)ting the Mistress of the House: Anne Clifford and Architectural Space," in *Women as Sites of Culture: Women's Roles in Cultural Formation from the Renaissance to the Twentieth Century*, ed. Susan Shifrin (Aldershot: Ashgate, 2002), 167–81, emphasizes the importance to Clifford of these architectural monuments and cites this passage, quoting from the edition of D. J. H. Clifford.

48 Spence, *Lady Anne Clifford*, 204, suggests that Clifford "deliberately re-created . . . a late medieval baronial context in which to spend her remaining years," as well as that her journeys from one castle to the next were patterned on royal progresses, those of Elizabeth or Anne of Denmark. He notes, 225, that "it took forty-eight double carts at 2s6d each to carry her goods from Appleby to Brough in September 1675."

49 On October 5, 1675, she records that "about 10 or 11 a clock in the forenoone, after I had layen in my chamber in Appleby Castle ever since ye 11th of May last, did I remove with my family from thence, by ye waies of Crackenthorp, Kirkby Thure, Temple Sowerby and Woodsyde into my Castle of Brougham in the same Countie, where I had not bin since ye 30th day of July 1673 till now; and where I now continued to lye as usuall in the chamber wherein my Noble father was borne and my Blessed Mother dyed till the – [blank in manuscript]."

50 D. J. H. Clifford, 154 and passim.

51 For example, she records with a distinct sense of loss the departure in June 1654 of her grandson: "the eighth day of this month was my Grandchild, the little Lord Compton carried away from mee by his Nurse" (122).

52 June 30, 1617: "still working & being extreamly melancholy & sad to see things go so ill with me, & fearing my Lord wou'd give all his land away from the Child."

53 Mihoko Suzuki, "Anne Clifford and the Gendering of History," *Clio* 30 (2001): 195–229, emphasizes the importance of Anne Clifford's female forebears, especially Idonea de Viteripont (d. 1235) and Isabella de Viteripont (1254–91) in her account of the Clifford line.

54 Chew, "Si(gh)ting the Mistress of the House," 171–74, notes the greater detail of the later accounts, and argues that "through her processions, Clifford both demonstrated and documented her control of all of these spaces."

55 These letters were dictated to her secretary, Edward Hasell, as she notes on Feb. 3, 1676: "this morning I set my hand to 4 good letters of Hasell's writing for mee, one to my Daughter Thanet, one to my Lord Northampton [widower of her daughter Isabella], one to my Grandchilde the Lady Alethea Compton, and one to Mr William Edge [the Receiver of her rents in Sussex; 233]; all in answer of letters I received from them by the last post" (246).

56 March 11, 1676, less than two weeks before her death.

57 Presumably bone-lace, defined by the *OED* as "lace, usually of linen thread, made by knitting upon a pattern marked by pins, with bobbins originally made of bone; formerly called bone-work lace." Bishop Rainbow, *A Sermon*, 35, recalls that "Before she began to build a Tower, . . . she first sat down and counted the cost, as our Saviour intimates wise Builders will do; she kept exact accounts weekly in Books of her own Method, and the Totals were duly signed with her own hand."

58 We know that Margaret Clifford compiled records to assist in the lawsuit after her husband's death; Acheson, 14; Spence, *Lady Anne Clifford*, 166 ff.

59 This is the Aunt Russell who, as Anne Clifford's guide to the court of Elizabeth, was so influential a figure in the 1603 memoir, and who around Michaelmas in 1603 was reported to be "something ill and melancholy" (D. J. H. Clifford, 27).

60 As noted in a history of Kenilworth in *The Penny Magazine*, July 31, 1835, "In Queen Elizabeth's time it was always called Killingworth."

61 Rainbow, *A Sermon*, 60–62, recounts the household devotional practices.

62 According to Rainbow, "She was absolute Mistriss of her Self, . . . and yet allowed a time for every purpose, for all Addresses, for any Person; none had access but by leave, when she called, but none were rejected; none must stay longer than she would; yet none departed unsatisfied. Like him at the Stern, she seem'd to do little or nothing, but indeed turn'd and steer'd the whole course of her affairs" (*A Sermon*, 53).

63 On July 27, 1617; John Donne, "A Valediction Forbidding Mourning," 35–36.

3 PYGMALION'S IMAGE: THE LIVES OF LUCY HUTCHINSON

1 Except for Cavendish's *True Relation,* which she took care to have published, all of the narratives I consider were written for a private audience.

2 The *Life of Colonel Hutchinson,* in the transcription by Julius Hutchinson, was first published in 1806, along with the fragmentary life of Lucy Hutchinson. *A True Relation of My Birth, Breeding, and Life* of Margaret

Cavendish, though originally published by her in a volume with *Nature's Pictures drawn by Fancies Pencil to the Life* (1656), was frequently published alongside *The Life of the thrice Noble . . . Prince, William Cavendishe, Duke, Marquess, and Earl of Newcastle*, which did not appear until a decade later. David Norbrook calls attention to a number of significant connections between Hutchinson and Cavendish in "Margaret Cavendish and Lucy Hutchinson: Identity, Ideology and Politics," *In-between: Essays and Studies in Literary Criticism* 9 (2000): 179–203. As Norbrook notes, 181, in the nineteenth century Sir Charles Firth published editions of both Hutchinson and Cavendish.

3 The "Life of Mrs. Lucy Hutchinson, Written by Herself: A Fragment," appears first in the editions of Keeble and Firth, though not in that of Sutherland.

4 The manuscript of the fragmentary autobiography is lost; all modern editions are based on Julius Hutchinson's 1806 transcription of the manuscript now in the Nottinghamshire County Archives. Just a few lines from the end of the present text Julius Hutchinson notes, "Many leaves were at this point torn from the ms"; N. H. Keeble, ed., *Memoirs of the Life of Colonel Hutchinson* (London: J. M. Dent, 1995), 345.

5 Norbrook, "Margaret Cavendish and Lucy Hutchinson," 197. N. H. Keeble, ed., *Memoirs*, 373, n. 324, and James Sutherland, in his edition of *Memoirs of the Life of Colonel Hutchinson* (London: Oxford University Press, 1973), xviii–xix, point to internal evidence for 1671 as the terminal date of composition; Sutherland thinks a date closer to 1664 than to 1671 is likely. The date of Lucy Hutchinson's death is not known, but she was still living in 1675 (Sutherland, ed., *Memoirs*, xix).

6 Lucy Hutchinson, "To My Children," in *Memoirs of the Life of Colonel Hutchinson*, ed. N. H. Keeble, 16–17. Unless otherwise noted, all further quotations from Hutchinson's life of herself or of her husband are from this edition, cited as Keeble. N. H. Keeble, "'The Colonel's Shadow': Lucy Hutchinson, Women's Writing and the Civil War," in *Literature and the English Civil War*, ed. Thomas Healy and Jonathan Sawday (Cambridge University Press, 1990), 229 and 236, emphasizes the public purpose of Lucy Hutchinson's memoir, which he sees as a Puritan answer to "the royalists' interpretation of providential design which the Restoration appeared to confirm."

7 Keeble, ed., *Memoirs*, 16.

8 Jelinek, "Introduction: Women's Autobiography and the Male Tradition," in Estelle Jelinek, ed., *Women's Autobiography: From Antiquity to the Present* (Boston: Twayne, 1986), 10, writes that "the stipulation that the autobiographical mode is an introspective and intimate one and that autobiographers write about their inner or emotional life" "is contrary to the evidence [and] constitutes an autobiographical fallacy of the first order."

9 "The Life of Mrs. Lucy Hutchinson, Written by Herself: A Fragment," as transcribed by Julius Hutchinson; Keeble, ed., *Memoirs*, 3.

10 See for example Hooker, *The Laws of Ecclesiastical Polity* 1. iii, on "The lawe which naturall agents have given them to observe": "Now if nature should intermit her course, and leave altogether, though it were but for a while, the observation of her own laws: if those principall and mother elements of the world, whereof all things in this lower world are made, should loose the qualities which now they have, if the frame of that heavenly arch erected over our heads should loosen and dissolve itself: if celestiall spheres should forget their wonted motions and by irregular volubility, turne themselves any way as it might happen: if the prince of the lightes of heaven which now as a Giant doth runne his unwearied course, should as it were through a languishing faintnes begin to stand and to rest himselfe: if the Moone should wander from her beaten way, the times and seasons of the yeare blend themselves by disordered and confused mixture, the winds breath out their last gaspe, the cloudes yeeld no rayne, the earth be defeated of heavenly influence, the fruites of the earth pine away as children at the withered breasts of their mother no longer able to yeeld them reliefe, what would become of man himselfe, whom these things now do all serve? See we not plainly that obedience of creatures unto the lawe of nature is the stay of the whole world?" (*Of the Laws of Ecclesiastical Polity . . . Books I to IV* (1593), ed. Georges Edelen. Folger Library Edition of the Works of Richard Hooker [Cambridge, MA: Belknap Press of Harvard University Press, 1977]; 1: 65–66). Joan Webber, *The Eloquent 'I' – Style and Self in Seventeenth-Century Prose* (Madison: University of Wisconsin Press, 1968), 8, emphasizes the Puritan autobiographer's tendency to begin with the literal facts, and to see his role as "to a large extent defined for him by his conception of history."

11 The language here recalls Matthew 10:29–31: "Are not two sparrows sold for a farthing? and one of them shall not fall on the ground without your Father. But the very hairs of your head are all numbered. Fear ye not therefore, ye are of more value than many sparrows."

12 This point is borne out by what she says about her parents. Despite the considerable detail in her account, she says she has not given them a full memorial: "since I shall detract from those I would celebrate by my imperfect commemorations, I shall content myself to sum up some few things *for my own use* [emphasis mine], and let the rest alone, . . ." (8).

13 I recall here advice to the fledgling writer: "Don't bite off the whole west coast if all you're going to chew is Seattle" (the pungent phrasing originated with my colleague Douglas Patey); or "Don't start with the opening scene of *Romeo and Juliet* if the assignment is to discuss Romeo's speech in 5.2."

14 Keeble, ed., *Memoirs*, 342, n. 4, suggests the influence of *Richard II* 2.1.40–58 on the patriotic sentiments of this passage.

15 As James Sutherland suggests in his note on this passage (*Memoirs*, 329), the disparity was more likely twenty-two than thirty-two years: "Since she was married to Sir Allen Apsley on 23 October 1615, and since her father died on 20 September 1594, she must have been much more than sixteen. It is most unlikely that Mrs. Hutchinson would make a mistake of such magnitude

about her mother's age, and the most obvious explanation is that the Rev. Julius Hutchinson's printer misread Mrs. Hutchinson's 26 for 16. Mrs. Hutchinson says that her mother's parents died when she was 'not above five years of age'. This would make the year of her birth 1589 – twenty-six years before her marriage in 1615."

16 *The Works of George Herbert*, ed. F. E. Hutchinson (Oxford: Clarendon Press, 1941; 1964). Since Lucy Hutchinson was an accomplished Latinist and translator of Lucretius, this passage was surely familiar to her. The passage in the *Aeneid*, Book 11, contains a double instance of positive omens. First, as Aeneas prepares to leave Troy:

> For there between his parents' hands and their faces
> From the tip of Iulus' [Ascanius'] cap a slender light
> Poured forth, soft flame quite harmless to the touch,
> That licked his hair and fed around his temples.
> We tried in our fear to shake out the burning hair
> And quench the holy fire with streams of water.

Then Anchises asks for another sign to confirm the first, and

> Suddenly thunder
> Crashed on the left, a star fell out of the sky
> And fled with its dazzling torch through the darkness of night.

These passages are taken from Vergil's *Aeneid,* trans. L. R. Lind (Bloomington: Indiana University Press, 1963), 2.722–27; 733–35. Perhaps the remembrance of the star of Bethlehem that guided the Magi to worship the Christ child in Bethlehem (Matt. 2:2) is a bit of a stretch even for so dramatic an account as this.

17 Lucy Hutchinson writes, "my father and mother fancying me then beautiful, and more than ordinarily apprehensive, applied all their cares, and spared no cost to improve me in my education, which procured me the admiration of those that flattered my parents" (14).

18 Williamson, *Lady Anne Clifford, Countess of Dorset, Pembroke, & Montgomery 1590-1676* (Kendal: Titus Wilson & Son, 1922), 66.

19 *The Memoirs of Anne, Lady Halkett and Ann, Lady Fanshawe,* ed. John Loftis (Oxford: Clarendon Press, 1979), 11.

20 Keeble, ed., *Memoirs,* 345, n. 33.

21 Ibid., notes 33 and 36.

22 Although Susan Cook, "'The Story I Most Particularly Intend': the Narrative Style of Lucy Hutchinson," *Critical Survey* 3 (1993): 275, believes that "the context in which [this break] occurs makes it likely that this is a form of self-censorship, coming at a point where Lucy has begun to relate her involvement with the romantic intrigues of the maidservants in her parents' home," it seems to me far more likely that a later reader removed these pages.

23 Keeble, ed., *Memoirs,* 345, n. 34.

24 Pepys records that the section was "so picquant, and wrote in English and most of it true, of the retirednesse of her life and how unpleasant it was, that

being writ in English and so in danger of being met with and read by others, I was vexed at it and desired her and then commanded her to teare it"; *The Diary of Samuel Pepys*, ed. R. C. Latham and W. Matthews, 11 vols. (London: G. Bell & Sons, 1970–83), IV: 9; cited by Sara Heller Mendelson, "Stuart Women's Diaries and Occasional Memoirs," in *Women in English Society, 1500–1800*, ed. Mary Prior (London: Methuen, 1985), 184.

25 Keeble, "'The Colonel's Shadow,'" 231.

26 Ibid., 238. Keeble argues that Hutchinson's strategy allows her to write authoritatively, and from a particular political perspective, while affirming wifely subordination and establishing apparent objectivity. I am more interested in the portrait she draws of herself within this relationship.

27 Indeed a less partial observer, contemplating a portrait of John Hutchinson, might find him to be long-faced, sharp-chinned, very severe, and possibly sanctimonious.

28 So complete is the history that it provides details often omitted in other accounts, although its bias toward Col. Hutchinson is also evident; see C. H. Firth, ed., *Memoirs of the Life of Colonel Hutchinson*, 2 vols. (London: John C. Nimmo, 1885), 1: xiv–xxii; Sutherland, ed., *Memoirs*, xi–xvi.

29 Cf. Northrop Frye, *The Secular Scripture: A Study of the Structure of Romance* (Cambridge, MA: Harvard University Press, 1976).

30 I refer, of course, to the pallor and faintness, not to the more bourgeois pretense of digestive difficulty. The passage continues on a more pathetic note: "for the distemper of his mind had infected his body with a cold sweat and such a dispersion of spirit that all the courage he could at present recollect was little enough to keep him alive" (48).

31 In Keeble's edition the text reads: "and certainly it was of the Lord, though he perceived it not, who had ordained him, through so many various providences, to be yoked with her in whom he found so much satisfaction" (47). The manuscript in the archives in Nottingham indicates this as a final version, but offers an intriguing alternate reading, which has been crossed out: "to be yoked with her [whom the Lord had chosen for him. Which and many years after when he found himself pleased in the low designation he hath acknowledged and resolved with himself how admirable it was brought about and praysed God for it whether she were so in herselfe or whether his greate thankefullnesse to God made him esteeme her, so he would often recounting Gods mercies sett this in the first ranke and] in whom he found so much satisfaction" (p. 51).

32 According to Keeble, "'The Colonel's Shadow,'" 232, "Lucy Hutchinson's conception of the feminine gender role was entirely traditional."

33 The manuscript version, cited above, n. 31, also wrestles with this issue of Lucy Hutchinson's innate worth and being and the extent to which John Hutchinson (or God?) is her maker: "for it whether she were so in herselfe or whether his greate thankefullnesse to God made him esteeme her, so he would often recounting Gods mercies sett this in the first ranke."

34 Keeble cites Antonia Fraser, *The Weaker Vessel* (New York: Knopf, 1984), 135, for this opinion, but Fraser is referring to Hutchinson's account of her own life rather than to the life of her husband.

35 James Sutherland, ed., *Memoirs*, xviii, writes: "she succeeded in buying a few more years of life for her husband, but she had cheated him of his martyrdom." But C. H. Firth, ed., *Memoirs*, I: xxi, is less certain that Lucy's letter of apology was absolutely against her husband's wishes: "the existence of a second petition, that to the House of Lords, dated six weeks later, seems to prove that Col. Hutchinson's share in this matter was not confined to the passive and silent acceptance of his wife's expedient."

36 Cook, "'The Story I Most Particularly Intend,'" 275.

4 ANN FANSHAWE, PRIVATE HISTORIAN

1 *The Memoirs of Ann, Lady Fanshawe* from *The Memoirs of Anne, Lady Halkett and Ann, Lady Fanshawe* (Oxford: Clarendon Press, 1979), ed. John Loftis, 101. The text is based on the manuscript in the British Library (Add. MS 41161). All further references to Ann Fanshawe's memoirs are to this edition, cited as Loftis.

2 The description, from the catalogue of the British Library, is quoted by Loftis, 91. As Loftis also notes, Ann Fanshaw deleted (by crossing out) a number of passages that seemed to her "indecorous, or too personal."

3 Loftis observes: "The nature of the Memoirs is conditioned by Lady Fanshawe's intention in writing them, an intention in which publication had no part. Those passages which may to us seem boastful should be read with an awareness that she envisaged, not an audience at large, but a family audience who would read the Memoirs in manuscript. She intended to provide her descendants with a record of their lineage" (xiv–xv).

4 Delany, *British Autobiography in the Seventeenth Century* (London: Routledge & Kegan Paul, 1969), 174.

5 Mary Beth Rose, *Gender and Heroism in Early Modern English Literature* (University of Chicago Press, 2002), 70. The discussion is part of a chapter entitled "Gender, Genre, and History: Female Heroism in Seventeenth-Century Autobiography," 55–84.

6 I concur with Gabriele Rippl, *Lebenstexte: Literarische Selbststilisierung englischer Frauen in der frühen Neuzeit* (Munich: Wilhelm Fink Verlag, 1998), 134, who points to the difficulty of finding a single generic category for Fanshawe's text.

7 The phrases that come to mind are "Remember now thy Creator in the days of thy youth . . ." (Ecclesiastes 12:1) and "Honour thy father and thy mother: that thy days may be long upon the land which the LORD thy God giveth thee" (generally construed as the fourth commandment; Exodus 20:12). There is also an echo of Paul's letter to the Philippians: "I have learned, in whatsoever state I am, therewith to be content" (Philippians 4:11).

8 Thinking of the present-day CEO, working out for an hour before heading to the office, one is struck by the very different ideal of calm, self-control, and measure in all things.

9 A similar hope is expressed at the end of the account of Sir Richard's family: "I hope in God the like paralell will be in you, which I heartly and dayly pray for" (108).

10 The story of God granting King Hezekiah fifteen more years of life, in answer to his prayer, is told in 2 Kings 20:1–6.

11 Keeble, ed., *Memoirs*, 14; cited above, p. 79.

12 Rose, *Gender and Heroism*, 66.

13 On the Fanshawes' attitudes toward Clarendon, see Loftis, xvi–xvii, 112 and n. 209.

14 The phrasing is that of Mary Beth Rose, *Gender and Heroism*, 66. Rippl, *Lebenstexte*, 182, also stresses that Fanshawe's goal is to present herself as a model Stuart wife and gentlewoman.

15 Although a pronounced feature of Margaret Hoby's diary, this sense of accountability to God is clearly not restricted to Puritans.

16 Ann Fanshawe is quoting (presumably by memory) from Hebrews 11:1: "Now faith is the substance of things hoped for, the evidence of things not seen."

17 Andrew Marvell expresses a similar conception of life as a stage in "Bermudas":

> What should we do but sing his praise
> That led us through the watery maze,
> Unto an isle so long unknown,
> And yet far kinder than our own
> Where he the huge sea-monsters wracks,
> That lift the deep upon their backs,
> He lands us on a grassy stage,
> Safe from the storms, and prelate's rage.
> (*Andrew Marvell*, ed. Frank Kermode and Keith Walker
> [Oxford University Press, 1990], 14)

18 Rose, *Gender and Heroism*, 66.

19 Cf. the serpent's temptation in *Paradise Lost* 5.74–76: "fair Angelic Eve, / . . . happy though thou art, / Happier thou may'st be, worthier canst not be"; *John Milton*, ed. Stephen Orgel and Jonathan Goldberg (Oxford University Press, 1990).

20 Although one may think first of Hotspur's refusal to tell his wife where he is going (in *1Henry IV*), Fanshawe's answer in fact recalls the words of another cavalier, "I could not love thee (Deare) so much, / Lov'd I not Honour more"; Richard Lovelace, "To Lucasta, Going to the Warres"; *The Poems of Richard Lovelace*, ed. C. H. Wilkinson (Oxford: Clarendon Press, 1930), 18.

21 Milton, *Paradise Lost* 4.490–91.

22 For example, regarding 1648 she writes, "My husband thought it convenient to send me into England again there to try what sums I could raise both for his subsistence abroad and mine at home; and though nothing was so

grievous to us both as parting, yet the necessity both of the publick and your
father's private affaires obliged us often to yeld to the trouble of absence, as at
this time" (122).
23 Emphasized in her designation of Sir Richard as "your father."
24 "Walking by the sea . . . 2 ships of the Dutch then in war with England shot
bullets at us so near that we heard them wiss by us, at which I called to my
husband to make haste back, and begun to run. But he altered not his pace,
saying if we must be kill'd, it were as good to be kill'd walking as running"
(120–21).
25 Others have viewed these passages more positively: B. G. MacCarthy, *The
Female Pen: Women Writers and Novelists 1621–1818* (Cork University Press,
1946–47; rpt. 1994), writes: "Like the great diaries [sic] she has an insatiable
appetite for curious facts" (92) and goes on to praise Fanshawe's "power of
natural realism" and the "vigorous simplicity of her style" (93).
26 Rippl, *Lebenstexte*, 169–82, emphasizes both travel literature, with its love of
detail, and the diplomat's report as models for Fanshawe's style in these
sections.
27 Translation of Horace, *Odes* 4.9.34–52.
28 Anne Halkett mentions the temptations offered to the young Prince Charles,
and credits his ability to withstand them to her father's tutelage; Loftis, 10.
29 Although Rose, *Gender and Heroism*, 69, says that her narrative trails off
inconclusively, it is the manuscript itself that breaks off – in mid-sentence at
the bottom of the page. It seems less likely that Fanshawe broke off just at
that point than that something is missing from the text itself.
30 Rose, *Gender and Heroism*, 70.

5 ROMANCE AND RESPECTABILITY: THE
AUTOBIOGRAPHY OF ANNE HALKETT

 1 Although Halkett did not give her text a title, and we have no evidence that
she intended it for publication, the term autobiography seems to me
appropriate in this case. The edition I have used throughout, *The Memoirs of
Anne, Lady Halkett and Ann, Lady Fanshawe*, ed. John Loftis (Oxford:
Clarendon Press, 1979), cited as Halkett, uses the looser designation *memoir*.
Mary Beth Rose, *Gender and Heroism in Early Modern English Literature*
(University of Chicago Press, 2002), uses the term autobiography in her
chapter on Halkett. Gabriele Rippl, *Lebenstexte: Literarische Selbststilisierung
englischer Frauen in der frühen Neuzeit* (Munich: Wilhelm Fink Verlag, 1998),
187–220, argues that Halkett draws on a variety of literary forms.
 2 Details of Anne Murray Halkett's life are taken from her autobiography and
the introductory materials in Loftis. There is also an account of Halkett's life
written by one "S. C.," drawing on the memoirs and designed to accompany
the publication of her devotional treatises in 1701 (published as *The Life of the
Lady Halkett* [Edinburgh, 1701]).

3 Halkett, 9. The reference in the 1662 *Book of Common Prayer* is part of the communion service; following absolution, "the priest shall say, 'If any man sin, we have an Advocate with the Father, Jesus Christ the righteous; and he is the propitiation for our sins.' St. John 2.1."

4 Paul Delany, *British Autobiography in the Seventeenth Century* (London: Routledge & Kegan Paul, 1969), 162, says, "Lady Halkett gives no motive for writing and does not seem to have planned to publish." But Rippl, *Lebenstexte*, 88, notes the numerous addresses to the reader in the text.

5 Halkett, 9. As in the Loftis edition, the text is printed here to indicate the fragmentary state of the MS.

6 As such it departs from the earlier stage of autobiography described by Donald Stauffer, *English Biography before 1700* (Cambridge, MA: Harvard University Press, 1930), 175, the notion that "the life of an individual might be expressed as the sum of his separate acts" leading to the "impersonal annals and chronicles of *res gestae*."

7 I shall say more later about the gaps in the manuscript: material is missing from the beginning and from the end, suggesting the ravages of time, and two leaves are torn out from the manuscript itself, suggesting more deliberate human intervention.

8 Rippl, *Lebenstexte*, 192–95, and Stauffer, *English Biography*, 212, emphasize the three romantic attachments as the chief structural principle; I see the tendentious nature of the self-presentation as a dominant shaping feature.

9 For decades, critics have seen Halkett's autobiography as a precursor to the eighteenth-century novel. See for example Stauffer, *English Biography*, 212. For Delany, *British Autobiography*, 162, Halkett is "a blend of Richardson and Sir Walter Scott"; for James Sutherland, *English Literature of the Late Seventeenth Century* (Oxford University Press, 1969), 263, Halkett's text "might have provided Samuel Richardson with all the material he could possibly need for another novel." All these statements indicate the crafted quality of Halkett's text. Sutherland states that Halkett's "fragmentary autobiography . . . was in print in the early eighteenth century," suggesting the possibility of influence on Richardson; in fact, what was in print was the biography by "S.C.," "a short extract, drawn out of large memoirs or Diaries, written by the worthy Lady," which depicts Halkett as an exemplary figure. Loftis, "Bampfield's Later Career: a Biographical Supplement" in *Colonel Joseph Bampfield's Apology*, ed. John Loftis and Paul H. Hardacre (Lewisburg: Bucknell University Press, 1993), 248, suggests that the biographer "had apparently seen the manuscript of her memoirs in a more complete state than now exists," and that the pages now missing were removed after Anne Halkett's death; 280, n. 11.

10 I'm grateful to Elizabeth Harries for the reminder of Mr. Knightley's words to Emma: "If I loved you less, I might be able to talk about it more" (III.13). Her question resembled mine: could Austen have read Halkett? Was this form of speech a cliché? Rippl, *Lebenstexte*, 195–212, emphasizes Halkett's use

of forms associated with the romance, though her discussion makes use of somewhat rigid generic categories.

11 Some readers have found the account so detailed that they have assumed a diary must be its basis; others find Halkett looking to fictional models to shape her autobiography. But Margaret Bottrall, *Every Man a Phoenix: Studies in Seventeenth-Century Autobiography* (London: John Murray, 1958), 152, asserts: "The kind of episode that she stored up in her memory or recorded in her journals was just the sort of thing that lingers in the mind of the average woman. Encounters with lovers and suitors, personal griefs and illnesses, conversations in which she scored successes, details of costume and gesture and manner – these are what seemed important to Anne Halkett when she came to write her life story." William Nelson, *Fact or Fiction: The Dilemma of the Renaissance Storyteller* (Cambridge, MA: Harvard University Press, 1973), 41–43, notes the tendency of storytellers from classical antiquity on to invent speeches appropriate to an occasion; cited in Lennard J. Davis, *Factual Fictions: The Origins of the English Novel* (New York: Columbia University Press, 1983), 67–68.

12 Gabriele Rippl, *Lebenstexte*, 183, citing Wayne Shumaker, *English Autobiography: Its Emergence, Materials, and Forms* (Berkeley: University of California Press, 1954), 65 ff., argues that Halkett bridges the gap between seventeenth-century romance and eighteenth-century novel; and Paul Salzman, *English Prose Fiction, 1558–1700* (Oxford: Clarendon Press, 1985), 181, in his discussion of the role of French heroic romances in the development of the novel, notes that "characters in the romances devoted a large amount of time to the analysis of delicate emotional dilemmas." Laurie Langbauer, *Women and Romance: The Consolations of Gender in the English Novel* (Ithaca and London: Cornell University Press, 1990), 1, points to the connection between romance and the emotional lives of women: "conceived as a mode of erotic wish-fulfillment, or as a prose form auxiliary to the novel, romance is thought somehow proper to women and usually derived accordingly." Lois Potter, *Secret Rites and Secret Writing: Royalist Literature, 1641–1660* (Cambridge University Press, 1980), 108, notes the connection with Cowley's play *The Guardian* (1641), where the blindfold stratagem is used.

13 The motif of conflict between parents and child over a marital partner is not only common in romance, but also occurs in Lucy Hutchinson's *Life of John Hutchinson*, with regard to herself; Hutchinson, ed. Keeble, 50.

14 Although one thinks most often of old Capulet's harshness – telling Juliet to "hang, beg, starve, die in the streets" (*Romeo and Juliet* 3.5.192) – it is Lady Capulet who comes closest to Mrs. Murray's phrase: "I would the fool were married to her grave!" (3.5.140).

15 Anne Halkett recounts that Thomas Howard had "resolved for a time to forbeare all converse with mee and to make love to all that came in his way; butt assured mee itt was only to make his friends thinke hee had forgot mee, and then hee might with the lese suspition prosecute his designe, which was never to love or marry any butt mee. And this . . . hee confirmed with all the

solemne oaths imaginable" (21). One could find a model here for Jane Austen's Frank Churchill and also for Wickham, although it is highly unlikely that Austen could have read Halkett's autobiography, which was not in print during her lifetime. The 1701 biographical account, by S.C., which draws on Halkett's text, makes only the briefest mention of her romantic adventures, instead emphasizing her piety.

16 See Salzman, *English Prose Fiction,* and Caroline Lucas, *Writing for Women: The Example of Woman as Reader in Elizabethan Romance* (Milton Keynes: Open University Press, 1989). On Elizabethan romances, Lucas says, "Critical histories . . . , which generally limit their attention to plot analysis, are particularly inappropriate, since any plot summary of Elizabethan romance inevitably distorts the experience of the reader because it leaves out the narrative technique, and the important role of rhetorically embellished speeches and debates" (43). One might cite, for example, the speeches of Camma in the first of the romances in Pettie's *Palace of Pleasure (A petite pallace of Pettie his pleasure,* London, 1576).

17 *Colonel Joseph Bampfield's Apology. . . 1685,* ed. Loftis and Hardacre, 21–22. Although it had been assumed by a number of scholars (including Loftis himself) that Bampfield was a double agent, for King and Parliament, the later work of Loftis and Hardacre, 21–24, strongly disputes that conclusion.

18 This problem is a common one in first-person narration; one need think only of the supposedly reformed Moll Flanders recounting with relish and intermittent penitence her previous life. But of course Moll Flanders, as Lennard Davis would remind us (*Factual Fictions,* ch. 1), is a fictional character. The problem of Bampfield's actions and reputation is even more complicated. In his edition of *Colonel Joseph Bampfield's Apology,* John Loftis argues that Bampfield was not, in fact, a dual agent and supplies other possible explanations for Charles II's antipathy to him. Loftis also provides a chronology suggesting that Bampfield himself may have believed, at least for a time, that his wife was dead (238–52) and that Anne Halkett herself may have been unfair to Bampfield. This view, as Loftis himself indicates, 13–14, differs markedly from the one articulated in his earlier edition of *The Memoirs of Anne, Lady Halkett* (1979). See also Sheila Ottway, "They Only Lived Twice: Public and Private Selfhood in the Autobiographies of Anne, Lady Halkett and Colonel Joseph Bampfield," in *Betraying Our Selves: Forms of Self-Representation in Early Modern English Texts,* ed. Henk Dragstra, Sheila Ottway, and Helen Wilcox (New York: St. Martin's Press, 2000), 136–47, esp. 142–46, who thinks Bampfield is more honorable than Halkett's narrative (and Loftis's edition of it) lead us to believe.

19 The child of Anne Howard, sister of Thomas Howard, her former suitor.

20 Even Loftis, in his concluding remarks on Bampfield (*Colonel Bampfield's Apology . . . and Bampfield's Later Career*), 249, admits that Bampfield "must have known the truth about his wife years before March 1653, when Anne learned that Catherine [his wife] was alive. He deceived Anne, not in the beginning, it would appear, but for a stretch of time before Anne read reports

that Catherine had come to London to undeceive those who thought she
had died."

21 Sir Charles Howard married Anne Howard, who was his cousin.

22 Paul Delany, *British Autobiography*, 162–63.

23 The account is detailed and romantic: C.B.'s letter is accompanied by the
letters of the seconds in the duel, and C.B. is reported to have said that "hee
was never ingaged in any imployment more contrary to his inclination then
to make use of his sword against him who drew his in the deffence of the
person hee loved beyond any living" (48–49).

24 I here differ from Rippl, *Lebenstexte*, who sees a quite clear plotting in the
text; I am struck both by Halkett's efforts in that direction and the limits of
her success.

25 "I began to reflect upon my owne misfortune in the unhapy report that was of
C. B.'s wife's beeing alive, and it was knowne to severalls aboutt the courtt
what my concerne in him was. This, with the unhandsome and unjust caracter
given both to him and my brother Will, made mee aprehend mightt make mee
nott bee so well looked upon by the King as otherways I might expect" (52).

26 For example in *A Journal of the Plague Year*, the narrator sees the accidents
that delayed his leaving London as "being from Heaven." Later, consulting
scripture for guidance, and coming by happenstance on a passage that reads
"There shall no evil befall thee, neither shall any plague come nigh thy
dwelling," he determines to stay; Defoe, *A Journal of the Plague Year*, ed.
Paula R. Backscheider (New York: Norton, 1992), 13, 15.

27 Like Ann Fanshawe "upon the stage to act what part God desined us"
(Loftis, ed., *Memoirs*, 113), Halkett from time to time interprets her life as a
drama directed by Divine Providence.

28 Both the impersonal language and the notion of the interested community
sound remarkably like Jane Austen. Halkett even anticipates some of the
irony of the opening of *Pride and Prejudice*: "It is a truth universally
acknowledged, that a single man in possession of a good fortune, must be in
want of a wife."

29 Loftis, *Colonel Joseph Bampfield's Apology*, 248, is inclined to believe that Anne
Murray and Joseph Bampfield went to the Netherlands to be married, in part
because a public declaration of their intention to marry (as required by law)
could have led to their arrest.

30 In the early modern period, equivocation was strongly associated with denial,
sometimes under torture, of a religious or political conviction punishable by
law; and the legitimacy of ambiguous statements, mental restrictions, and
unexpressed qualifications was debated. See Albert R. Jonsen and Stephen
Toulmin, *The Abuse of Casuistry: A History of Moral Reasoning* (Berkeley:
University of California Press, 1988), 195–215. According to one theory, "One
speaks a sentence that literally does not express the state of affairs, but by
adding a qualification in his mind, the speaker rendered the spoken statement
true 'as far as he and God were concerned'" (202). Of the several instances of
equivocation cited by the *OED*, perhaps most pertinent is one from

Richardson's *Pamela* (1741), as Mr. B complains to the heroine: "You won't tell a downright fib for the world; but for equivocation! No Jesuit ever went beyond you."

31 Martin de Azpilcueta (1493–1586); cited by Margaret Ferguson, *Dido's Daughters: Literacy, Gender, and Empire in Early Modern England and France* (University of Chicago Press, 2003), 276–77.

32 Keith Thomas, "Cases of Conscience in Seventeenth-Century England," in *Public Duty and Private Conscience in Seventeenth-Century England: Essays Presented to G. E. Aylmer*, ed. John Morrill, Paul Slack, and Daniel Woolf (Oxford: Clarendon Press, 1993), 51. Thomas, 52, sees this transition as "the origin of the modern, more secular, belief that, whatever we do, we retain our moral integrity so long as we obey our consciences."

6 MARGARET CAVENDISH: SHY PERSON TO BLAZING EMPRESS

1 As noted by Sidonie Smith, "The Ragged Rout of Self: Margaret Cavendish's *True Relation* and the Heroics of Self-Disclosure," in *A Poetics of Women's Autobiography: Marginality and the Fictions of Self-Representation* (Bloomington: Indiana University Press, 1987), 87, Cavendish first wrote her own autobiographical sketch, and later wrote the biography of her husband, to which *A True Relation* was then appended. Whereas Smith, 100, sees this as "her story [becoming] a satellite revolving around the body of man's story," I take the order of composition to be as important as the later form of publication.

2 For Cavendish's biography, see Douglas Grant, *Margaret the First* (University of Toronto Press, 1957); Kathleen Jones, *A Glorious Fame: The Life of Margaret Cavendish, Duchess of Newcastle, 1623–1673* (London: Bloomsbury, 1988); Anna Battigelli, *Margaret Cavendish and the Exiles of the Mind* (Lexington: University Press of Kentucky, 1998); and Katie Whitaker, *Mad Madge* (New York: Basic Books, 2002).

3 Kate Lilley, Introduction to Margaret Cavendish, *The Blazing World and Other Writings* (Harmondsworth: Penguin, 1994), xvii. Lilley focuses on two stories, "The Contract" and "Assaulted and Pursued Chastity," noting strong similarities to the Cavendishes' own history: a "young and wealthy heroine" is married to a man, "desirable and sexually libertine," who was "initially married to [a] wealthy, older [widow]." "The narrative denouement requires the removal of the present wife, respectively through annulment and death, and the reform of the rakish husband by the virtuous, beautiful and brilliantly accomplished heroine. William Cavendish was just such a dissolute and successful younger brother, whom Margaret Cavendish married after the death of his first wife, a rich widow" (xvi–xvii).

4 *A True Relation*, in *Paper Bodies: A Margaret Cavendish Reader*, ed. Sylvia Bowerbank and Sara Mendelson (Peterborough, Ontario: Broadview Press, 2000), 63. All further references to *A True Relation* are to this edition.

5 The phrase is from Enobarbus, who hopes to be like one who follows "a fall'n lord . . . / And earns a place i' th' story"; *Antony and Cleopatra* 3.13.46; *The Riverside Shakespeare*, ed. G. Blakemore Evans, 2nd edn. (Boston: Houghton Mifflin, 1997). See also Line Cottegnies, "The 'Native Tongue' of the 'Authoress': the Mythical Structure of Margaret Cavendish's Autobiographical Narrative," in *Authorial Conquests: Essays on Genre in the Writings of Margaret Cavendish*, ed. Line Cottegnies and Nancy Weitz (Madison, NJ: Fairleigh Dickinson University Press, 2003), 104, on Cavendish's "awareness of identity as a literary construct."

6 Cottegnies, "The 'Native Tongue,'" 110, finds in this narrative a "loose chronological . . . [and] a quasi-mythical structure."

7 Mary Beth Rose, *Gender and Heroism in Early Modern English Literature* (University of Chicago Press, 2002), 63.

8 As Bowerbank notes, *Paper Bodies*, 44 n. 3, "Because Thomas, the eldest son, was born before Cavendish's father was allowed to return from exile and marry her mother, the Lucas estate was inherited by John, the second (but first legitimate) son." For a more sober and substantive account than that offered by Cavendish herself, see Sara Heller Mendelson, *The Mental World of Stuart Women* (Amherst: University of Massachusetts Press, 1987), 12–31, as well as the discussions of Cavendish cited in n. 2 above.

9 On the matter of education for women, see Margaret P. Hannay, "'O Daughter Heare': Reconstructing the Lives of Aristocratic Englishwomen," in *Attending to Women in Early Modern England*, ed. Betty S. Travitsky and Adele F. Seeff (Newark: University of Delaware Press, 1994), 35–63. Margaret Lucas's formal education seems to have been remarkably slight even for her time; see, for example, Lisa T. Sarasohn, "A Science Turned Upside Down: Feminism and the Natural Philosophy of Margaret Cavendish," *Huntington Library Quarterly* 47 (1984): 292.

10 An Epistle, preceding *Nature's Pictures* in *The Life of William Cavendish, Duke of Newcastle, to which is added The True Relation of My Birth, Breeding, and Life by Margaret, Duchess of Newcastle*, ed. C. H. Firth (London: George Routledge and Sons [1886]), 152.

11 In the twenty-two pages of *A True Relation*, there are ten instances of *bashful* or *bashfulness*.

12 Mendelson, *Mental World*, 21–24, cites the couple's correspondence, Cavendish's fictional works, and the reaction of others at court. She asserts that "however strong her attachment to Newcastle, Margaret's role was not as innocent as her memoirs would lead us to believe," and that both Newcastle's associates and his children from his first marriage thought that "Margaret was a designing young woman determined to throw herself in his path" (21). Smith, *A Poetics of Women's Autobiography*, chapter 5, finds competing models – masculine and feminine – behind several of the contradictions in Cavendish's autobiography. She argues, "For Cavendish, the representation of herself as foolish, uncomfortable, ignorant, fearful, bashful, and speechless in public testifies to her superior virtue, the basis on which her true merit as model woman

rests" (92–93). Hero Chalmers, "Dismantling the Myth of 'Mad Madge': the Cultural Context of Margaret Cavendish's Authorial Self-Presentation," *Women's Writing* 4 (1997): 329, notes that Cavendish herself links "bashfulness" with aristocratic status and ideals, citing *The World's Olio* (1655), 88. Judith Kegan Gardiner, "'Singularity of Self': Cavendish's *True Relation*, Narcissism, and the Gendering of Individualism," *Studies in English Literary Culture, 1660–1700* 21 (1997): 52–65, calls Cavendish a "bashful exhibitionist," and interprets her bashfulness as narcissism (55). Cottegnies, "The 'Native Tongue,'" 112–13, associates Cavendish's conflicting self-images with the personal crises of Rousseau's *Confessions*.

13 In fact, not quite the end, for Cavendish goes on to refrain from commending her sisters, although "many would say they were very handsome," and to compare their beauty unfavorably with that of their mother.

14 See my discussion of Burton in *Generating Texts: The Progeny of Seventeenth-Century Prose* (Charlottesville: University Press of Virginia, 1996), 105–27.

15 See for example Mendelson, *Mental World*, 12–24; 51–52.

16 This may help explain why Mary Evelyn found her so disagreeable. She recounts, "I found Doctor Charlton with her, complimenting her wit and learning in a high manner; which she took to be so much her due that she swore if the schools did not banish Aristotle and read Margaret, Duchess of Newcastle, they did her wrong, and deserved to be utterly abolished. My part was not yet to speak, but admire; especially hearing her go on magnifying her own generous actions, stately buildings, noble fortune, her lord's prodigious losses in the war, his power, valour, wit, learning, and industry,–what did she not mention to his or her own advantage? . . . Never did I see a woman so full of herself, so amazingly vain and ambitious"; Mary Evelyn to Ralph Bohun, c. 1667, in *The Diary and Correspondence of John Evelyn*, ed. William Bray (London, 1857), IV: 9; cited in *Paper Bodies*, ed. Bowerbank and Mendelson, 92.

17 Cavendish's delight in singularity of dress resembles that found in the exchange between the Duchess and the Empress in *The Description of a New World, Called the Blazing World*, in *Paper Bodies*, ed. Bowerbank and Mendelson, 245. All further references to *The Blazing World* are to this edition.

18 Jean Gagen, "Honor and Fame in the Works of the Duchess of Newcastle," *Studies in Philology* 56 (1959): 532–33, says "the Duchess of Newcastle was her own favorite character, and she stalked through her plays and narratives in numerous transparent disguises." Helen Wilcox concurs: "it would be quite possible to claim . . . that all of Cavendish's work was in some serious sense autobiographical"; "Margaret Cavendish and the Landscapes of a Woman's Life," in *Mapping the Self: Space, Identity, Discourse in British Auto/Biography*, ed. Frédéric Regard (Publications de l'Université de Saint-Etienne, 2003), 84.

19 Paul Salzman, *English Prose Fiction, 1558–1700* (Oxford: Clarendon Press, 1985), 298, describes *The Blazing World* as "a most unusual blend of imaginary voyage, utopia, and autobiography," noting also that it "may

irritate students of serious utopias" (295). See also Nicole Pohl, "'Of Mixt Natures': Questions of Genre in Margaret Cavendish's *The Blazing World*," in *A Princely Brave Woman: Essays on Margaret Cavendish, Duchess of Newcastle*, ed. Stephen Clucas (Aldershot: Ashgate, 2003), 63, who argues that "although the superficial structure of . . . *The Blazing World* . . . displays a triangular design, the text consists of a multiplicity of genres, a multiplicity of viewpoints, and uses rhetorical figures that confront conventional binarisms."

20 Lisa T. Sarasohn, "A Science Turned Upside Down," 289–307, sets Cavendish's attitudes toward atomism and materialism in the context of the thought of Hobbes, Descartes, and Gassendi. See also John Rogers, *The Matter of Revolution: Science, Poetry and Politics in the Age of Milton* (Ithaca: Cornell University Press, 1996); and Lee Cullen Khanna, "The Subject of Utopia: Margaret Cavendish and Her *Blazing-World*," in *Utopian and Science Fiction by Women: Worlds of Difference*, ed. Jane L. Donawerth and Carol A. Kolmerten (Syracuse University Press, 1994), 15–34.

21 *Blazing World*, 162. In *A True Relation*, Cavendish says, "I had a naturall stupidity towards the learning of any other Language, than my native tongue" (59–60).

22 Pepys and Evelyn depicted Cavendish as credulous rather than comprehending. On these early reports, see Sylvia Bowerbank, who argues that Cavendish's views of science were in fact far more advanced than is generally believed, and presents *The Blazing World* as a response to Bacon's *New Atlantis*; Introduction to *Paper Bodies*, 24–34. Bowerbank also cites Marjorie Nicolson, *Pepys's Diary and the New Science* (Charlottesville: University of Virginia Press, 1965), 104–14; and Sarasohn, "A Science Turned Upside-Down," 290–91, notes the similarities of Cavendish's views to those of respected thinkers of the day. Eve Keller, "'Producing Petty Gods': Margaret Cavendish's Critique of Experimental Science," *ELH* 64 (1997): 447–71, argues that in both *Observations on Experimental Philosophy* and *The Blazing World* (which were published together in 1666), Cavendish mounts a critique of science as "a discipline of self-interested, and even egoistic, construction, rather than one of rational discovery or passive revelation" (456).

23 Generally the Empress receives very respectful attention. The one exception, when the Worm-men laugh at her question regarding colorless minerals and creatures within the earth, seems to signify for Cavendish the rigor and delight of intellectual engagement: "The Emperess was so wonderfully taken with this discourse of the Worm-men, that she not onely pardoned the rudeness they committed in laughing at first at her question, but yielded a full assent to their opinion, which she thought the most rational that ever she had heard yet; and then proceeding in her questions, enquired further . . ." (180).

24 Like *A True Relation*, which was published in the same volume as a work of a different sort (in that case *Nature's Pictures* represented the fantasy world, and *A True Relation* the more factual), *The Blazing World* accompanies a work, Cavendish's *Observations upon Experimental Philosophy*, that addresses the other end of the spectrum of reason and fantasy; the two were published

together in 1666. Cristina Malcolmson, in "'The Explication of Whiteness and Blackness': Skin Color and the Physics of Color in the Works of Robert Boyle and Margaret Cavendish," in *Fault Lines and Controversies in the Study of Seventeenth-Century English Literature*, ed. Claude J. Summers and Ted-Larry Pebworth (Columbia: University of Missouri Press, 2002), esp. 199–203, argues for the close relationship between Cavendish's scientific and fictional interests. Lisa T. Sarasohn, "*Leviathan* and the Lady: Cavendish's Critique of Hobbes in the *Philosophical Letters*," in *Authorial Conquests*, ed. Cottegnies and Weitz, 40–58, argues for a considerably more active stance on Cavendish's part, as does Brandie R. Siegfried, "Anecdotal and Cabalistic Forms in *Observations upon Experimental Philosophy*," also in *Authorial Conquests*, ed. Cottegnies and Weitz, 59–79.

25 Cavendish stresses the desirability of monarchy ("to have but one Soveraign, one Religion, one Law, and one Language, so that all the World might be but as one united Family, without divisions"; 229) and suggests that the desire for change in a world that "was very well and wisely order'd and governed at first, when I came to be Emperess thereof" (229), is rather whimsical and arbitrary.

26 See Sarah Hutton, "Science and Satire: the Lucianic Voice of Margaret Cavendish's *Description of a New World Called the Blazing World*," in *Authorial Conquests*, ed. Cottegnies and Weitz, 161–78.

27 A more widely known model might be Bottom who, in *A Midsummer Night's Dream*, 1.2, is eager to play Pyramus, Thisby, and the Lion. Line Cottegnies, "The 'Native Tongue,'" 114, offers a more serious account: "Cavendish almost schizophrenically adopts two different perspectives on herself at once, immortalizing a posthumous figure of herself but above all celebrating herself as the author manipulating the text."

28 For example, Dorothy Osborne's famous comment to William Temple: "You need not send me my Lady Newcastle's book at all for I have seen it, and am satisfied that there are many soberer people in Bedlam; I'll swear her friends are much to blame to let her go abroad." Letter to William Temple on April 14 1653, from *Letters of Dorothy Osborne*, ed. G. C. Moore Smith (Oxford: Clarendon Press 1928), 41; quoted in Grant, *Margaret the First*, 126.

29 In the incident recounted in *A True Relation*, 51, cited above, p. 142.

30 "Had my Lord Wealth [the Duchess replies to the Emperor], I am sure he would not spare it, in rendering his Buildings as Noble as could be made" (246).

31 Douglas Bush, *English Literature of the Earlier Seventeenth Century, 1600–1660* (Oxford: Clarendon Press, 1962), 24; Salzman, *English Prose Fiction*, 295. See also the summary by Sarah Hutton, "Science and Satire," 161 ff. These comments were made before Cavendish acquired her own society, her own website, and her own following of inquiring scholars. Stephen Clucas, Introduction to *A Princely Brave Woman*, argues for the importance of reading Margaret Cavendish in context.

32 In *Timber, or Discoveries*, Jonson said of Shakespeare, "His wit was in his owne power; would the rule of it had beene so too. Many times hee fell into

those things, could not escape laughter: As when hee said in the person of *Caesar*, one speaking to him; *Caesar, thou dost me wrong.* Hee replyed: *Caesar did never wrong, but with just cause:* and such like; which were ridiculous" (in *Ben Jonson*, ed. C. H. Herford, Percy and Evelyn Simpson [Oxford: Clarendon Press, 1947]; VIII: 584). Interestingly enough, Cavendish says something rather like this about her own anger in *A True Relation*, asserting, "I am seldom angry, . . but when I am angry, I am very angry, but yet it is soon over, and I am easily pacified, if it be not such an injury as may create a hate" (61).

CONCLUSION

1 Hunter, *Before Novels: The Cultural Contexts of Eighteenth-Century English Fiction* (New York: Norton, 1990), 312.
2 Patricia Crawford, "Public Duty, Conscience, and Women in Early Modern England," in *Public Duty and Private Conscience in Seventeenth-Century England*, ed. John Morrill, Paul Slack, and Daniel Woolf (Oxford: Clarendon Press, 1993), 57, has argued that "the public and private in early modern England were permeable concepts in thought, and slippery concepts in practice – both the public and the private were constantly under negotiation and debate; secondly, that the public sphere was not an entirely male space, and that some females shared responsibility for the discharge of public duties; and, thirdly, that women used religious beliefs and arguments about conscience to justify action in the public sphere."
3 See chapter 6, n. 28, above.

Bibliography

PRIMARY SOURCES

MANUSCRIPT SOURCES

British Library, London

MS Egerton 2614 The Diary of Lady Margaret Hoby.

MS Harley 6177 A Summary of the Lives of the Veteriponts, Cliffords, and Earls of Cumberland, and of Lady Countess Dowager Anne Clifford. . . copied from the original MS by Henry Fisher Dec. 1737.

Add. 21425 Anne Clifford, correspondence.

Add. 34105 f. 62 Extracts from Anne Clifford's memoirs.

Add. 4116 Memoirs of Ann, Lady Fanshawe.

Add. 32376 Autobiography of Anne, Lady Halkett.

Add. 25901 Life of Colonel Hutchinson.

Add. 46172 ff. 93–96 Lucy Hutchinson, Note-book.

Add 39779 ff. 42–47 Fragment of notebook.

Cumbria Record Office: Kendal

WD/Hoth 10 Anne Clifford, Great Books of Record, 3 volumes (2 copies).

WD/Hoth/A988/17 Anne Clifford's Account books.

WD/Hoth/Box 44 Letters.

Cumbria, Penrith

MS in possession of Mr. R. B. Hasell-McCosh of Dalemain House, Penrith; Anne Clifford's last days.

Nottingham County Archives

DDHU4 Lucy Hutchinson, Memoirs of the Life of Colonel Hutchinson.

PRINTED SOURCES

Austen, Jane. *Emma* (1816), ed. David Lodge. London: Oxford University Press, 1971.

Pride and Prejudice (1814), ed. R. W. Chapman, 3rd edn. Oxford University Press, 1932.

Bampfield, Joseph. *Colonel Joseph Bampfield's Apology . . . 1685*, ed. John Loftis and Paul H. Hardacre, and "Bampfield's Later Career: a Biographical Supplement" by John Loftis. Lewisburg: Bucknell University Press, 1993.

The Book of Common Prayer. London: Printed by John Bill and Christopher Barker, 1662.

Cavendish, Margaret. *Margaret Cavendish: Sociable Letters*, ed. James Fitzmaurice. New York: Garland, 1997.

The Blazing World and Other Writings, ed. Kate Lilly. Harmondsworth: Penguin, 1994.

The Life of William Cavendish, Duke of Newcastle, to which is added The True Relation of My Birth, Breeding, and Life by Margaret, Duchess of Newcastle, ed. C. H. Firth. London: George Routledge & Sons [1886].

Observations upon Experimental Philosophy, ed. Eileen O'Neill. Cambridge University Press, 2001.

Paper Bodies: A Margaret Cavendish Reader, ed. Sylvia Bowerbank and Sara Mendelson. Peterborough, Ontario: Broadview Press, 2000.

Political Writings, ed. Susan James. Cambridge University Press, 2003.

Clifford, Anne. *The Diary of Anne Clifford 1616–1619: A Critical Edition*, ed. Katherine Acheson. New York: Garland, 1995.

The Diaries of Lady Anne Clifford, ed. D. J. H. Clifford. Stroud: Sutton, 1990.

Lives of Lady Anne Clifford, Countess of Dorset, Pembroke and Montgomery (1590–1676) and of her parents, summarized by herself, ed. Julius Parnell Gilson. London and Aylesbury: Roxburghe Club, 1916.

Congreve, William. *The Way of the World*. London: Jacob Tonson, 1700.

Defoe, Daniel. *A Journal of the Plague Year* (1722), ed. Paula R. Backscheider. New York: Norton, 1992.

Moll Flanders (1722), ed. James Sutherland. Boston: Houghton Mifflin, 1951.

Donne, John. *Devotions upon Emergent Occasions*, ed. Anthony Raspa. Montreal: McGill–Queen's University Press, 1975.

Donne's Poetical Works, ed. H. J. C. Grierson. 2 vols. Oxford: Clarendon Press, 1912.

Eliot, T. S. *The Complete Poems and Plays, 1909–1950*. New York: Harcourt Brace, 1958.

Evelyn, John. *The Diary and Correspondence of John Evelyn*, ed. William Bray. London, 1857.

Fanshawe, Ann. *The Memoirs of Ann, Lady Fanshawe wife of the Right Honble. Sir Richard Fanshawe, Bart., 1600–72, reprinted from the original manuscript in the possession of Mr. Evelyn John Fanshawe of Parsloes*. London: John Lane, 1907.

The Memoirs of Anne, Lady Halkett and Ann, Lady Fanshawe, ed. John Loftis. Oxford: Clarendon Press, 1979.

Halkett, Anne. *The Autobiography of Anne, Lady Halkett*, ed. John Gough Nicols. Westminster: Camden Society, 1875.

Herbert, George. *The Works of George Herbert*, ed. F. E. Hutchinson. Oxford: Clarendon Press, 1941.

Hoby, Margaret. *Diary of Lady Margaret Hoby 1599–1605*, ed. Dorothy M. Meads. London: George Routledge & Sons, 1930.

The Private Life of an Elizabethan Lady: The Diary of Lady Margaret Hoby 1599–1605, ed. Joanna Moody. Stroud: Sutton, 1998; pb. 2001.

Hooker, Richard. *Of the Laws of Ecclesiastical Polity . . . Books I to IV* (1593), ed. Georges Edelen. Folger Library Edition of the Works of Richard Hooker. Vol. 1. Cambridge, MA: Belknap Press of Harvard University Press, 1977–93.

Hutchinson, Lucy. *Lucy Hutchinson's Translation of Lucretius: De rerum natura*, ed. Hugh de Quehen. London: Duckworth, 1996.

Memoirs of the Life of Colonel Hutchinson, Governor of Nottingham by His Widow Lucy, ed. C. H. Firth. 2 vols. London: John C. Nimmo, 1885.

Memoirs of the Life of Colonel Hutchinson, written by His Widow Lucy. London: Kegan Paul, Trench, Truebner, 1904.

Memoirs of the Life of Colonel Hutchinson by Lucy Hutchinson, ed. N. H. Keeble. London: J. M. Dent, 1995.

Memoirs of the Life of Colonel Hutchinson, with the fragment of an autobiography of Mrs. Hutchinson, ed. James Sutherland. London: Oxford University Press, 1973.

Order and Disorder, ed. David Norbrook. Oxford: Blackwell, 2001.

Jonson, Ben. *Timber, or Discoveries*. In *Ben Jonson*, ed. C. H. Herford, Percy and Evelyn Simpson. Vol. VIII. Oxford: Clarendon Press, 1947.

Lovelace, Richard. *The Poems of Richard Lovelace*, ed. C. H. Wilkinson. Oxford: Clarendon Press, 1930.

Marvell, Andrew. *Andrew Marvell*, ed. Frank Kermode and Keith Walker. Oxford University Press, 1990.

Milton, John. *John Milton*, ed. Stephen Orgel and Jonathan Goldberg. Oxford University Press, 1990.

Osborne, Dorothy. *The Letters of Dorothy Osborne to William Temple*, ed. G. C. Moore Smith. Oxford: Clarendon Press, 1928.

Pettie, George. *A Petite Pallace of Pettie His Pleasure Containing Many Pretie Histories by Him Set Forth. . .* 2 vols. London: Chatto and Windus, 1908.

Pepys, Samuel. *The Diary of Samuel Pepys*, ed. R. C. Latham and W. Matthews. 11 vols. London: G. Bell & Sons, 1970–83.

Rainbow, Edward. *A Sermon Preached at the funeral of the Right Honorable Anne, Countess of Pembroke, Dorset, and Montgomery . . .* by the Right Reverend. . . Edward Lord Bishop of Carlisle. London: R. Royston, 1677.

Richardson, Samuel. *Pamela* (1741). New York: Norton, 1958.

Clarissa (1747–8). Harmondsworth: Penguin, 1985.

S. C. *The Life of the Lady Halkett.* Edinburgh: printed for Mr. Andrew Symson and Mr. Henry Knox, 1701.

Shakespeare, William. *The Riverside Shakespeare*, 2nd. edn. Ed. G. Blakemore Evans, et al. Boston: Houghton Mifflin, 1997.

Stuart, Arbella. *The Letters of Lady Arbella Stuart*, ed. Sara Jayne Steen. New York: Oxford University Press, 1994.

Vergil. *The Aeneid*, trans. L. R. Lind. Bloomington: Indiana University Press, 1963.

Walton, Izaak. *The Lives of John Donne, Sir Henry Wotton, Richard Hooker, George Herbert & Robert Sanderson*, ed. G. Saintsbury. London: Oxford University Press, 1927.

Wilson, Katharina M. and Frank J. Warnke, eds. *Women Writers of the Seventeenth Century.* Athens: University of Georgia Press, 1989.

Woolf, Virginia. *A Room of One's Own* (1929). New York: Harcourt, Brace, and World, 1957.

The Common Reader. London: Hogarth Press, 1929.

SECONDARY SOURCES

Acheson, Katherine Osler. "The Modernity of the Early Modern: The Example of Anne Clifford." In *Discontinuities*, ed. Comensoli and Stevens. 27–51.

Andersen, Jennifer, and Elizabeth Sauer, eds. *Books and Readers in Early Modern England: Material Studies.* Philadelphia: University of Pennsylvania Press, 2002.

Battigelli, Anna. *Margaret Cavendish and the Exiles of the Mind.* Lexington: University Press of Kentucky, 1998.

Beasley, Faith E. *Revising Memory: Women's Fiction and Memoirs in Seventeenth-Century France.* New Brunswick: Rutgers University Press, 1990.

Beilin, Elaine. *Redeeming Eve: Women Writers of the English Renaissance.* Princeton University Press, 1987.

Benstock, Shari, ed. *The Private Self: Theory and Practice of Women's Autobiographical Writings.* London: Routledge, 1988.

Blodgett, Harriet. *Centuries of Female Days: Englishwomen's Private Diaries.* New Brunswick, NJ: Rutgers University Press, 1988.

Botonaki, Effie. "Seventeenth-Century Englishwomen's Spiritual Diaries: Self-examination, Covenanting, and Account Keeping." *The Sixteenth-Century Journal* 30 (1999): 3–21.

Bottrall, Margaret. *Every Man a Phoenix: Studies in Seventeenth-Century Autobiography.* London: John Murray, 1958.

Bowerbank, Sylvia. "The Spider's Delight: Margaret Cavendish and the Female Imagination." *English Literary Renaissance* 14 (1984): 392–408.

Brant, Clare, and Diane Purkiss, eds. *Women, Texts and Histories, 1575–1760.* London: Routledge, 1992.

Bridenthal, Renate, and Claudia Koonz, eds. *Becoming Visible: Women in European History.* Boston: Houghton Mifflin, 1977.

Brodsky, Bella, and Celeste Schenck, eds. *Life/Lines: Theorizing Women's Autobiography*. Ithaca and London: Cornell University Press, 1988.

Broughton, Trev Lynn, and Linda Anderson, eds. *Women's Lives / Women's Times: New Essays on Auto/Biography*. Albany: State University of New York Press, 1997.

Brown, Sylvia. "Margaret Cavendish: Strategies Rhetorical and Philosophical Against the Charge of Wantonness, Or Her Excuses for Writing So Much." *Critical Matrix: Princeton Working Papers in Women's Studies* 6 (1991): 20–45.

Bruss, Elizabeth. *Autobiographical Acts: The Changing Situation of a Literary Genre*. Baltimore: Johns Hopkins University Press, 1976.

Bush, Douglas. *English Literature in the Earlier Seventeenth Century, 1600–1660*. 2nd edn. Oxford: Clarendon Press, 1962.

Cerasano, S. P., and Marion Wynne-Davies, eds. *Gloriana's Face: Women, Public and Private, in the English Renaissance*. Detroit: Wayne State University Press, 1992.

Certeau, Michel de. *The Practice of Everyday Life*, trans. Steven F. Rendall. Berkeley: University of California Press, 1984.

Chalmers, Hero. "Dismantling the Myth of 'Mad Madge': the Cultural Context of Margaret Cavendish's Authorial Self-Presentation." *Women's Writing* 4 (1997): 323–40.

Chew, Elizabeth V. "Si(gh)ting the Mistress of the House: Anne Clifford and Architectural Space." In *Women as Sites of Culture*, ed. Shifrin. 167–81.

Cline, Cheryl. *Women's Diaries, Journals, and Letters: An Annotated Bibliography*. New York: Garland, 1989.

Clucas, Stephen, ed. *A Princely Brave Woman: Essays on Margaret Cavendish, Duchess of Newcastle*. Aldershot: Ashgate, 2003.

Coleman, Linda S., ed. *Women's Life-Writing: Finding Voice/Building Community*. Bowling Green, OH: Bowling Green State University Popular Press, 1997.

Coleman, Patrick, Jayne Lewis, and Jill Kowalik, eds. *Representations of the Self from the Renaissance to Romanticism*. Cambridge University Press, 2000.

Collinson, Patrick. *The Birthpangs of Protestant England: Religious and Cultural Change in the Sixteenth and Seventeenth Centuries*. New York: St. Martin's Press, 1988.

Comensoli, Viviana, and Paul Stevens, eds. *Discontinuities: New Essays on Renaissance Literature and Criticism*. University of Toronto Press, 1998.

Cook, Susan. "'The Story I Most Particularly Intend': the Narrative Style of Lucy Hutchinson." *Critical Survey* 3 (1993): 271–77.

Cottegnies, Line, and Nancy Weitz, eds. *Authorial Conquests: Essays on Genre in the Writings of Margaret Cavendish*. Madison, NJ: Fairleigh Dickinson University Press, 2003.

"The Garden and the Tower: Pastoral Retreat and Configurations of the Self in the Auto/Biographical Works of Margaret Cavendish and Lucy Hutchinson." In *Mapping the Self*, ed. Regard. 125–44.

Crawford, Patricia. "Public Duty, Private Conscience, and Women in Early
    Modern England." In *Public Duty and Private Conscience in Seventeenth-
    Century England*, ed. Morrill, Slack, and Woolf. 57–76.
    "Women's Published Writings 1600–1700." In *Women in English Society,
    1500–1800*, ed. Prior. 211–82.
Crawford, Patricia M. *Women and Religion in England, 1500–1720*. London:
    Routledge, 1993.
Cressy, David. *Literacy and the Social Order: Reading and Writing in Tudor and
    Stuart England*. Cambridge University Press, 1980.
Culley, Margo, ed. *American Women's Autobiography: Fea(s)ts of Memory*.
    Madison: University of Wisconsin Press, 1992.
Davis, Lennard. *Factual Fictions: The Origins of the English Novel*. New York:
    Columbia University Press, 1983.
Daybell, James, ed. *Early Modern Women's Letter Writing, 1450–1700*.
    Basingstoke: Palgrave, 2001.
Delany, Paul. *British Autobiography in the Seventeenth Century*. London:
    Routledge & Kegan Paul, 1969.
De Man, Paul. "Autobiography as De-facement." *Modern Language Notes* 94
    (1979): 919–30.
Dolan, Frances. "Reading, Work, and Catholic Women's Biographies." *English
    Literary Renaissance* 31 (2003): 343–72.
    ,"Reading, Writing, and Other Crimes." In *Feminist Readings of Early Modern
    Culture*, ed. Traub, Kaplan, and Callaghan. 142–67.
Donovan, Josephine. *Women and the Rise of the Novel, 1405–1726*. New York: St.
    Martin's Press, 1999.
Dragstra, Henk, Sheila Ottway, and Helen Wilcox, eds. *Betraying Our Selves:
    Forms of Self-Representation in Early Modern English Texts*. New York: St.
    Martin's Press, 2000.
Eakin, Paul J. *Fictions in Autobiography*. Princeton University Press, 1985.
    Touching the World: Reference in Autobiography. Princeton University Press,
    1992.
Egan, Susanna. *Patterns of Experience in Autobiography*. Chapel Hill: University
    of North Carolina Press, 1984.
Ezell, Margaret J. M. *The Patriarch's Wife: Literary Evidence and the History of the
    Family*. Chapel Hill: University of North Carolina Press, 1987.
    "The Posthumous Publication of Women's Manuscripts and the History of
    Authorship." In *Women's Writing and the Circulation of Ideas*, ed. Justice
    and Tinker. 121–36.
    Writing Women's Literary History. Baltimore: Johns Hopkins University Press,
    1993.
Farrell, Kirby, Elizabeth H. Hageman, and Arthur F. Kinney, eds. *Women in the
    Renaissance*. Amherst: University of Massachusetts Press, 1988.
Ferguson, Margaret W. *Dido's Daughters: Literacy, Gender, and Empire in Early
    Modern England and France*. University of Chicago Press, 2003.

"Moderation and its Discontents: Recent Work on Renaissance Women." *Feminist Studies* 20 (1994): 349–66.

"A Room Not Their Own: Renaissance Women as Readers and Writers." In *The Comparative Perspective on Literature*, ed. Koelb and Noakes. 93–116.

Ferguson, Margaret W., Maureen Quilligan, and Nancy J. Vickers, eds. *Rewriting the Renaissance: The Discourses of Sexual Difference in Early Modern Europe.* University of Chicago Press, 1986.

Ferguson, Moira. "A 'Wise, Wittie and Learned Lady': Margaret Lucas Cavendish." In *Women Writers of the Seventeenth Century*, ed. Wilson and Warnke. 305–18.

Findley, Sandra, and Elaine Hobby. "Seventeenth-Century Women's Autobiography." In *1642: Literature and Power in the Seventeenth Century: Proceedings of the Essex Conference on the Sociology of Literature, July 1980*, ed. Francis Barker et al. Colchester: Essex University Press, 1981. 11–36.

Fisher, Sheila, and Janet E. Halley, eds. *Seeking the Woman in Late Medieval and Renaissance Writings: Essays in Feminist Contextual Criticism.* Knoxville: University of Tennessee Press, 1989.

Fitzmaurice, James. "Autobiography, Parody and the *Sociable Letters* of Margaret Cavendish." In *A Princely Brave Woman*, ed. Clucas. 69–83.

"Fancy and the Family: Self-characterizations of Margaret Cavendish." *Huntington Library Quarterly* 53 (1990): 199–209.

Fleishmann, Avrom. *Figures of Autobiography.* Berkeley: University of California Press, 1983.

Fletcher, Anthony. *Gender, Sex, and Subordination in England, 1500–1800.* New Haven: Yale University Press, 1995.

Fraser, Antonia. *The Weaker Vessel.* New York: Knopf, 1984.

Frye, Northrop. *The Secular Scripture: A Study of the Structure of Romance.* Cambridge, MA: Harvard University Press, 1976.

Frye, Susan, and Karen Robertson, eds. *Maids and Mistresses: Cousins and Queens: Women's Alliances in Early Modern England.* New York: Oxford University Press, 1999.

Gagen, Jean. "Honor and Fame in the Works of the Duchess of Newcastle." *Studies in Philology* 56 (1959): 519–38.

Gallagher, Catherine. "Embracing the Absolute: Margaret Cavendish and the Politics of the Female Subject in Seventeenth-Century England." In *Early Women Writers: 1600–1720*, ed. Pacheco. 133–45; rpt. of "Embracing the Absolute: the Politics of the Female Subject in Seventeenth-Century England." *Genders* 1 (1988): 24–31.

Gardiner, Judith Kegan. "'Singularity of Self': Cavendish's *True Relation*, Narcissism, and the Gendering of Individualism." *Studies in English Literary Culture, 1660–1700* 21 (1997): 52–65.

Gilmore, Leigh. *Autobiographics: A Feminist Theory of Women's Self-Representation.* Ithaca: Cornell University Press, 1994.

Goldberg, Jonathan. *Desiring Women Writing: English Renaissance Examples.* Stanford University Press, 1997.

Goreau, Angeline. *The Whole Duty of a Woman: Female Writers in Seventeenth-Century England.* Garden City, New York: Doubleday–Dial, 1985.

Graham, Elspeth, Hilary Hinds, Elaine Hobby, and Helen Wilcox, eds. *Her Own Life: Autobiographical Writings by Seventeenth-Century Englishwomen.* London: Routledge, 1989; rpt. 1992.

Graham, Elspeth. "Women's Writing and the Self." In *Women and Literature in Britain, 1500–1700,* ed. Wilcox. 209–33.

Grant, Douglas. *Margaret the First: A Biography of Margaret Cavendish, Duchess of Newcastle.* University of Toronto Press, 1957.

Greer, Germaine. "The Tulsa Center for the Study of Women's Literature: What We Are Doing and Why We Are Doing It." *Tulsa Studies in Women's Literature* 1 (1982): 5–26.

Grundy, Isobel, and Susan Wiseman, eds. *Women, Writing, History, 1640–1740.* Athens: University of Georgia Press, 1992.

Guibbory, Achsah. *The Map of Time: Seventeenth-Century English Literature and Ideas of Pattern in History.* Urbana: University of Illinois Press, 1986.

Gunn, Janet Varner. *Autobiography: Toward a Poetics of Experience.* Philadelphia: University of Pennsylvania Press, 1982.

Gusdorf, Georges. "Conditions and Limits of Autobiography." In *Autobiography: Essays Theoretical and Critical,* ed. Olney. 28–48.

Hackett, Helen. *Women and Romance Fiction in the English Renaissance.* Cambridge University Press, 2000.

Hageman, Elizabeth H. "Recent Studies in Women Writers of the English Seventeenth Century [1604–1674]." *English Literary Renaissance* 18 (1988): 138–67.

"Recent Studies in Women Writers of Tudor England." *English Literary Renaissance* 17 (1987): 409–25.

Hallett, Nicky. "Anne Clifford as Orlando: Virginia Woolf's Feminist Historiology and Women's Biography." *Women's History Review* 4 (1995): 505–24.

Hannay, Margaret P. "'O Daughter Heare': Reconstructing the Lives of Aristocratic Englishwomen." In *Attending to Women in Early Modern England,* ed. Travitsky and Seeff. 35–63.

Hannay, Margaret Patterson, ed. *Silent but for the Word: Tudor Women as Patrons, Translators, and Writers of Religious Works.* Kent, OH: Kent State University Press, 1985.

Hart, Francis R. "Notes for an Anatomy of Modern Autobiography." *New Literary History* 1 (1970): 485–511.

Haselkorn, Anne M., and Betty S. Travitsky, eds. *The Renaissance Englishwoman in Print: Counterbalancing the Canon.* Amherst: University of Massachusetts Press, 1990.

Healy, Thomas, and Jonathan Sawday, eds. *Literature and the English Civil War.* Cambridge University Press, 1990.

Heilbrun, Carolyn G. *Writing a Woman's Life.* New York: Norton, 1988.

Henderson, Katherine Usher, and Barbara F. McManus. *Half Humankind: Contexts and Texts of the Controversy about Women in England, 1540–1640.* Urbana: University of Illinois Press, 1985.

Hobby, Elaine. *Virtue of Necessity: English Women's Writing, 1649–88.* London: Virago Press, 1988.

Holmes, Martin. *Proud Northern Lady: Lady Anne Clifford, 1590–1676.* London and Chichester: Phillimore, 1975.

Houlbrooke, Ralph A. *The English Family, 1450–1700.* London: Longman, 1984.

Houlbrooke, Ralph, ed. *English Family Life, 1576–1716: An Anthology from Diaries.* Oxford: Basil Blackwell, 1988.

Howarth, William J. "Some Principles of Autobiography." In *Autobiography: Essays Theoretical and Critical,* ed. Olney. 84–114.

Hull, Suzanne W. *Chaste, Silent, and Obedient: English Books for Women 1475–1640.* San Marino, CA: Huntington Library, 1982.

Hunter, J. Paul. *Before Novels: The Cultural Contexts of Eighteenth-Century English Fiction.* New York: Norton, 1990.

Hutton, Sarah. "Science and Satire: the Lucianic Voice of Margaret Cavendish's *Description of a New World Called the Blazing World.*" In *Authorial Conquests,* ed. Cottegnies and Weitz. 161–78.

Imbrie, Ann E. "Defining Nonfiction Genres." In *Renaissance Genres,* ed. Lewalski. 45–69.

Jagodzinski, Cecile M. *Privacy and Print: Reading and Writing in Seventeenth-Century England.* Charlottesville: University Press of Virginia, 1999.

Jelinek, Estelle C. *The Tradition of Women's Autobiography: From Antiquity to the Present.* Boston: Twayne, 1986.

Jelinek, Estelle C., ed. *Women's Autobiography: Essays in Criticism.* Bloomington: Indiana University Press, 1980.

Jones, Ann Rosalind, and Peter Stallybrass. *Renaissance Clothing and the Materials of Memory.* Cambridge University Press, 2000.

Jones, Kathleen. *A Glorious Fame: The Life of Margaret Cavendish, Duchess of Newcastle, 1623–1673.* London: Bloomsbury, 1988.

Jonsen, Albert R. and Stephen Toulmin. *The Abuse of Casuistry: A History of Moral Reasoning.* Berkeley: University of California Press, 1988.

Jordan, Constance. *Renaissance Feminism: Literary Texts and Political Models.* Ithaca: Cornell University Press, 1990.

Jowitt, Claire. "Imperial Dreams? Margaret Cavendish and the Cult of Elizabeth." *Women's Writing* 4 (1997): 383–99.

Justice, George L., and Nathan Tinker, eds. *Women's Writing and Circulation of Ideas: Manuscript Publication in England, 1550–1800.* Cambridge University Press, 2002.

Keeble, N. H. "'The Colonel's Shadow': Lucy Hutchinson, Women's Writing and the Civil War." In *Literature and the English Civil War,* ed. Healy and Sawday. 227–47.

The Cultural Identity of Seventeenth-Century Woman. London: Routledge, 1994.

"Obedient Subjects? The Loyal Self in Some Later Seventeenth-Century Royalist Women's Memoirs." In *Culture and Society in the Stuart Restoration,* ed. Maclean. 201–18.

Kegl, Rosemary. "'The world I have made': Margaret Cavendish, Feminism, and the *Blazing-World.*" In *Feminist Readings of Early Modern Culture,* ed. Traub, Kaplan, and Callaghan. 119–41.

Keller, Eve. "Producing Petty Gods: Margaret Cavendish's Critique of Experimental Science." ELH 64 (1997): 447–71.

Kelly, Joan. "Did Women Have a Renaissance?" In *Women, History, and Theory: The Essays of Joan Kelly.* University of Chicago Press, 1984. 19–50.

Khanna, Lee Cullen. "The Subject of Utopia: Margaret Cavendish and Her *Blazing-World.*" In *Utopian and Science Fiction by Women: Worlds of Difference,* ed. Jane L. Donawerth and Carol A. Kolmerten. Syracuse University Press, 1994. 15–34.

King, Sigrid, ed. *Pilgrimage for Love: Essays in Early Modern Literature in Honor of Josephine A. Roberts.* Tempe, Arizona: Arizona Center for Medieval and Renaissance Studies, 1999.

Koelb, Clayton and Susan Noakes, eds. *The Comparative Perspective on Literature: Approaches to Theory and Practice.* Ithaca: Cornell University Press, 1988.

Krontiris, Tina. *Oppositional Voices: Women as Writers and Translators of Literature in the English Renaissance.* London: Routledge, 1992.

Lamb, Mary Ellen. "The Agency of the Split Subject: Lady Anne Clifford and the Uses of Reading." *English Literary Renaissance* 22 (1992): 347–68.

"Margaret Hoby's Diary: Women's Reading Practices and the Gendering of the Reformation Subject." In *Pilgrimage for Love,* ed. King. 63–94.

"The Sociality of Margaret Hoby's Reading Practices and the Representation of Reformation Interiority." *Critical Survey* 12 (2000): 17–32.

Langbauer, Laurie. *Women and Romance: The Consolations of Gender in the English Novel.* Ithaca and London: Cornell University Press, 1990.

Langford, Rachel, and Russell West, eds. *Marginal Voices, Marginal Forms: Diaries in European Literature and History.* Amsterdam: Rodopi, 1999.

Lejeune, Philippe. *On Autobiography,* ed. Paul John Eakin; trans. Katherine Leary. Minneapolis: University of Minnesota Press, 1989.

"The Practice of the Private Journal: Chronicle of an Investigation (1986–1998)." In *Marginal Voices, Marginal Forms,* ed. Langford and West. 185–211.

Leslie, Marina. "Gender, Genre, and the Utopian Body in Margaret Cavendish's *Blazing World.*" *Utopian Studies* 7 (1996): 6–24.

Lewalski, Barbara Kiefer, ed. *Renaissance Genres: Essays on Theory, History, and Interpretation.* Cambridge, MA: Harvard University Press, 1986.

"Rewriting Patriarchy and Patronage: Margaret Clifford, Anne Clifford, and Aemilia Lanyer." *Yearbook of English Studies* 21 (1991): 87–106.

Writing Women in Jacobean England. Cambridge, MA and London: Harvard University Press, 1993.

Lilley, Kate. "Blazing Worlds: Seventeenth-Century Women's Utopian Writing." In *Women, Texts and Histories, 1575–1760,* ed. Brant and Purkiss. 102–33.

"Contracting Readers: 'Margaret Newcastle' and the Rhetoric of Conjugality." In *A Princely Brave Woman,* ed. Clucas. 19–39.

Lucas, Caroline. *Writing for Women: The Example of Woman as Reader in Elizabethan Romance.* Milton Keynes: Open University Press, 1989.

MacCarthy, B. G. *The Female Pen: Women Writers and Novelists.* Cork University Press, 1946–47; rpt. New York University Press, 1994.

Maclean, Gerald, ed. *Culture and Society in the Stuart Restoration: Literature, Drama, History.* Cambridge University Press, 1995.

MacLean, Ian. *The Renaissance Notion of Woman: A Study in the Fortunes of Scholasticism and Medical Science in European Intellectual Life.* Cambridge University Press, 1980.

Malcolmson, Cristina. "'The Explication of Whiteness and Blackness': Skin Color and the Physics of Color in the Works of Robert Boyle and Margaret Cavendish." In *Fault Lines and Controversies in the Study of Seventeenth-Century English Literature,* ed. Claude J. Summers and Ted-Larry Pebworth. Columbia: University of Missouri Press, 2002. 187–203.

Mandel, Barrett J. "Full of Life Now." In *Autobiography: Essays Theoretical and Critical,* ed. Olney. 49–72.

Marshall, Sherrin, ed. *Women in Reformation and Counter-Reformation Europe.* Bloomington: Indiana University Press, 1989.

Maslen, R. W. *Elizabethan Fictions: Espionage, Counter-Espionage, and the Duplicity of Fiction in Early Elizabethan Prose Narratives.* Oxford: Clarendon Press, 1979.

Mason, Mary G. "The Other Voice: Autobiographies of Women Writers." In *Autobiography: Essays Theoretical and Critical,* ed. Olney. 207–35.

Matchinske, Megan. *Writing, Gender and State in Early Modern England.* Cambridge University Press, 1998.

Matthews, William. *British Diaries: An Annotated Bibliography of British Diaries Written between 1492 and 1942.* Berkeley: University of California Press, 1950.

Maus, Katherine Eisaman. "Proof and Consequences: Inwardness and Its Exposure in the English Renaissance." *Representations* 34 (1991): 29–52.

McKeon, Michael. *The Origins of the English Novel, 1600–1740.* Baltimore: Johns Hopkins University Press, 1987.

Mendelson, Sara Heller. "Stuart Women's Diaries and Occasional Memoirs." In *Women in English Society, 1500–1800,* ed. Prior. 181–210.

The Mental World of Stuart Women. Amherst: University of Massachusetts Press, 1987.

Mendelson, Sara, and Patricia Crawford. *Women in Early Modern England.* Oxford: Clarendon Press, 1997.

Miller, Nancy K. "Emphasis Added: Plots and Plausibilites in Women's Fictions." *PMLA* 96 (1981): 36–48.

"Representing Others: Gender and Subjects of Autobiography." *Differences* 6 (1994): 1–27.

Miller, Naomi J. *Changing the Subject: Mary Wroth and Figurations of Gender in Early Modern England.* Lexington: University Press of Kentucky, 1996.

Morrill, John, Paul Slack, and Daniel Woolf, eds. *Public Duty and Private Conscience in Seventeenth-Century England.* Oxford: Clarendon Press, 1993.

Morris, John N. *Versions of the Self: Studies in English Autobiography from John Bunyan to John Stuart Mill.* New York: Basic Books, 1966.

Mueller, Janel M. *The Native Tongue and the Word: Developments in English Prose Style, 1380–1580.* University of Chicago Press, 1984.

Nelson, William. *Fact or Fiction: The Dilemma of the Renaissance Storyteller.* Cambridge, MA: Harvard University Press, 1973.

Nicolson, Marjorie. *Pepys's Diary and the New Science.* Charlottesville: University Press of Virginia, 1965.

Norbrook, David. "Margaret Cavendish and Lucy Hutchinson: Identity, Ideology and Politics." *In-between: Essays and Studies in Literary Criticism* 9 (2000): 179–203.

Nussbaum, Felicity A. *The Autobiographical Subject: Gender and Ideology in Eighteenth-Century England.* Baltimore: Johns Hopkins University Press, 1989.

O'Connor, Mary. "Representations of Intimacy in the Life-Writing of Anne Clifford and Anne Dormer." In *Representations of the Self,* ed. Coleman, Lewis, and Kowalik. 79–96.

Olney, James, ed. *Autobiography: Essays Theoretical and Critical.* Princeton University Press, 1980.

"Autobiography and the Cultural Moment: a Thematic, Historical, and Bibliographical Introduction." In Olney, ed., *Autobiography.* 3–27.

Memory and Narrative: The Weave of Life-Writing. University of Chicago Press, 1998.

Metaphors of Self: The Meaning of Autobiography. Princeton University Press, 1972.

Orlin, Lena Cowen. *Private Matters and Public Culture in Post-Reformation England.* Ithaca: Cornell University Press, 1994.

Otten, Charlotte F., ed. *English Women's Voices: 1540–1700.* Miami: Florida International University Press, 1992.

Ottway, Sheila. "They Only Lived Twice: Public and Private Selfhood in the Autobiographies of Anne, Lady Halkett and Colonel Joseph Bampfield." In *Betraying Our Selves,* ed. Dragstra, et al. 136–47.

Pacheco, Anita, ed. *Early Women Writers: 1600–1720.* London: Longman, 1998.

Paloma, Dolores. "Margaret Cavendish: Defining the Female Self." *Women's Studies* 7 (1980): 55–66.

Pearson, Jacqueline. "Women Reading, Reading Women." In *Women and Literature in Britain, 1500-1700,* ed. Wilcox. 80–99.

Pohl, Nicole. "'Of Mixt Natures': Questions of Genre in Margaret Cavendish's *The Blazing World.*" In *A Princely Brave Woman,* ed. Clucas. 51–68.

Pointon, Marcia. *Strategies for Showing: Women, Possession, and Representation in English Visual Culture: 1665–1800.* Oxford University Press, 1997.

Pollock, Linda, ed. *With Faith and Physic: The Life of a Tudor Gentlewoman: Lady Grace Mildmay 1551–1620.* New York: St. Martin's Press, 1995.

Pomerleau, Cynthia. "The Emergence of Women's Autobiography in England." In *Women's Autobiography,* ed. Jelinek. 21–38.

Ponsonby, Arthur. *English Diaries.* London: Methuen, 1923.

Potter, Lois. *Secret Rites and Secret Writings: Royalist Literature, 1641–1660.* Cambridge University Press, 1989.

Prior, Mary, ed. *Women in English Society, 1500–1800.* London: Methuen, 1985.

Regard, Frédéric, ed. *Mapping the Self: Space, Identity, Discourse in British Auto/ Biography.* Publications de l'Université de Saint-Étienne, 2003.

Ricoeur, Paul. *Time and Narrative,* trans. Kathleen McLaughlin and David Pellauer. 3 vols. University of Chicago Press, 1984–88.

Rippl, Gabriele. *Lebenstexte: Literarische Selbststilisierung englischer Frauen in der frühen Neuzeit.* Munich: Wilhelm Fink Verlag, 1998.

Rogers, John. *The Matter of Revolution: Science, Poetry and Politics in the Age of Milton.* Ithaca: Cornell University Press, 1996.

Rose, Mary Beth. *Gender and Heroism in Early Modern English Literature.* University of Chicago Press, 2002.

Rose, Mary Beth, ed. *Women in the Middle Ages and the Renaissance: Literary and Historical Perspectives.* Syracuse University Press, 1986.

Sackville-West, Vita. *Knole and the Sackvilles.* London, 1922.

Salzman, Paul. *English Prose Fiction, 1558–1700.* Oxford: Clarendon Press, 1985.

Sarasohn, Lisa T. "*Leviathan* and the Lady: Cavendish's Critique of Hobbes in the *Philosophical Letters.*" In *Authorial Conquests,* ed. Cottegnies and Weitz. 40–58.

"A Science Turned Upside Down: Feminism and the Natural Philosophy of Margaret Cavendish." *Huntington Library Quarterly* 47 (1984): 289–307.

Schlaeger, Jürgen. "Parallel Explorations: Exploring the Self in the Late Sixteenth and Early Seventeenth Centuries." In *Mapping the Self,* ed. Regard. 33–54.

"Self-Exploration in Early Modern English Diaries." In *Marginal Voices, Marginal Forms,* ed. Langford and West. 22–36.

Schleiner, Louise. *Tudor and Stuart Women Writers.* Bloomington: Indiana University Press, 1994.

Seelig, Sharon Cadman. *Generating Texts: The Progeny of Seventeenth-Century Prose.* Charlottesville: University Press of Virginia, 1996.

Sharpe, Kevin. *Reading Revolutions: The Politics of Reading in Early Modern England.* New Haven: Yale University Press, 2000.

Sherman, Sandra. "Trembling Texts: Margaret Cavendish and the Dialectic of Authorship." *English Literary Renaissance* 24 (1994): 184–210.

Sherman, Stuart. *Telling Time: Clocks, Diaries, and English Diurnal Form, 1660–1785.* University of Chicago Press, 1996.

Shifrin, Susan, ed. *Women as Sites of Culture: Women's Roles in Cultural Formation from the Renaissance to the Twentieth Century.* Aldershot: Ashgate, 2002.

Shuger, Debora. "Life-Writing in Seventeenth-Century England." In *Representations of the Self,* ed. Coleman, Lewis, and Kowalik. 63–78.

Shumaker, Wayne. *English Autobiography: Its Emergence, Materials, and Forms.* Berkeley: University of California Press, 1954.

Siegfried, Brandie R. "Anecdotal and Cabalistic Forms in *Observations upon Experimental Philosophy.*" In *Authorial Conquests,* ed. Cottegnies and Weitz. 59–79.

Smith, Barbara, and Ursula Appelt, eds. *Write or Be Written: Early Modern Women Poets and Cultural Constraints.* Aldershot: Ashgate, 2001.

Smith, Hilda. "Feminism and the Methodology of Women's History." In *Liberating Women's History,* ed. Berenice A. Carroll. Urbana: University of Illinois Press, 1976. 368–84.

Smith, Hilda L. *Reason's Disciples: Seventeenth-Century English Feminists.* Urbana: University of Illinois Press, 1982.

Smith, Sidonie. *A Poetics of Women's Autobiography: Marginality and the Fictions of Self-Representation.* Bloomington: Indiana University Press, 1987.

Smith, Sidonie and Julia Watson. *Reading Autobiography: A Guide for Interpreting Life Narratives.* Minneapolis: University of Minnesota Press, 2001.

Spacks, Patricia Meyer. *The Female Imagination.* New York: Alfred A. Knopf, 1975.

Imagining a Self: Autobiography and Novel in Eighteenth-Century England. Cambridge, MA: Harvard University Press, 1976.

Spence, Richard T. *Lady Anne Clifford: Countess of Pembroke, Dorset and Montgomery (1590–1676).* Stroud, Gloucestershire: Sutton, 1997.

Spender, Dale. *Mothers of the Novel.* London: Pandora, 1986.

Spufford, Margaret. *Small Books and Pleasant Histories: Popular Fiction and its Readership in Seventeenth-Century England.* London: Methuen, 1981.

Stanton, Domna C. *The Female Autograph: Theory and Practice of Autobiography from the Tenth to the Twentieth Century.* University of Chicago Press, 1987; orginally New York Literary Forum, 1984.

Stauffer, Donald A. *The Art of Biography in Eighteenth-Century England.* Princeton University Press, 1941.

English Biography Before 1700. Cambridge, MA: Harvard University Press, 1930.

Steen, Sara Jayne. "Women Writers of the Seventeenth Century, 1604–1674." *English Literary Renaissance* 24 (1994): 243–74.

Sturrock, John. *The Language of Autobiography: Studies in the First Person Singular.* Cambridge University Press, 1993.

Sutherland, Christine Mason. "Aspiring to the Rhetorical Tradition: a Study of Margaret Cavendish." In *Listening to Their Voices,* ed. Wertheimer. 255–71.

Sutherland, James. *English Literature of the Late Seventeenth Century*. Oxford University Press, 1969.

Suzuki, Mihoko. "Anne Clifford and the Gendering of History." *Clio* 30 (2001): 195–229.

Swaim, Kathleen M. *Pilgrim's Progress, Puritan Progress: Discourses and Contexts*. Urbana: University of Illinois Press, 1993.

Thomas, Keith. "Cases of Conscience in Seventeenth-Century England." In *Public Duty and Private Conscience in Seventeenth-Century England*, ed. Morrill, Slack, and Woolf. 29–56.

Todd, Janet. *The Sign of Angellica: Women, Writing, and Fiction, 1660–1800*. New York: Columbia University Press, 1989.

Tomlinson, Sophie. "My Brain the Stage: Margaret Cavendish and the Fantasy of Female Performance." In *Women, Texts and Histories, 1575–1760*, ed. Brant and Purkiss. 134–63.

Traub, Valerie, Lindsay M. Kaplan, and Dympna Callaghan, eds. *Feminist Readings of Early Modern Culture*. Cambridge University Press, 1996.

Travitsky, Betty S., and Adele F. Seeff, eds. *Attending to Women in Early Modern England*. Newark: University of Delaware Press, 1994.

Trubowitz, Rachel. "The Reenchantment of Utopia and the Female Monarchical Self: Margaret Cavendish's *Blazing World*." *Tulsa Studies in Women's Literature* 11 (1992): 229–46.

Ulrich, Laurel Thatcher. *A Midwife's Tale: The Life of Martha Ballard, Based on Her Diary, 1785–1812*. New York: Alfred A. Knopf, 1990.

Wagner, Geraldine Muñoz. "Engendering a Bodily Subjectivity: Romance Literatures and the Lives of Seventeenth Century Women." Ph.D. Thesis, Brown University, 2000.

Wall, Wendy. *The Imprint of Gender: Authorship and Publication in the English Renaissance*. Ithaca: Cornell University Press, 1993.

Waller, Gary F. "Struggling into Discourse: the Emergence of Renaissance Women's Writing." In *Silent but for the Word*, ed. Hannay. 238–56.

Walker, Kim. "'Busie in my Clositt': Letters, Diaries, and Autobiographical Writing." In Walker, *Women Writers of the English Renaissance*. New York: Twayne, 1996. 26–46.

Warnicke, Retha. *Women of the English Renaissance and Reformation*. Westport, CT: Greenwood Press, 1983.

Watkins, Owen C. *The Puritan Experience: Studies in Spiritual Autobiography*. New York: Schocken, 1972.

Webber, Joan. *The Eloquent 'I' – Style and Self in Seventeenth-Century Prose*. Madison: University of Wisconsin Press, 1968.

Wertheimer, Molly Meijer. *Listening to Their Voices: The Rhetorical Activities of Historical Women*. Columbia: University of South Carolina Press, 1997.

Wheale, Nigel. *Writing and Society: Literacy, Print and Politics in Britain, 1590–1660*. London: Routledge, 1999.

Whitaker, Katie. *Mad Madge*. New York: Basic Books, 2002.

Wiesner, Merry E. *Women and Gender in Early Modern Europe.* 2nd edn. Cambridge University Press, 2000.

Wilcox, Helen. "Her Own Life, Her Own Living? Text and Materiality in Seventeenth-Century Englishwomen's Autobiographical Writings." In *Betraying Our Selves*, ed. Dragstra, et al. 105–19.

"Margaret Cavendish and the Landscapes of a Woman's Life." In *Mapping the Self*, ed. Regard. 73–88.

"Private Writing and Public Function: Autobiographical Texts by Renaissance Gentlewomen." In *Gloriana's Face*, ed. Cerasano and Wynne-Davies. 47–62.

Wilcox, Helen, ed. *Women and Literature in Britain, 1500–1700.* Cambridge University Press, 1996.

Willen, Diane. "Godly Women in Early Modern England: Puritanism and Gender." *Journal of Ecclesiastical History* 43 (1992): 561–80.

"Women and Religion in Early Modern England." In *Women in Reformation and Counter-Reformation Europe*, ed. Marshall. 140–65.

Williams, George H., and Angel M. Mergal, eds. *Spiritual and Anabaptist Writers.* Philadelphia: Westminster Press, 1957.

Williamson, G[eorge] C. *George, Third Earl of Cumberland, 1558–1605, His Life and His Voyages.* Cambridge University Press, 1920.

Lady Anne Clifford, Countess of Dorset, Pembroke, & Montgomery 1590–1676. Kendal: Titus Wilson & Son, 1922.

Wilson, Katharina M., and Frank J. Warnke, eds. *Women Writers of the Seventeenth Century.* Athens: University of Georgia Press, 1989.

Wiseman, Susan. "Gender and Status in Dramatic Discourse: Margaret Cavendish, Duchess of Newcastle." In *Women, Writing, History, 1640–1740*, ed. Grundy and Wiseman. 159–77.

Woodbridge, Linda. *Women and the English Renaissance: Literature and the Nature of Womankind, 1540–1620.* Urbana: University of Illinois Press, 1984.

Wrightson, Keith. *English Society, 1580–1680.* New Brunswick, NJ: Rutgers University Press, 1982.

Wynne-Davies, Marion. "'How Great is Thy Change': Familial Discourses in the Cavendish Family." In *A Princely Brave Woman*, ed. Clucas. 40–50.

Ziegler, Georgianna N. "Women Writers of Tudor England, 1485–1603." *English Literary Renaissance* 24 (1994): 229–42.

Index